TEST ITEMS

Charles P. Crouch
Georgia Southern University

A HISTORY OF WESTERN SOCIETY

Sixth Edition

John P. McKay
University of Illinois at Urbana-Champaign

Bennett D. Hill
Georgetown University

John Buckler
University of Illinois at Urbana-Champaign

Houghton Mifflin Company   Boston   New York

COPYRIGHT © HOUGHTON MIFFLIN COMPANY. ALL RIGHTS RESERVED.

Copyright © 1999 by Houghton Mifflin Company. All rights reserved.

Houghton Mifflin Company hereby grants you permission to reproduce the Houghton Mifflin material contained in this work in classroom quantities, solely for use with the accompanying Houghton Mifflin textbook. All reproductions must include the Houghton Mifflin copyright notice and no fee may be collected except to cover the cost of duplication. If you wish to make any other use of this material, including reproducing or transmitting the materials or portions thereof in any form or by any electronic or mechanical means including any information storage or retrieval system, you must obtain written permission from Houghton Mifflin Company, unless such use is expressly permitted by federal copyright law. If you wish to reproduce material acknowledging a rights holder other than Houghton Mifflin Company, you must obtain permission from the rights holder. Address inquiries to College Permissions, Houghton Mifflin Company, 222 Berkeley Street, Boston, MA 02116-3764.

Printed in the U.S.A.

ISBN: 0-395-904390

123456789-PP-02 01 00 99 98

Contents

Introduction   iv
Chapter 1   Near Eastern Origins   1
Chapter 2   Small Kingdoms and Mighty Empires in the Near East   9
Chapter 3   The Legacy of Greece   17
Chapter 4   Hellenistic Diffusion   26
Chapter 5   The Rise of Rome   34
Chapter 6   The Pax Romana   42
Chapter 7   The Making of Europe   50
Chapter 8   The Carolingian World: Europe in the Early Middle Ages   59
Chapter 9   Revival, Recovery, and Reform   67
Chapter 10   Life in Christian Europe in the High Middle Ages   75
Chapter 11   The Creativity and Vitality of the High Middle Ages   84
Chapter 12   The Crisis of the Later Middle Ages   94
Chapter 13   European Society in the Age of the Renaissance   103
Chapter 14   Reform and Renewal in the Christian Church   113
Chapter 15   The Age of European Expansion and Religious Wars   122
Chapter 16   Absolutism and Constitutionalism in Western Europe (ca. 1589-1715)   132
Chapter 17   Absolutism in Eastern Europe to 1740   141
Chapter 18   Toward a New World-view   150
Chapter 19   The Expansion of Europe in the Eighteenth Century   159
Chapter 20   The Changing Life of the People   167
Chapter 21   The Revolution in Politics, 1775-1815   175
Chapter 22   The Revolution in Energy and Industry   185
Chapter 23   Ideologies and Upheavals, 1815-1850   194
Chapter 24   Life in the Changing Urban Society   202
Chapter 25   The Age of Nationalism, 1850-1914   210
Chapter 26   The West and the World   218
Chapter 27   The Great Break: War and Revolution   226
Chapter 28   The Age of Anxiety   235
Chapter 29   Dictatorships and the Second World War   244
Chapter 30   Cold War Conflicts and Social Transformations, 1945-1985   253
Chapter 31   Revolution, Reunification, and Rebuilding, 1985 to the Present   262
Unit, Midterm, and Final Examination Questions   270
Answer Key for Multiple-Choice Questions   278

COPYRIGHT © HOUGHTON MIFFLIN COMPANY. ALL RIGHTS RESERVED.

INTRODUCTION

Test Items provides identifications, essay questions, and multiple-choice questions for each chapter of a *A History of Western Society*, by John P. McKay, Bennett D. Hill and John Buckler. In addition, questions for unit, midterm, and final examinations are provided. An answer key for the multiple-choice questions can be found at the end of the book.

The questions, which are drawn from the text, tables, maps, and other features, vary in purpose. The essay questions test students' understanding of specific concepts, and the ability to synthesize facts with those concepts, in the text. The multiple-choice and identification questions are designed to evaluate the students' knowledge of facts and concepts and also to increase their analytical skills. Every attempt has been made to focus on substantive issues and to provide straightforward, unambiguous answers to the multiple-choice questions. The test items also differ in their level of difficulty. You are encouraged to select items best suit your own emphases and pedagogical interests; of course, your philosophy of testing will influence your choice of items.

Other useful questions for testing and discussion can be found in the two-volume *Study Guide* to *A History of Western Society*.

CHAPTER 1

NEAR EASTERN ORIGINS

Key Terms

1. historical fact
2. *civilis*
3. *Homo sapiens*
4. tribe
5. patriarch
6. Ebla
7. "Iceman"
8. Mesopotamia
9. Semitic
10. Sargon
11. Hammurabi's Code
12. Kassites
13. Marduk
14. cuneiform
15. *Epic of Gilgamesh*
16. pharaoh
17. Hyksos
18. Akhenaten
19. Indo-European
20. *pankus*

Essay Questions

21. History is the effort to reconstruct the past, to discover what people thought and did. Historians base their reconstruction of the past on facts and interpretation. How does this process work? What types of sources do historians use? How do they evaluate the accuracy of those sources? In what ways has the practice of history changed over time?

    This question asks the student, in essence, to define what is meant by the term "history." After providing a definition, the essay should include a discussion of how a discrete piece of information becomes a historical fact and how the historical facts are then molded together, based on the conceptual framework of individual historians, to become what we call history. A good answer should also include a discussion of the two main divisions in the types of sources used, primary

primary and secondary; this discussion should also indicate the various types of primary and secondary materials utilized by historians, such as physical artifacts, written records, accounts of later historians, and modern scholarly products. A good essay should include a brief discussion of the ways in which a historian is able to evaluate, internally and externally, the accuracy of both primary and secondary sources. Finally, the essay should describe the complementary development of the information age and social history and how this has changed the way in which historians reconstruct the past.

22. The real transformation in human existence occurred when large numbers of people began to rely primarily on the crops they grew and the animals they domesticated. Describe the manner in which this transformation took place. Discuss the consequences of this transformation.

This essay should describe how early humans made the transition from hunting and gathering to a settled lifestyle, based on agriculture; it should include mention of the gradual and often incomplete nature of this transformation. Most importantly, the essay should include a thorough discussion of the consequences, including such things as population growth, emergence of trading, rise of towns and cities, and changes in kinship and other societal organizations.

23. Egypt and Mesopotamia were both sites of ancient civilizations. Describe each of these civilizations in terms of its political structure, religion, society, and culture. How can we account for the similarities and differences between these two?

For this question, a basic description of each civilization is necessary. For politics, this description should include governmental organization, political and geographic unity, role of the military, and role of the priesthood. For religion, include role and power of the priesthood, types and attitudes of the gods, view of the afterlife. For society, the good essay should include the social structure, slavery, family, and gender. The description of culture should include such things as art and folk tales. Following the descriptions of the two civilizations, the similarities and differences between each should be acknowledged. Finally, these differences and similarities must be explained, based upon such factors as historical development and geography.

24. One of the most salient features of the history of the Ancient Near East was the cultural endurance of Sumerian and Egyptian civilizations and the prolific cross-cultural interaction amongst the peoples of the region. How did the process of what the textbook refers to as "cultural endurance and dissemination" work? How can we explain the endurance of the older civilizations, while at the same time acknowledging the adoptions and adaptations which occurred not only amongst newly-arrived peoples and neighboring societies but also in the well-established Sumerian and Egyptian societies?

The description of the process should stress the appeal of Sumerian and Egyptian culture (religion, technology, alphabet, art, literature, etc.) on newcomers and neighbors; examples include but are not limited to: Semites, Eblaites, Kassites, Hyksos. The essay should next describe the cross-fertilization of cultures: Egypt and Nubia, southern Syria, Palestine, Hyksos; Sumer and Semites, northern Syria. The essay should then attempt to assess the appeal of Sumerian and Egyptian culture: utility of written language, elegance of literature, usefulness of political organization, etc. Finally, the essay should conclude with a discussion of the ways in which peoples borrow and adapt that which most responds to their own societal needs and desires.

25. Sumerian society was complex, with its members divided into distinct categories. Describe these

social categories in terms of membership, wealth and power, duties, functions, and obligations. How does the Law Code of Hammurabi reflect this social stratification?

This question asks the student to outline and describe the social structure of Sumerian society. The Law Code of Hammurabi should be used to provide the supporting examples for the essay's descriptions.

26. Geographical factors seemed to have enormous impact on political and economic development in Egypt and Mesopotamia. Describe these factors and assess their influence. What impact did geography have on religion in each of these areas? What other factors seemed to have an impact on the development of these ancient civilizations?

One of the major themes of this chapter is the impact of the physical environment, (typography and climate) on human civilization; this essay is designed to underscore that theme. To answer this question well, an essay should first describe the respective environments of Mesopotamia and Egypt. Next, the impact of geography on political, economic and religious developments in each civilization should be carefully assessed. The role of migration should be discussed thoroughly, especially the cross-fertilization of culture and technology; a thoughtful essay should also indicate the role of geography on migration. Finally, a summation of the importance of geography on the development of these civilizations, indicated by the discussion of the differences between the two, should conclude the essay.

Multiple-Choice Questions

27. The study of history is the effort to
    a. memorize names, dates, and events.
    b. reconstruct the past to discover how people lived.
    c. provide a guide for modern-day policy making.
    d. discover the uniqueness of each era.

28. The primary building block of Mesopotamian architecture was
    a. mud bricks.
    b. granite.
    c. limestone.
    d. concrete.

29. Akhenaten's experiment with monotheism failed because
    a. its elaborate ritual was too confusing.
    b. the hated and corrupt priesthood endorsed it.
    c. it had no connection with the Egyptian past.
    d. it did not gain the support of the pharaoh.

30. Charles Darwin's theory of evolution
    a. claimed that human beings and apes are descended from common ancestors.
    b. was overturned by the discovery of the Neanderthal man.
    c. was roundly criticized by the scientific community.
    d. attempted to reconcile the biblical account of the creation with that of modern evolution theory.

31. Paleolithic hunters were successful because of
    a. their bravery.
    b. their weaponry.
    c. the abundance of animals.
    d. their social organization.

32. The evidence provided by the discovery of the "Iceman" indicates that
    a. the nomadic way of life was completely destroyed by the transformation to systematic agriculture.
    b. the development of systematic agriculture occurred first in Europe.
    c. nomadic life coincided peacefully with the emerging agricultural settlements.
    d. Neolithic peoples relied exclusively on hunting and gathering to survive.

33. In Paleolithic times, the tribe was governed by the
    a. elders.
    b. patriarch.
    c. matriarch.
    d. warriors.

34. The primary responsibility of Paleolithic women was
    a. bearing children.
    b. gathering nuts and fruits.
    c. tending the fire.
    d. cultivating crops.

35. The Tigris and Euphrates Rivers supplied all of the following *except*
    a. fish.
    b. water for irrigation.
    c. building materials.
    d. an easy communication network.

36. The emergence of towns and cities in the Neolithic Age was a product of
    a. systematic agriculture.
    b. larger, healthier populations.
    c. the large-scale exchange of goods.
    d. mass migrations.

37. The transformation from a nomadic to a settled lifestyle
    a. had little impact on the extended family.
    b. weakened the bonds of the nuclear family.
    c. weakened the bonds of the extended family.
    d. had little impact on the agricultural system.

38. The most important aspect of the prosperity evidenced by the emergence of urban centers during the Neolithic era was the
    a. development of new military techniques and technology.
    b. architectural advances made in building design and construction.
    c. dramatic increase in population.
    d. decline of violent collective behavior, such as war.

39. The division of labor within Neolithic towns resulted from
    a. agricultural surplus.
    b. urbanization.
    c. military conquest.
    d. development of metalworking technology.

40. All of the following were products of systematic agriculture *except*
    a. the division of labor.
    b. the dissolution of the nuclear family.
    c. a healthier population.
    d. a dramatic increase in population.

41. After initially adopting a settled agricultural lifestyle, Neolithic farmers increased their productivity by
    a. having larger families.
    b. instituting agricultural slavery.
    c. developing religions that worshiped agricultural gods rather than hunting gods.
    d. using bigger, stronger domesticated animals and improved tools.

42. When the Sumerians migrated into Mesopotamia, the native Semites
    a. assimilated the newcomers.
    b. were destroyed.
    c. adopted the Sumerian culture.
    d. emigrated from the Near East.

43. The legacy of the Kassites to the development of western civilization was their
    a. invention of iron-working technology.
    b. domestication of animals.
    c. preservation and transmission of Mesopotamian culture
    d. religious and political unification of Egypt.

44. The harsh environment of Mesopotamia produced a religion that featured
    a. a benevolent Supreme Being, with a completely spiritual manifestation.
    b. cruel anthropomorphic gods.
    c. a very weak priesthood.
    d. a monotheistic theology and an anthropomorphic god.

45. Sumerian society was
    a. dominated by the priesthood.
    b. composed of two social groupings: nobles and slaves.
    c. complex, with various social categories.
    d. fluid, with a high degree of social mobility.

46. In Sumer a person could become a slave for all of the following reasons *except*
    a. race.
    b. crime.
    c. bad debts.
    d. fortunes of war.

COPYRIGHT © HOUGHTON MIFFLIN COMPANY. ALL RIGHTS RESERVED.

47. Hammurabi's political success resulted from his
    a. destruction of the Sumerian concept of urban kingship.
    b. conquest of Egypt.
    c. destruction of existing Mesopotamian culture and establishment of the ascendency of Babylonian culture.
    d. linking the concepts of Semitic tribal chief with that of Sumerian urban kingship.

48. One major drawback to the complex system of writing known as *pictographs* was that it
    a. did not include numbers.
    b. could not represent abstract ideas.
    c. was too complex.
    d. was not logical.

49. The key theme of the *Epic of Gilgamesh* is the
    a. search for immortality.
    b. battle between good and evil.
    c. creation of men and women.
    d. destruction of the world.

50. The relationship between Egypt and the peoples of southern Syria and Palestine was generally based on
    a. shared ethnic roots.
    b. trade.
    c. imperialistic conquest by the Egyptians.
    d. military alliances against the Mesopotamians.

51. Hammurabi's code was designed to
    a. regulate the relationships among his people.
    b. intimidate the common people in order to prevent social upheaval.
    c. protect the position of nobles and priests.
    d. increase the power of the nobility over the priesthood.

52. Under Hammurabi's code, the purpose of the dowry was to
    a. ensure equality between husband and wife.
    b. protect the rights and status of married women.
    c. make it easier for husbands to divorce their wives.
    d. protect inheritance rights of all of a family's children.

53. Mesopotamian and Egyptian religions differed in that
    a. one was monotheistic and one was polytheistic.
    b. Egypt lacked an organized priesthood.
    c. the priests in Mesopotamia had little political power.
    d. Egyptian gods were benevolent, while Mesopotamian gods were harsh.

54. The most important factor in the political unification of Egypt was
    a. a powerful pharaoh.
    b. economic self-sufficiency.
    c. geography.
    d. the social structure.

55. Hammurabi secured Babylon's cultural ascendancy through
    a. military conquest.
    b. economic domination.
    c. universalization of Babylonian gods.
    d. control of irrigation.

56. The Egyptian concept of kingship was
    a. derived from the Nubians.
    b. closely connected with the Nile Valley.
    c. imposed by the Romans.
    d. similar to the typical concept of a single person ruling a political entity.

57. Egyptian religion was
    a. shaped by Nubian religious beliefs.
    b. greatly influenced by Mesopotamian religion.
    c. independent of the political development of Egypt.
    d. permeated by the cyclical patterns of the Nile River.

58. Egyptian society was characterized by
    a. the absence of any slavery.
    b. an unusual amount of social mobility.
    c. a rigid caste system.
    d. the equality of all beneath the pharaoh.

59. In the "Individual and Society" section of the text, the story of Ah-Mose the Egyptian represents
    a. Egyptian destruction of the Hyksos.
    b. the role of the pharoah in Egyptian society.
    c. the monotheistic experiments of Akhenaton.
    d. rigidity of the social system in Egypt.

60. Near Eastern peoples originally developed writing to
    a. write poetry.
    b. compose theological studies.
    c. keep accurate records.
    d. understand their history.

61. Hittite society was characterized by
    a. social mobility.
    b. very little economic differentiation.
    c. a strong aristocracy.
    d. its ability to resist the superior Mesopotamian culture.

62. The technological base of Hittite success was their
    a. extensive use of calvary.
    b. mastery of siege techniques and technology.
    c. adoption of bronze military technology from the Egyptians.
    d. introduction of iron technology to war and agriculture.

CHAPTER 2

SMALL KINGDOMS AND MIGHTY EMPIRES IN THE NEAR EAST

Key Terms

1. Kushites
2. Nebuchadnezzar
3. Sargon II
4. Medes
5. Baal
6. Babylonian Captivity
7. Solomon
8. Judah
9. Covenant
10. Jeremiah
11. frieze
12. Ugarit
13. Cyrus the Great
14. satrap
15. Ahriman
16. Magi
17. *Zend Avesta*
18. Royal Road
19. Talmud
20. Zoroaster

Essay Questions

21. Compare the two great empires—Assyrian and Persian—that emerged after the thirteenth century B.C. How were they created? How were they ruled? How do historians explain the differences and similarities between them?

    In this comparative essay, the student should describe the establishment of both empires, including the role of geography, social structure, economic factors, military effectiveness, and individual rulers. Next, the answer should describe the different ways by which the Assyrians and Persians controlled their empires. Finally, the essay must attempt to explain why the Assyrians and the Persians ruled their respective empires in such different manners; in this part of the essay, consideration of the role of individual rulers, especially Cyrus, and the impact of geography would be very illustrative. The thoughtful essay might also indicate the more effective governmental strategy and why it was more effective.

22. Describe and discuss the evolution of Hebrew society. What were the benefits and costs of this evolution? How did it affect the family? How would you assess the impact social evolution had on the Jewish religion, being sure to include a discussion of Samuel's sermon to the Hebrews on kingship, in "Listening to the Past"?

This essay should describe the evolution of the Hebrews from a nomadic to a settled society, being sure to indicate the impact of older, well-established cultures on the Hebrews. Second, the essay must assess the impact of the transformation to a settled lifestyle on Hebrew society, including political development, social stratification, land ownership, wealth concentration. Of special interest is the impact on the family and on women for which the Bible provides substantial documentation; the essay should discuss marriage, property and inheritance rights, role of nuclear family, divorce, family size, etc. Finally, an assessment of the transformation's impact on religion is necessary; one must discuss the Hebrew religion before the Hebrews adopted a settled lifestyle and then how the religion was transformed, being sure to include references to Samuel's sermon, the Torah, and the Talmud.

23. Compare the Jewish religion with Zoroastrianism. What are the key features of each? What distinguished these two religions from earlier Mesopotamian religion? How have these two religions influenced our own time?

This essay should include a description of the major beliefs of each religion, including such things as views of the afterlife, nature of good and evil, and the relationship between God and believers, being sure to indicate similarities and differences. Next, the essay should indicate the major break with older religions. Finally, the essay should indicate the modern-day reflections of these two religions.

24. The Persian Empire was one of the greatest of all time. Describe its creation and governance and assess critically the reasons for the success of this far-flung empire.

For this essay, one should begin with a description of Iranian geography and early Iranian society. Next, one should discuss the political evolution of the Medes, including the role of migration and invasion, into a single, unified kingdom. Third, the essay should describe the development of the Persian Empire under Cyrus and his successors, including both Cyrus's view of empire and how this view was transformed into actual policies; there should also be a description of the extent of the empire. Finally, based upon the discussion of Cyrus's views and policies, the essay should then offer an explanation for the success of this world empire.

25. Describe and discuss the evolution of the Jewish religion, including the nature of Yahweh and the Covenant. In what ways did the Hebrew religion affect their society? How does Samuel's sermon to the Israelites (in "Listening to the Past") exemplify critical elements of both Jewish religion and politics?

In this essay, the student should discuss the special nature of Yahweh, the evolution of Yahweh, and the Covenant between Yahweh and the Hebrews. Second, the essay should provide an explanation for the development. Next, the role of religion in the development of Jewish society should be explored in depth, using the Bible judiciously to provide evidence. Finally, Samuel's sermon should be assessed to underscore not only the Covenant, but also the interrelationship between religious and earthly affairs.

26. What was the role of women in Hebrew society? How and why did the adoption of a settled lifestyle affect women?

The essay should describe the position of women in Hebrew society, in both the nomadic and settled periods. This description should be followed by a discussion of why adoption of a settled lifestyle would result in changes; this discussion should not only reveal something about the role of women in such societies, but also about these types of society in general.

27. While the collapse of the great empires Egypt and Mesopotamia (see chapter 1) certainly resulted in a great deal of chaos, the resulting era was also one of cultural diffusion and recovery. How does the example of Ugarit exemplify the political and cultural realities in the aftermath of the collapse of the New Kingdom in Egypt and Hittites in Mesopotamia?

First, one should identify the general characteristics of the small, independent states of the regions: economic viability, shared culture, etc. Second, the essay should describe Ugarit's political, cultural, and social institutions. Next, there should be an indication of the applicability of Ugarit's example. Finally, one should emphasize the preservation of the shared cultural heritage of the Ancient Near East.

Multiple-Choice Questions

28. Egypt was reunified in the 8th century B.C. by the
    a. Phoenicians.
    b. Sea Peoples.
    c. Kushites.
    d. Hebrews.

29. A critical factor in the evolution of the Jewish religion was the
    a. influence of Zoroaster.
    b. influence of Akhenaten.
    c. adoption of a settled lifestyle.
    d. political oppression of the Assyrians.

30. The Hebrews were able to establish themselves in Palestine
    a. through a series of wars.
    b. by forming an alliance with Egypt.
    c. through intermarriage with the Philistines.
    d. because it was unpopulated at the time.

31. In "Listening to the Past," Samuel urges his fellow Hebrews to
    a. attack the Assyrians.
    b. adhere to the Covenant.
    c. worship Baal.
    d. reject the religion of Zoroaster.

32. The Phoenicians' greatest cultural achievement was the
    a. invention of settled agriculture.
    b. development of a sun-based calendar.
    c. adoption of monotheistic religion.
    d. creation of an alphabet.

33. According to modern scholars, the Old Testament of the Bible was
    a. written by a single author in the fifth century B.C.
    b. composed in stages, over many years and by many authors.
    c. largely fictitious.
    d. a collection of stories gathered by Moses.

34. According to the text, Baal represents the
    a. collapse of Egyptian authority.
    b. wisdom and leniency with which the Persians ruled their empire.
    c. appeal of established cultures to newcomers, such as the Hebrews in Palestine.
    d. power of the Covenant between the Hebrews and Yahweh.

35. The story of the Egyptian bureaucrat Wen-Amon, recounted in the "Individuals in Society" section, is representative of all of the following *except*
    a. decline of Egyptian power.
    b. spread of Zoroastrianism into Egypt.
    c. continued respect of many for the past greatness of Egypt.
    d. continued arrogance of Egyptian officials.

36. During the Babylonian Captivity, the Hebrew religion
    a. was redefined and established.
    b. almost disappeared.
    c. was exposed to Zoroastrianism.
    d. was adopted by the Chaldeans.

37. After Solomon's death, the Hebrew kingdom
    a. continued to consolidate politically.
    b. became a powerful empire.
    c. devolved into a tribal-based society.
    d. split into two separate nations.

38. Many Hebrews resented Solomon for all of the following reasons *except*
    a. his acceptance of other religions.
    b. higher taxes.
    c. his failure to unite the Hebrew kingdom.
    d. his use of forced labor.

39. A fundamental concept of the Jewish religion, the Covenant
    a. implied a deep bond among the Hebrew people.
    b. recognized the diversity of the gods.
    c. implied an agreement between the Hebrews and their god.
    d. recognized that Yahweh was the chief god of the Hebrews.

40. The Jewish Talmud is
    a. the Jewish name for the Bible.
    b. the collection of civil and ceremonial law.
    c. an early version of the Old Testament.
    d. the governing council of the Jewish religion.

41. The most important difference between Yahweh and Mesopotamian gods was Yahweh's
    a. indifference.
    b. spiritual nature.
    c. vengeful character.
    d. care for the individual.

42. In his sermons, the prophet Jeremiah called for
    a. mercy and justice.
    b. harsher punishments for sinners.
    c. a religious crusade against the Persians.
    d. a return to the nomadic life.

43. The most importance source for our knowledge of Hebrew society has been
    a. archaeological excavations.
    b. the Bible.
    c. governmental records.
    d. personal letters and diaries.

44. The most important social institution in Hebrew society was the
    a. family.
    b. village.
    c. nation.
    d. kingdom.

45. As Jews became more urbanized, the role of women in society
    a. became more important.
    b. was more restricted.
    c. was relatively unchanged.
    d. was relegated to religious functions.

46. In ancient Israel, the education of children
    a. was left entirely up to the mother.
    b. took place in organized schools.
    c. was the same for both boys and girls.
    d. was the responsibility of both mothers and fathers.

14 / Small Kingdoms and Mighty Empires in the Near East

47. The dietary rules of the Jews
    a. actually contradict Mosaic law.
    b. are no longer practiced by Orthodox Jews today.
    c. were designed to promote economic activity.
    d. represent the relationship between the Torah and the Talmud.

48. The town of Ugarit is an excellent example of
    a. an imperial capital.
    b. the decline of independent cities and towns in this era.
    c. the harshness with which the Assyrians ruled their empire.
    d. the independent, economically vibrant, yet small state that thrived in this era.

49. The family farm, an important tradition to the Hebrews, was threatened by the
    a. Assyrian invasion of Palestine.
    b. increasing prosperity of the Hebrew society.
    c. development of the Jewish religion.
    d. influx of nomadic tribes into Palestine.

50. The most important factor promoting Assyrian political cohesion and military might was
    a. their warlike religion.
    b. the underdevelopment of Assyrian commerce.
    c. the constant threat of invasion.
    d. the collapse of the Hebrew kingdom.

51. The key reason for the Assyrians' success in conquering and controlling their empire was their
    a. sophisticated and effective military organization.
    b. shrewd diplomacy.
    c. brutality.
    d. respect for and acceptance of other cultures.

52. The destruction of the Assyrian Empire paved the way for the emergence of
    a. many small kingdoms.
    b. Egyptian imperialism.
    c. the Persian Empire.
    d. the Hebrew nation.

53. Assyrian artistic technique known as "frieze" was
    a. a symbolic representation of Assyrian gods.
    b. a series of episodes depicting some event.
    c. characterized by stylized portrayals of lovers.
    d. lost following the collapse of the Assyrian Empire.

54. The Chaldean kings of Babylonia, in their effort to solidify and consolidate power,
    a. neglected commercial and religious aspects of their society.
    b. rejected their own past and adopted much of Medean culture and practices.
    c. sought an alliance with the Assyrians.
    d. consciously attempted to emulate the greatness of Hammurabi's era.

55. The Persians gained a decisive military advantage over the prehistoric natives of Iran by the use of
    a. bronze weaponry.
    b. horses.
    c. siege machinery.
    d. infantry.

56. The early Iranian economy featured all of the following *except*
    a. large-scale, plantation-based agriculture.
    b. brisk trade with outsiders.
    c. prosperous and sturdy peasant-based agriculture.
    d. mining and horse-breeding.

57. The Persian Empire was the creation of
    a. Darius the Great.
    b. Croesus the Rich.
    c. Sargon the Great.
    d. Cyrus the Great.

58. The key government officials in the Persian *satrapies* included all of the following *except*
    a. governor.
    b. high priest.
    c. military commander.
    d. tax collector.

59. Two characteristics that lift Cyrus above the common level of warrior-king were his concept of empire and
    a. concern for economic development.
    b. effective use of military power.
    c. enlightened governance of his empire.
    d. creation of an efficient bureaucracy.

60. The Magi were
    a. provincial governors of the Persian Empire.
    b. evil gods that attempted to make humans evil.
    c. members of the royal council of the Persian kings.
    d. Iranian priests.

61. The collection of religious hymns and poems from Persia is known as the
    a. *Talmud*.
    b. *Torah*.
    c. *Wen-Amon*.
    d. *Zend Avesta*.

62. Ahuramazda and Ahriman
    a. represented good and evil.
    b. were the two largest satrapies in the Persian Empire.
    c. wrote the *Zend Avesta*.
    d. were the most influential disciples of Zoroaster.

63. Zoroaster taught that
    a. life is a constant struggle between good and evil.
    b. humans are mere pawns, manipulated by the gods.
    c. priests should have power over political leaders.
    d. there is only one god.

64. All of the following contributed to the effective governance of the Persian Empire *except*
    a. good communication.
    b. effective administrative structures.
    c. governmental terrorism.
    d. respect for local customs.

65. Zoroastrianism
    a. was imposed throughout the Persian Empire by the emperor.
    b. continued to influence religious thought for centuries.
    c. had little impact beyond its time and place of origin.
    d. was very pessimistic about people and the afterlife.

History and Geography

66. Describe the climate and topography of the Iranian plateau. How did this affect the development of Iranian society and politics?

67. Invasion and migration had a great impact on not only the creation of empires but also on cultural development of the region. Discuss briefly the role of migration and invasion on the spread of Egyptian culture and Hebrew religion.

68. Examine the map of the Persian empire (Map 2.3). What areas did the empire include? Can we call the Persian empire a "world empire"?

CHAPTER 3

THE LEGACY OF GREECE

Key Terms

1. liminal
2. *Theogony*
3. Sophocles
4. Linear B
5. Homer
6. Lycurgus
7. polis
8. acropolis
9. democracy
10. hoplites
11. Solon
12. boule
13. Archilochus
14. Delian League
15. Herodotus
16. Sappho
17. Pre-Socratics
18. Sophists
19. *The Republic*
20. Olympic Games
21. Philip of Macedon

Essay Questions

22. Greek civilization was rocked continually by destructive wars. Using specific examples from the Second Messenian War, the Persian wars, and the Peloponnesian War, discuss and analyze the causes and consequences of this pattern. In general, how did warfare affect the development of Greek civilization?

    This essay attempts to analyze the impact of warfare on the development of both domestic political development and relations among the various city-states of Greece. The wars, despite the differences in causes and consequences among the three, can reveal the role of warfare on Greek civilization. Finally, a good essay should address the role of warfare not only in the development

18 / The Legacy of Greece

of both domestic politics and relations among the city-states, but also the effect on the Greeks themselves.

23. Athens and Sparta are often presented as the models of Greek political development: one militaristic and aristocratic, the other intellectual and democratic. How accurate is this appraisal? To answer this question, one should begin with a description of the social and political evolution of both city-states. What similarities and differences do you find? How do you account for the differences?

    For this essay, the student should describe rather fully the development of Athenian and Spartan political and social institutions; this should include such aspects as: the Lycurgan regime of Sparta and the various reforms in Athens; the suppression of individualism in Sparta and its exaltation in Athens; and the militarism and exclusivity of both. The essay should indicate the differences between each as well as the similarities. Most importantly, the good essay will provide the reasons behind the divergences and congruencies, which can be applied to an understanding of Greek history in general.

24. "Art is the mirror of Life." How did Greek artists, architects, and writers reflect the society in which they lived? What were the basic themes of their endeavors?

    In this essay, the student should first identify the basic themes of Greek artistic endeavor, such as individualism, energy, rationalism, and humanism. The essay should include examples from both the Lyric Age (Archilochus, Sappho) and Periclean Athens (Acropolis, plays of Aeschylus and Sophocles). Finally, the essay should indicate the societal reflection in art: Archilochus and patriotism and the energy of colonization; Sappho and personal individualism; the Acropolis and rationalism and the glorification of human achievements; Athenian theater and its roots in the political events of Athens.

25. "Perhaps the greatest legacy of Greece is intellectual." Trace the development of philosophy and science from the pre-Socratic origins through Aristotle. What were the most significant developments? What was the general principle which guided Greek philosophers?

    For this question, the student should provide a narrative of the development of Greek science and philosophy from Thales to Aristotle; this section should include such things as the belief in basic elements, boundless nature of the universe, evolution, atomic theory, ethics (Aesop), medicine, Sophist concentration on logic and study of human beings, Socratic method, Platonic dualism and political thought, and the impressive achievements of Aristotle in natural science and political philosophy. The good essay should stress the Greek belief that the universe could be explained and understood, that is, rational thought; second, the essay should emphasize the Greek concentration on the study of human beings.

26. Like Mesopotamian society, Greek civilization lacked political unity. Why? How did disunity affect the development of Greek society in general? What, if any, were the factors that fostered homogeneity?

    To explain the lack of political unity, one should emphasize the geography of the Greek peninsula. Next, the distinctiveness and independence of the Greek city-states should be discussed, using Athens and Sparta as examples; the Peloponnesian War and the Macedonian conquest of Greece can also be used to indicate the independent nature of Greek civilization. Finally, the Olympic

Games, language, and philosophical inquiry can all be used as an example of unity.

27. Describe the political development of Athens from the reforms of Solon through Pericles' reign. What factors motivated reformers? To what extent was Athens a true democracy?

    This essay should begin with a description of the evolution of the Athenian political system. This should include: the conditions prior to Solon's efforts, Solon's reforms relative to debt and slavery, his division of Athenian society; Pisistratus' use of the common people against his aristocratic enemies; and Cleisthenes' reforms. Motivation should next be considered, from Solon's concern for the Athenian polis to the political struggles between rival leaders. Next, the essay should consider the imperialistic nature of Athens following the defeat of the Persians, specifically the role of Cimon in turning the Delian League into a vehicle for Athenian expansion and Pericles' use of League funds for the beautification of Athens. Finally, one should assess the nature of the Athenian polity in terms of which segments of society had a voice in political affairs, which segments did not, and which Athenians actually exercised political power.

28. The city-state has been called a "community of citizens." How does this definition reflect the reality of the situation in Greek city-states? Who were the citizens and what rights and responsibilities did they possess? What segments of the population were not considered citizens? What rights and duties did these people have?

    In this essay, one should first define the concept of citizenship and then identify those groups in society which were citizens and those which were not. For those groups which were not citizens, the student should describe their legal protections and responsibilities. Finally, returning to the definition of citizenship, a connection should be made between citizenship and the ownership of property, place of birth, and military service.

29. What was the role of women, in terms of opportunities and obligations, in Greek city-states? How did social status affect those opportunities and obligations? How did Athenian women differ from Spartan women? How does the example of Aspasia underscore the generalizations made in the textbook?

    This question requires a description of the life led by Greek women; this should include household duties, marriage, citizenship, property rights, seclusion of upper-class women, ability of and necessity for lower-class women to appear in public. The concept of liminal power must be discussed. The more active and open public life of Spartan women should be assessed, with the explanation of this development addressed, especially the Lycurgan regime and its imposition of militaristic duties on all Spartans. The "Individuals in Society" feature on Aspasia should be mentioned as an example of a person rising to the highest rank in society.

30. The polis was the quintessential Greek political structure. What were the roots of this form of polity? What were the general characteristics of the polis?

    A brief mention of the misinterpretation of the term "polis" as city-state should start the essay. Next, the essay should place the origins in the upheavals of the late Mycenaean period, with the role and preservation of local governmental and social, economic, and religious institutions and functions stressed. The impact of the Dorians follows. The rural-urban nature should be described, with the significant religious role of the countryside mentioned.

Multiple-Choice Questions

31. According to the text, prehistoric Minoan civilization was
    a. quite warlike.
    b. poor and agrarian.
    c. wealthy and peaceful.
    d. democratic.

32. Aristotle's *Politics* portrays the polis as
    a. the degeneration of kingdoms.
    b. a natural, almost biological, development.
    c. the most perfect form of political organization imaginable.
    d. an unexpected and unnatural evolution of political structures.

33. The geography of Greece
    a. had little impact on the development of Greek society.
    b. was a divisive force in Greek life.
    c. unified the Greek city-states.
    d. had a positive influence on Greek intellectual life.

34. The Mycenaean civilization was probably destroyed by
    a. natural catastrophe.
    b. foreign invasions.
    c. slave revolts.
    d. internecine wars.

35. The works of Homer
    a. were realistic accounts of Greek history.
    b. described the development of Greek religion.
    c. portrayed engaging but flawed human beings.
    d. provided a blueprint for future political development.

36. Hesiod's *Works and Days* indicates that he
    a. had faith in divine justice.
    b. believed the gods to be cruel and uncaring.
    c. believed there to be no ethical basis for existence.
    d. hated and feared the gods.

37. During the late Mycenaean period, towns and villages
    a. had developed a number of distinct, local institutions.
    b. had virtually disappeared throughout Greece.
    c. were unified under the king of Mycenae.
    d. were administered by Persian satraps.

38. In the early polis, the *chora* (countryside) was characterized by all of the following *except*
    a. food production.
    b. forming the territorial possessions of the polis.
    c. site of religious shrines and sanctuaries.
    d. location of the marketplace.

39. For protection, Greek city-states relied on
    a. large, professional standing armies.
    b. a militia of citizens from all socio-economic levels.
    c. the harsh geographic reality of Greece.
    d. armies of slaves and mercenaries.

40. Tyranny
    a. was the site of the Athenian temple to Athena.
    b. is the seizure of power by unconstitutional means.
    c. is the most efficient form of government.
    d. was rare in the Greek polis.

41. The man most responsible for turning the Delian League into a vehicle of Athenian imperialism was
    a. Pericles
    b. Solon.
    c. Cimon.
    d. Philip.

42. The greatest weakness of the Greek city-state was
    a. its size.
    b. the loose requirements of citizenship.
    c. its individualism.
    d. the rigidity of its political constitutions.

43. Sappho is best known for her
    a. erotic poetry.
    b. scientific theories.
    c. epic sagas.
    d. religious poems.

44. Greek colonies
    a. were quickly conquered by native warrior-states.
    b. remained under the rule of the founding city.
    c. adapted to local customs and culture.
    d. spread Greek culture throughout the Mediterranean world.

45. The Lycurgan regime in Sparta resulted in
    a. a society ruled by an aristocratic, warrior elite.
    b. increasingly democratic institutions, resembling Athens.
    c. a tyrannical overthrow of the old constitution.
    d. the erosion of Spartan military power.

46. Spartan women
    a. were sheltered from the harshness of the Lycurgan regimen.
    b. enjoyed a more active and public life than most other Greek women.
    c. were responsible only for having babies.
    d. were more oppressed than most other Greek women.

47. Towns and villages of the late Mycenaean period had all of the following *except*
    a. importance, economically.
    b. a cult of their own deity.
    c. a strong military presence.
    d. a social system.

48. Solon's reforms in Athens
    a. established democracy in Athens.
    b. established social equality.
    c. gave commoners a place in the assembly.
    d. abolished slavery.

49. The most significant institution created by Cleisthenes' political reforms was the
    a. boule.
    b. polis.
    c. ostracism.
    d. archon.

50. Underlying Athenian democracy was the belief that
    a. there was a union between the citizen and the state.
    b. the state exists for itself.
    c. the state exists for the good of the citizen.
    d. political power belongs in the hands of the aristocrats.

51. The Greeks' defeat of the Persians
    a. lessened the individualism of the Greek polis.
    b. allowed the Greeks to develop their own civilization.
    c. destroyed the Persian Empire.
    d. weakened Athens.

52. The pan-Hellenic alliance was designed to
    a. fight the Persians.
    b. write a constitution for all Greece.
    c. organize Greek migration.
    d. destroy Athenian imperialism.

53. Thucydides attributed the brutality of the Athenians during the Peloponnesian War to the
    a. high stakes of the war.
    b. length of the war.
    c. cruelty of the gods.
    d. ambition of the people.

54. The Acropolis has been called the epitome of Greek art and spirit because
    a. all of the buildings were dedicated to the gods.
    b. of its immense buildings.
    c. it expresses the Greeks' fascination with the human and rational.
    d. it expresses the Greeks' fascination with the polis.

55. Greek artists attempted to evoke human
    a. dignity.
    b. frailty.
    c. passion.
    d. sexuality.

56. In general the themes explored by Athenian dramatists included all of the following *except*
    a. romantic love stories.
    b. religion and society.
    c. the relationship between society and the individual.
    d. the nature of good and evil.

57. Most Athenians supported themselves as
    a. craftsmen.
    b. farmers.
    c. unskilled laborers.
    d. tradesmen.

58. Slavery in Athens
    a. never replaced free labor.
    b. was quite rare.
    c. supplied the manual labor force.
    d. was harsh.

59. The main source of legal and social protection for Athenian women was
    a. the legal code.
    b. a tradition of respect for women.
    c. her dowry.
    d. the bride's gift.

60. The anthropological term *liminal* refers to the
    a. secondary status of women in Athens.
    b. representation of women in Greek art.
    c. dowry rites of Athenian women.
    d. vital but unofficial role of women in Athenian society.

61. Each Greek polis had its own minor deities and cults, which
    a. made the inhabitants more religious.
    b. gave the priesthood a strong political position.
    c. enhanced civic pride.
    d. confused the people about whom to worship.

62. The most important function of the athletic contests held at Olympia was to
    a. bring Greeks together culturally and religiously.
    b. create a pan-Hellenic trading network.
    c. find the greatest athletes.
    d. increase the friction between rival city-states.

63. Sophists believed that
    a. all areas are the proper subject of study.
    b. human beings are the only proper subject of study.
    c. natural science is the only proper subject of study.
    d. logic is the only proper subject of study.

64. According to Socrates, human beings can find true happiness only
    a. through good citizenship.
    b. through philosophy.
    c. by pursuing excellence.
    d. by being happily married.

65. Plato's great contribution to philosophy was
    a. the founding of the Academy.
    b. the atomic theory.
    c. publishing the dialogues of Socrates.
    d. the theory of eternal forms.

66. Herodotus' main theme was the
    a. decline of Greek values.
    b. past glories and heroes of Greek Dark Ages.
    c. conflict between east and west.
    d. role of the gods in everyday life.

67. Pericles paid for his extensive building program through
    a. higher taxes.
    b. loans.
    c. appropriating Delian League funds.
    d. his private fortune.

68. Draco's law code embodied the ideal that
    a. the wealthy should make the law.
    b. leniency is more effective than harshness.
    c. law codes of all city-states should be uniform.
    d. the law belonged to the citizens.

69. The culmination of Pre-Socratic thought was the theory that
    a. four substances -- air, fire, earth, water -- make up the universe.
    b. one god had created the world.
    c. the universe was complex and unknowable.
    d. humans had achieved physical perfection.

70. The ideal state described by Aristotle's *Politics* depended upon
    a. a strong military.
    b. a thriving economy.
    c. educated and tolerant citizens and leaders.
    d. rigid social structure, based on wealth.

71. The most important factor in the success of Philip II of Macedon in Greece resulted from
    a. his generalship.
    b. internecine warfare among the Greeks.
    c. superior military technology.
    d. the treachery of Athens and Sparta.

72. In the Funeral Oration, presented in the "Individuals in Society" feature, Pericles' depiction of the proper Athenian lady
    a. was a woman who stayed at home.
    b. accurately described Aspasia, his lover.
    c. urged women to play a more active role in the affairs of the polis.
    d. urged women to reject traditional morals in order to attract new husbands.

History and Geography

73. Describe the geography of the areas inhabited by the Greeks. How did geography affect the development of Greek civilization?

74. After examining Map 3.2, indicate the spread of Greek colonization. What were the causes of this colonization?

75. Describe the physical attributes of a typical polis and explain the influence of geography on this layout.

CHAPTER 4

HELLENISTIC DIFFUSION

Key Terms

1. Battle of Ipsus
2. Ay Khanoum
3. koine
4. politeuma
5. Great Silk Road
6. Tyche
7. mystery religions
8. Samian pottery
9. Diogenes of Sinope
10. Stoics
11. Epicureans
12. Aristarchus of Samos
13. New Comedy
14. *Elements of Geometry*
15. Archimedes
16. Theophrastus
17. Dogmatic school
18. Empiric school
19. natural law
20. Celtiberians

Essay Questions

21. The Hellenistic civilization saw the spread of cities founded by Alexander and his successors. What was the role and impact of these new cities?

    The student should discuss the urban nature of the Hellenistic world. This discussion should include the motivation behind the founding of the new cities and the growth of established cities, the official functions of the cities, their role in the spread of Greek ideas and peoples, and their importance in the emergence of the trading networks in this era. A good essay should also mention how the urbanized Hellenistic world facilitated Roman conquest of the Mediterranean world.

22. "Perhaps the greatest consequence of Alexander's conquest was economic." Discuss this

statement. In what ways did the pattern of economic activity change in the Hellenistic era? What were the long-range consequences of this change?

To answer this question, one should describe and analyze the emergence of trade, especially in commodities such as grain and potteries, as a consequence of the growth of urban civilization. This can be compared to the more self-sufficient nature of previous civilizations in the region. Long-range consequences would include such things as the spread of Greek culture, exemplified by the use of koine as the lingua franca of the Mediterranean world and the use of the Attic standard for coinage, large-scale agriculture, slave and other forms of cheap labor, which suppressed technological innovation, and the unification of the Mediterranean world.

23. In the Hellenistic period, women enjoyed a new prominence. How had their life chances improved? How does Plutarch's description of Queen Mother Cratesicleia support or detract from this assertion? What caused the improvement?

For this question, one should focus on the enhanced opportunities, in education, medicine, and literature, for women of the upper classes, based upon economic circumstances and political evolution. Spartan legal traditions concerning property rights should be cited. The story of Cratesicleia not only indicates the role of women, albeit passively, in Hellenistic politics and diplomacy, but also the liminal power of women in this era. Despite legal handicaps, the participation of women in economic affairs was the primary reason for this change.

24. "Despite its undeniable brilliance, Hellenistic science was remarkable for its impracticality." Who were the great thinkers of the period and what were their contributions? Why was Hellenistic science so impractical?

In addition to a narrative describing the various thinkers and inventors of the Hellenistic age (Aristarchus, Ptolemy, Euclid, Eratosthenes, Theophrastus, Archimedes and both schools of medical thought), a good essay should provide an explanation for why Hellenistic science had no practical applications, a function of the cheapness of human labor at the time.

25. "The Hellenistic city offered cultural and economic opportunities but did not foster a sense of united, integrated enterprise." How accurate is this assessment?

First, one should describe briefly the classic Hellenic polis. Next, one should discuss the origins of the Hellenistic cities: Greek monarchs' needs for loyal bureaucrats and soldiers. A description of the new cities - cultural offerings, architecture, economic opportunities - along with a discussion of the constitutional arrangements should then follow: institutions of the classical polis without the sovereignty. The generalized dislocation of the period should be used to emphasize the lack of civic loyalty evident in the Hellenistic cities.

26. The Hellenistic period saw a substantial "democratization" of philosophy. Describe this democratization of philosophy and offer a well-supported conclusion as to why more and more people in this era turned to philosophy for comfort. What other alternatives existed which offered solace to the confused and concerned of the Hellenistic era?

First, the essay should describe the major schools of thought in the Hellenistic era: Cynicism, Epicureanism, and Stoicism. Following this description, the essay should then turn to an analysis of why more people needed the "consolation of philosophy": failure of new Hellenistic cities to meet the emotional needs of their citizens, role of Tyche, near constant warfare, the harshness of life for most people. The essay should then discuss the emergence of mystery religions, including a brief description of the general characteristics of these religions, as an alternative to the schools of philosophy discussed earlier.

Multiple-Choice Questions

27. Alexander's campaign into Asia Minor was
    a. only a campaign of conquest.
    b. primarily a religious pilgrimage.
    c. a military campaign and an expedition of discovery.
    d. a complete failure.

28. Alexander's expedition eastward halted at the Hyphasis River because the
    a. Macedonian army mutinied.
    b. powerful Indian army repulsed the Macedonians.
    c. young emperor died.
    d. omens from the gods were unfavorable.

29. The evidence against the view that Alexander was tolerant and humane includes all of the following *except* the
    a. murder of an official who had saved his life.
    b. assassination of his father and brothers.
    c. assassination of several officials.
    d. slaughter of Iranians and Indians.

30. The greatest consequence of Alexander's conquests was the
    a. destruction of the Persian Empire.
    b. opening of the East to the spread of Hellenism.
    c. knowledge he gathered during his campaigns.
    d. establishment of trade with India.

31. The Battle of Ipsus
    a. resulted in the Macedonian conquest of India.
    b. launched Alexander's campaign against the Persian Empire.
    c. ended with the death of Alexander the Great.
    d. determined that no one general would rule Alexander's empire.

32. The political history of the Hellenistic period was dominated by Greek leagues and
    a. sovereign city-states.
    b. the Macedonian Empire.
    c. great monarchies.
    d. small kingdoms.

33. The evidence from Ay Khanoum indicates that
    a. natives quickly assimilated Greek immigrants.
    b. Greeks and natives embraced aspects of each other's culture.
    c. native culture was completely destroyed.
    d. Hellenistic cities had little impact in the East.

34. The mass-manufactured pottery so popular during the Hellenistic period was known as
    a. Attic standard pottery.
    b. Tyche-style pottery.
    c. Samian pottery.
    d. Archimedian pottery.

35. Vitally important to the success of the Seleucid dynasty was the
    a. establishment of a state religion.
    b. adoption of Eastern culture.
    c. abolition of slavery.
    d. establishment of military colonies.

36. The Hellenistic city
    a. was completely subordinate to its king.
    b. had limited autonomy.
    c. had a complicated, formal relationship with its king.
    d. was an independent city-state.

37. The role of women in Hellenistic society
    a. was more limited than that of Hellenic women.
    b. improved for upper-class and royal women.
    c. improved for women of all social classes.
    d. suffered as a result of increased commercial activity.

38. The Hellenization of Easterners in the successor states can best be described as
    a. thorough.
    b. brutal.
    c. a veneer.
    d. uneven.

39. Luxury items became more of a necessity than a luxury as a result of
    a. royal decrees.
    b. increased volume of trade.
    c. population decline.
    d. population growth.

40. The bureaucracies of the Hellenistic kingdoms usually were recruited from
    a. Rome.
    b. Persia.
    c. Greece.
    d. local, native populations.

30 / Hellenistic Diffusion

41. The term "koine" refers to
    a. Greco-Macedonian immigrants to the new cities in the East.
    b. political organization which governed Jewish affairs.
    c. the philosophical belief that fate, Tyche, ruled the world.
    d. a common dialect that developed during the Hellenistic period.

42. For the most part, Jews in Hellenistic cities were
    a. rarely Hellenized.
    b. ruthlessly oppressed.
    c. thoroughly Hellenized.
    d. enslaved.

43. The political corporation formed by the Jews in Hellenistic cities was known as the
    a. Tyche.
    b. koine.
    c. politeuma.
    d. ghetto.

44. The expansion of commerce in the Hellenistic world was a product of all of the following *except*
    a. standard coinage.
    b. increased geographical knowledge.
    c. agricultural surpluses.
    d. peace.

45. The most important commodity in the Hellenistic period was
    a. grain.
    b. wine.
    c. fish.
    d. gold.

46. In the Hellenistic world, slavery was
    a. important for maintaining the army.
    b. suppressed by all the successor dynasties.
    c. strictly an urban phenomenon.
    d. vitally important to the economy.

47. The uniqueness of Hellenistic culture lay in its
    a. complete Greekness.
    b. fusion of Greek and Eastern cultures.
    c. adoption by the Romans.
    d. destruction of native religions.

48. The lack of mechanization in Hellenistic industries was a product of
    a. abundant cheap labor.
    b. the dominance of agriculture.
    c. the few, and mediocre, scientists.
    d. the fear of rebellion by the unemployed.

49. The Ptolemaic dynasty in Egypt discouraged slavery and the slave trade because
    a. of the dynasty's philosophical distaste for the trade in human beings.
    b. the dynasty's religion forbade slavery.
    c. slaves would have competed with free labor.
    d. Egyptian priests warned of divine retribution.

50. Over time the Greeks sought spiritual solace in all of the following *except*
    a. philosophy.
    b. Tyche.
    c. Judaism.
    d. mystery religions.

51. Hellenistic kings did not spread Greek religion because
    a. they considered religion to be a private matter.
    b. many had adopted Eastern religions.
    c. they feared the reaction of local populations.
    d. they were jealous of the power of the Greek priesthood.

52. The primary advantage of the mystery religions over the old Greek cults was that
    a. they typically worshiped a female god.
    b. their initiation rites were simple.
    c. they appealed to all groups in society.
    d. the new religions were supported by the kings.

53. All of the following were traits of the mystery religions *except*
    a. a community of initiates united with their god.
    b. a promise of eternal life for the soul after death.
    c. emotional intensity.
    d. the use of human sacrifice.

54. The widespread study of philosophy during the Hellenistic period was a product of all of the following *except* the
    a. decline of the polis.
    b. greater intellectual curiosity of the people.
    c. instability of life.
    d. decline of traditional religion.

55. Dogmatism was
    a. a school of philosophy.
    b. the successor dynasty in Macedonia.
    c. the belief that fate was cruel and vindictive.
    d. a school of medical thought and practice.

56. The Cynics believed in
    a. nothing.
    b. tradition.
    c. rejecting material goods.
    d. the sanctity of Greek religion.

57. Euclid is most famous for his work in
    a. astronomy.
    b. mathematics.
    c. medicine.
    d. law.

58. Epicureans advocated
    a. pleasure in moderation.
    b. sensual dissipation.
    c. violent emotion.
    d. active political involvement.

59. Menander's plays were typified by all of the following *except* that they were
    a. based on domestic situations.
    b. realistic.
    c. skillfully constructed.
    d. based on tragic and/or political plays from the Classical period.

60. The most significant achievement of the Stoics was the concept of
    a. natural law.
    b. living in accordance with nature.
    c. a universal political state.
    d. passive resistance.

61. The prominence of women in Hellenistic society was largely due to
    a. the natural law philosophy of the Stoics.
    b. their domination of mystery religions.
    c. their increased participation in economic affairs.
    d. a decline in the male population.

62. The greatest library of the Hellenistic era could be found in the city of
    a. Athens.
    b. Alexandria.
    c. Ay Khanoum.
    d. Persepolis.

63. The greatest thinker of the Hellenistic period was
    a. Archimedes.
    b. Euclid.
    c. Theophrastus.
    d. Eratosthenes.

64. During the Hellenistic period, the western Mediterranean was dominated by all of the following groups, at one time or another, *except*
    a. Berbers.
    b. Macedonians.
    c. Phoenicians.
    d. Celtiberians.

65. The Dogmatic school of medicine based its medical research on
    a. speculation and study of anatomy.
    b. observation and herbal lore.
    c. syllogistic method.
    d. observation of disease symptoms.

66. The major consequences of the conquests of Alexander and the creation of the successor kingdoms included all of the following *except*
    a. a resurgence of monarchical government.
    b. the active role of royal women in politics.
    c. the weakening of Greek culture.
    d. an era of peace and stability.

67. The Hellenistic period provided the basis for all of the following *except*
    a. the destruction of the civilizations of the Near East.
    b. the rise of Christianity.
    c. a new cosmopolitan society.
    d. the Roman Empire.

History and Geography

68. What was the extent of Alexander's empire? What was the geographic basis of the successor kingdoms into which the empire was divided after his death?

69. How did the Hellenistic world become more unified during this era?

70. Describe the various commodities which were part and parcel of the commercial trading network of the Hellenistic world. (Do not limit yourself to thinking in purely materialistic terms.) How did this commercial network enhance the unification of the Mediterranean world?

CHAPTER 5

THE RISE OF ROME

Key Terms

1. Latium
2. Etruscans
3. Senate
4. plebeians
5. *civitas sine suffragio*
6. tribune
7. law of equity
8. Law of the Twelve Tables
9. Hannibal
10. Pyrrhus
11. Cato the Elder
12. paterfamilias
13. *Mare nostrum*
14. Scipionic Circle
15. latifundia
16. Tiberius Gracchus
17. Sulla
18. Gaius Marius
19. Julius Caesar
20. Spartacus

Essay Questions

21. Imperial conquests between 282 and 146 B.C. brought new ideas and new ways of doing things into Roman society, creating a sharp contrast with traditional values and practices. Two men, Cato and Scipio Aemilianus, are excellent examples of the old and the new. Compare the lifestyles of these individuals. How does the account of popular religion and magic in "Listening to the Past" illustrate the traditional lifestyle? How can we account for the transformation from the traditional to the new lifestyle?

    For this essay, one should describe how each man lived, including such things as foods eaten, physical setting, role of family, kinship, religious practices, education, and recreation. A description of the curses found in "Listening to the Past" provides more evidence about the traditional lifestyle; a good essay should demonstrate the difference between the superstitions of traditional religion and the rational philosophy of the Greeks. The explanation for the transformation lies in the acquisition of empire, especially Greece and the Hellenistic cities.

22. With their victory in the Punic Wars, the Romans were able to transform the Mediterranean into *mare nostrum*, "our sea." How did this come about? Trace the conflict between Rome and Carthage from beginning to end. Why did the Romans prevail?

    First, there should be a concise narrative of the history of the Punic Wars. Second, the causes of Roman victory should be discussed, including the traditional Roman values and practices such as tenacity (the building of a fleet is a good example) and bravery, and also Roman skill as politicians and diplomats, through the creation of alliances with the other Italian peoples.

23. The Roman Republic underwent two great social upheavals: the Struggle of the Orders and the civil wars of the late Republic. Compare these two upheavals in terms of causes, participants, and results. Who profited in each case? Was Rome better off after each upheaval? Explain your answer.

    Initially, the answer should describe both upheavals: for the Struggle of the Orders, include the plebeians' desire to share in the political process, their leverage from serving in the army during the early wars, the general strike, patricians and plebeians, the various legal and constitutional reforms which resulted; for the problems of the late Republic, include the problems of governing the empire, unhappiness of Italian allies, growth of large-scale agriculture, impoverishment of many Romans, role of army generals, personal ambitions of many reformers. In conclusion, one should discuss the improvement and solidification of the Roman constitution resulting from the Struggle of the Orders, without widespread violence, while at the end of the Republic, political violence (ushered in by the assassinations of the Gracchi) became the order of the day, ultimately destroying the Republic.

24. "The acquisition of empire spelled doom for the Republic." Assess the validity of this quote. To answer this question effectively, one should consider the problems resulting from the wars of conquest (282-146 B.C.) and the attempts to solve these serious problems.

    In this essay, one should fully describe the problems (burgeoning slavery, decline of the free peasant farmer, economic competition from the provinces, enhanced political power of the generals, increased influence of Greek culture) of empire. Second, the reforming efforts of such men as the Gracchi, Gaius Marius, Sulla, and Julius Caesar must be described and analyzed for their effectiveness in dealing with the problems. Finally, one should assess the relationship between the fragility of constitutional governments and the impact of overseas conquest.

25. "Rome's great achievement lay in the ability of the Romans not only to conquer peoples but to incorporate them into the Roman system." Discuss this statement, supporting your conclusions. Do you think the statement is accurate? Why or why not?

    This question asks the student to describe Roman relations with the peoples they conquered, including other Italians, Greeks, Hellenistic kingdoms, Iberians, and northern Europeans. The answer should discuss the Roman practice of extending at least partial rights of citizenship to those peoples the Romans considered civilized, Roman alliances with other peoples, and the Roman policy of attempting to avoid formal annexation unless it was deemed necessary. The extension of full citizenship, by Julius Caesar, to the provincial subjects should conclude this discussion. A thoughtful essay should also compare the Roman practice with that of the Greeks, to show the unique and wise nature of the Roman system.

26. If any one word could adequately describe the Romans, it would be *imperialistic*. Discuss the Romans imperialism to 27 B.C. What motivated Roman conquests? How did Roman policies differ regarding the civilized East and the barbarian West?

First, one should describe Roman conquests up to the end of the Republic. Next, the essay should assess the motivation behind such conquests, especially the Roman perception of the necessity for such conquests to insure the security of Rome and how this became a seemingly constant need as the empire grew; the ambitions of individual generals in the late Republic should also be considered. Roman military colonization efforts should also be discussed, both those in Italy in the third century B.C. and those established in the late Republic by Julius Caesar. Finally, Roman policies in the civilized East and barbarian West should be described: reluctance to conquer in the East compared to the policy of conquest in the West and why this was considered necessary.

27. The family was a very important institution in traditional Roman society. Describe this institution. What was the daily life of a Roman family like? What was the role of religion? What was the role of women in the family? How did the family reflect Roman values?

One must first describe the paterfamilias and his relationship with other family members. A discussion of treatment and education of children should follow. Next, daily life should be described, found in the section on Cato. Religion, including role of the paterfamilias in religious observances, household gods, festivals and curses, should be discussed. Finally, the role of women, especially the mother, should be described; a thoughtful essay should compare the role of the mother to that of the paterfamilias. Those aspects of the family which underscore traditional Roman values should be identified: importance of order, obedience, and hard work.

Multiple-Choice Questions

28. The geography of Italy
    a. was very harsh.
    b. pushed Romans to expand into the Adriatic Sea.
    c. encouraged Romans to look to the Mediterranean Sea.
    d. fostered political fragmentation.

29. All of the following statements about Etruscan society are accurate *except* that
    a. its cities resembled Greek city-states.
    b. the Etruscans migrated to the Italian peninsula from Mesopotamia.
    c. the Etruscans imported luxury goods from the eastern Mediterranean.
    d. the Etruscans formed a loosely organized league of cities which dominated the peninsula.

30. The religious leaders of the Celts were known as the
    a. Druids.
    b. Etruscans.
    c. Fasces.
    d. Magi.

31. The Romans, unlike the Greeks, were masterful
    a. warriors.
    b. politicians.
    c. diplomats.
    d. sailors.

32. Roman roads, which were used well into the medieval era, facilitated all of the following *except*
    a. easy and relatively rapid communication between Rome and its colonies.
    b. quick movement of troops.
    c. growth of trade.
    d. expansion of slavery in the Roman Republic.

33. The Republic official whose function was to oversee the administration of justice and interpret the law was the
    a. censor.
    b. praetor.
    c. aedile.
    d. consul.

34. In the early Republic, Roman society was divided into
    a. patricians and plebeians.
    b. Romans and non-Romans.
    c. urban and rural dwellers.
    d. citizens and slaves.

35. Before the Struggle of the Orders, plebeians' voice in government was articulated by the
    a. Senate.
    b. Comitia curiata.
    c. Pomerium.
    d. Concilium plebis.

36. The Senate's importance was primarily a product of
    a. the senators' wealth.
    b. its stability and continuity.
    c. the weakness of the other political institutions.
    d. its control of the army.

37. Roman law had as its underlying principle the
    a. concept of social justice.
    b. protection of citizens' lives and property.
    c. prevention of social and political upheaval.
    d. separation of political powers.

38. The law of equity stipulates that legal decisions should be based on
    a. the good of the state.
    b. that which pleases the prince is law.
    c. what is believed to be right and just to all parties
    d. the social status of the litigants in a particular case.

39. By the late Republic, Roman jurists were reaching decisions based on *ius*
    a. *civile*.
    b. *senatium*
    c. *criminale*.
    d. *naturale*.

40. During the Struggle of the Orders, the plebeians' leverage stemmed from their
    a. control of agriculture.
    b. increasing wealth.
    c. importance to the army.
    d. control of the urban economy.

41. The main issue in the Struggle of the Orders was the
    a. plebeians' efforts to obtain recognition of their rights.
    b. abolition of the latifundia and state ownership of land.
    c. extension of citizenship to non-Romans.
    d. reform of slavery in Rome.

42. The Struggle of the Orders resulted in
    a. anarchy and class warfare.
    b. greater unity of all Romans.
    c. plebeian control of Rome.
    d. the abolition of the Republic.

43. The challenge to Roman control of the Mediterranean came from
    a. Ptolemaic Egypt.
    b. Carthage.
    c. Alexandria.
    d. the Etruscans.

44. The Carthaginian general who brought the Second Punic War to the gates of Rome was
    a. Scipio Africanus.
    b. Pyrrhus.
    c. Tarquin the Proud.
    d. Hannibal.

45. In Roman law, the term *ius gentium* refers to
    a. business and property law.
    b. the concept of equity.
    c. a universal law, applied to all people.
    d. lawyers and judges.

46. The term *mare nostrum* refers to the
    a. impact of Hellenism on Roman society.
    b. legal status of Roman mothers.
    c. Roman conquest of the Mediterranean world.
    d. alliance between Rome and the rest of the Italian peninsula.

47. The most important factor causing change in the late Republic was
    a. the acquisition of empire.
    b. the Struggle of the Orders.
    c. the advent of Christianity.
    d. enlightened reformers.

48. In Roman families the paterfamilias was the
    a. family farm.
    b. family council, composed of all adult males.
    c. oldest dominant male, with near absolute power.
    d. marriage contract between husband and wife.

49. In traditional Roman families, the mother was expected to display all of the following virtues *except*
    a. fidelity.
    b. intellectual curiosity.
    c. dedication to the family.
    d. modesty.

50. With the acquisition of empire, slavery became
    a. limited to Africans.
    b. unnecessary.
    c. more widespread.
    d. economically unimportant.

51. The text uses the lives of Cato the Elder and Scipio Aemilianus to illustrate the
    a. difference between patrician and plebeian lifestyles.
    b. lifestyles of the patrician elites in the cities.
    c. impact of the Struggle of the Orders.
    d. changes that resulted from Roman conquests.

52. The life of Scipio Aemilianus illustrates the
    a. unchanging nature of everyday life in Rome.
    b. lifestyle of patrician families.
    c. influence of Hellenism on Roman patricians.
    d. urban lifestyle of the common people of Rome.

53. The wars of conquest resulted in all of the following *except*
    a. the destruction of Hellenic culture.
    b. agitation by Italians for full citizenship.
    c. impoverishment of the Roman farmer-soldier.
    d. extensive use of slaves in all aspects of the economy.

54. All of the following were reforms associated with the Struggle of the Orders *except*
    a. Law of the Twelve Tables.
    b. Licinian-Sextian Rogations.
    c. tribunes.
    d. comitia centuriata.

55. The Scipionic Circle refers to the
    a. increasing influence of Hellenism in Roman society and culture.
    b. reformers who sought to address the problems of the late Republic.
    c. Italian allies closest to Rome.
    d. reforms which were the climax of the Struggle of the Orders.

56. The term *latifundia* refers to
    a. land conquered by Roman armies.
    b. a new social class created by imperial expansion.
    c. huge agricultural estates.
    d. the military reforms of Marius.

57. The most divisive and explosive issue resulting from the wars of conquest was that of
    a. citizenship for non-Romans.
    b. the spread of Greek influence.
    c. the spread of slavery.
    d. land reform.

58. The main feature of the reform program of Tiberius Gracchus was
    a. providing free bread to the poor of Rome.
    b. distributing public land to impoverished Romans.
    c. the abolition of the Senate.
    d. establishing colonies of ex-soldiers throughout the empire.

59. The murder of Tiberius Gracchus
    a. illustrated the hatred between the classes.
    b. triggered an era of political violence.
    c. was engineered by his rival, Julius Caesar.
    d. showed the growing influence of Hellenistic political solutions.

60. The slave revolt led by Spartacus
    a. led to the collapse of Sulla's constitution and renewal of civil war.
    b. had virtually no impact on the course of events in the late Republic.
    c. resulted in fundamental reforms in the institution of slavery.
    d. was used by Julius Caesar as a justification for his seizure of power.

61. The innovations in military recruitment of Gaius Marius
    a. were approved by the Senate.
    b. were designed to prevent civil war.
    c. created private armies loyal to their generals, not Rome.
    d. reestablished the Roman army as a citizen-soldier institution.

62. Cicero, featured in "Individuals in Society," is best remembered for his
    a. military conquests.
    b. literary achievements.
    c. political career.
    d. sweeping reform plans.

63. Historically, the most important aspect of Sulla's efforts at restoring the republican constitution was his
    a. restoration of traditional powers to the Senate.
    b. allowing access to public office to Italians previously excluded.
    c. assumption of the role of dictator.
    d. abolition of slavery.

64. The most important consequence of the reforms of Julius Caesar was the
    a. destruction of the Republic.
    b. continuation of civil war.
    c. gradual acceptance of Christianity.
    d. creation of an empire of citizens, not subjects.

65. The curses reproduced in "Listening to the Past" called for all of the following *except*
    a. victory over Rome's military rivals.
    b. the punishment of a lover.
    c. insuring the defeat of a chariot racer.
    d. the punishment of a thief.

History and Geography

66. How did geography affect the expansion of Rome?

67. Describe the geography of the Italian peninsula. What were the special features of the area in which Rome was located?

68. After studying Map 5.2, explain why Rome and Carthage would be natural rivals and why the Roman victory in the Punic Wars led to the establishment of Roman control of the Mediterranean world.

CHAPTER 6

THE PAX ROMANA

Key Terms

1. Livy
2. pax Romana
3. princeps civitatus
4. Lyons
5. Pontius Pilate
6. Zealots
7. John the Baptist
8. *Gospels*
9. *Georgics*
10. Paul of Tarsus
11. chariot racing
12. Tacitus
13. Late antiquity
14. Gaul
15. Ambrose of Milan
16. Diocletian
17. "barracks emperors"
18. Goths
19. Constantinople
20. martyrs

Essay Questions

21. One of the most important events that occurred during the time of the Roman Empire was the birth of Christianity. Describe the evolution of Christianity. How do historians explain the success of early Christianity?

    The essay should begin with a description of the origins of Christianity in both Hebrew religion and the various messianic movements of that era. This should include a discussion of the relationship between the Jews and the Romans as well as the existence of the various mystery religions. Next, the essay should discuss the theological contributions of Jesus and his teachings, being sure to indicate both the unique and typical aspects of this movement compared to existing Hebrew religion and other messianic movements. The role of Paul in transforming Christianity into a religious movement for both Jews and Gentiles must be considered; his earlier contact with Stoic philosophy and his fundamental reorientation of the religion must be discussed. Finally, the essay should explain the success of Christianity, by considering the universal message of the religion, its leadership, and the social conditions of the Mediterranean world at the time.

22. Essential to the efficient operation of the state is an able, dedicated, and loyal bureaucracy. Trace the evolution of the Roman bureaucracy. How effective was it?

    This essay should provide a narrative of the evolution of the imperial bureaucracy from its origins under Augustus through the collapse of the empire. The discussion should include the membership of the bureaucracy and how it changed, its functions, and its strengths and weaknesses. The essay should include a discussion of the role of the bureaucracy in maintaining the integrity of the empire, despite the failings of individual emperors and increasing pressure from invasions.

23. By late antiquity, Christianity was the dominant religion in the Mediterranean world. Why?

    This essay should include a discussion of the attractions of early Christianity: emotional appeal of promised salvation, forgiveness, acceptance of Gentile women, sense of community, sense of purpose, egalitarianism, and inspired leadership and evangelism of Paul of Tarsus. Next, the essay should assess factors which, in later years, would insure Christianity's triumph: exclusivity, the resulting repression, and martyrdom which attracted more adherents; egalitarianism in an era of increasing poverty for many; community feeling in an alienating urban environment; the increasingly important role of Christian leaders in the secular arena; official recognition by Roman emperors.

24. The relationship between Rome and the provinces was complex and would have an impact long after the Empire in the West had ceased to exist. Describe this relationship, being sure to note regional differences. How pervasive was "Romanization"? What were the long-term consequences of this relationship?

    The essay should begin with a description of the spread of Roman culture during the early empire, with Lyons serving as a good example of the process of Romanization. A thoughtful essay would discuss the role of imperial policy in the emergence of Christianity. Transformation of the army under the Flavians should also be mentioned. Next the essay should emphasize both the regional variations in the relationship: east and west of the Rhine in Europe; Asia Minor and north Africa; west Africa, and discuss the reasons behind these differences. Finally, the essay should include a discussion of the retention of native culture and the degree of assimilation, regionally.

25. The history of the Roman Empire is marked by periods of civil war and then reform. How did the reformers—Augustus Caesar, the Antonines, Diocletian, and Constantine—respond to the civil wars? Why did civil wars continue to recur?

    The essay should begin with a brief description of the periods of civil war and reform. Second, the reforms (constitutional, administrative, military, financial) should be described, including an assessment of the effectiveness of the reforms in relation to the problems which the reforms were to address. Third, one should indicate the problems facing the empire, especially the role of the army in political affairs, socio-economic changes, and the entry of new peoples into the empire.

26. Describe the evolution of the agrarian sector of Roman economy and society during the period of the Roman Empire. How and why did the major changes occur? What was the long-term impact of these changes?

    The first of these changes was the emergence of the small tenant farmer as the backbone of Roman agriculture, resulting from the prosperity of the era of the five good emperors. The second change was brought on by both an era of civil war and a vast influx of barbarian invasions, during which the villa became the basis of rural political and economic life; the resulting impoverishment of many farmers, aggravated by the efforts of tax collectors, in essence, reduced free farmers to serfdom. Thus the two developments together laid the foundation of medieval agriculture: manor agriculture dominated by strong landlords exercising great power over an enserfed peasant population.

27. The culture and society of the Roman Empire often are portrayed as lascivious, cruel, bloodthirsty, and extravagant. How accurate is this portrayal?

    For this essay, one should discuss the entertainment spectacles of the empire, including not only gladiatorial contests but also chariot racing; reference should be made to the fact that such extravaganzas did not attract every Roman citizen. Second, one should address the efforts of the emperors to both care for and divert the population of Rome, as both benevolence and as a form of social control. A discussion of the ebb and flow of the persecution of Christians would be a useful addition to the essay.

Multiple-Choice Questions

28. Ovid's *Fasti* described the
    a. Augustan constitution.
    b. popular culture of imperial Rome.
    c. rise of Christianity.
    d. anarchy of the "year of four emperors."

29. Pontius Pilate was most concerned with
    a. crushing all religious challenges to Judaism.
    b. suppressing the Jews.
    c. maintaining law and order.
    d. reforming the provincial administration.

30. The literary flowering of the pax Romana included all of the following *except*
    a. Virgil.
    b. Caligula.
    c. Horace.
    d. Livy.

31. The worst defect of the Augustan settlement was the
    a. use of slaves in the bureaucracy.
    b. army's ability to interfere in politics.
    c. establishment of a monarchical form of government.
    d. suppression of Christianity.

32. The most powerful institution in the Roman Empire was the
    a. bureaucracy.
    b. senate.
    c. church.
    d. army.

33. The most important source of information on the life of Jesus is the
    a. biography written by Paul of Tarsus.
    b. Roman census records.
    c. oral tradition of early Christianity.
    d. four gospels of the New Testament.

34. The main source of Augustus's power was his position as
    a. commander of the army.
    b. chief priest of the state religion.
    c. First Citizen.
    d. head tribune.

35. The early followers of Jesus, before the conversion of Paul of Tarsus, were mostly
    a. Gentiles.
    b. Essenes.
    c. Hellenized Jews.
    d. Romanized Semitic peoples.

36. *Roma et Augustus* refers to the
    a. history of Augustus's reign by Tacitus.
    b. epic poem of Augustus's deeds by Virgil.
    c. concept of empire.
    d. cult of the emperor and the state.

37. The example of the city of Lyons represents the
    a. fate of a rebellious city.
    b. spread of Christianity into Gaul.
    c. process of assimilation between Roman and native culture.
    d. collapse of Roman authority on the northern frontier.

38. During the reign of Augustus, Roman territorial expansion was
    a. concentrated in Europe.
    b. concentrated in Africa.
    c. ended.
    d. was concentrated in Asia Minor.

39. During the Golden Age, the funerary inscriptions on the graves of ordinary Romans indicate that
    a. many Romans detested the Augustan settlement.
    b. many had converted to Christianity.
    c. they were an industrious and affectionate people.
    d. these people were brutal and imperialistic.

40. Virgil's *Georgics* is a poetic work about
    a. everyday life on a farm.
    b. the mythical founding of Rome.
    c. the accomplishments of Augustus.
    d. the collapse of the Republic.

41. The main theme of Livy's *Ab Urbe Condita* was the
    a. disastrous impact of Christianity.
    b. greatness of the Republic
    c. usurpation of the Republic by Augustus.
    d. beauty and fulfillment of rural life.

42. The Zealots
    a. believed that Jesus was the messiah.
    b. wanted to expel the Romans from Judea.
    c. were followers of a new mystery religion.
    d. felt Christ's message applied only to Jews.

43. All of the following represent social, political, and religious unrest in Jewish society prior to the birth of Jesus *except*
    a. the Apocalypse of Baruch.
    b. the Zealots.
    c. Zoroastrianism.
    d. John the Baptist.

44. Paul of Tarsus believed that
    a. Christ's teachings should be proclaimed to all.
    b. Christianity should be used to defeat Rome.
    c. Christ's message applied only to Jews.
    d. Christians should avoid contact with pagans.

45. Some scholars have argued that Paul of Tarsus's concept of the universal nature of Christianity was influenced by the
    a. Zoroastrians.
    b. Stoics.
    c. Essenes.
    d. Gentiles.

46. The bureaucracy created by the Emperor Claudius was made up of
    a. ex-officers and soldiers of the army.
    b. professionally trained jurists.
    c. his own ex-slaves.
    d. almost entirely patricians.

47. The "year of the four emperors" (A.D. 69) was the result of
    a. barbarian invasions.
    b. Christian efforts to overthrow the Empire.
    c. a devastating plague that swept through Rome that year.
    d. the Roman army's ability to interfere in politics.

48. During the age of the five good emperors, the Roman army was
    a. a source of economic stability and Romanization.
    b. the cause of ongoing political unrest in the provinces.
    c. composed of citizen-soldiers from Italy, with Roman officers.
    d. greatly reduced in size and political influence.

49. The most popular form of entertainment in Rome was
    a. gladiatorial competitions.
    b. chariot racing.
    c. drama.
    d. eating and drinking.

50. During the second century A.D., the manufacturing centers of the empire
    a. remained concentrated in Italy.
    b. shifted to the east.
    c. suffered greatly from barbarian invasions.
    d. became concentrated in Gaul and Germany.

51. During the tumultuous third century, ordinary people's greatest problems were caused by all of the following *except*
    a. evangelic Christians.
    b. barbarian invaders.
    c. imperial soldiers.
    d. local officials.

52. Diocletian's reforms were designed to deal with the size of the empire and
    a. the problem of barbarian invasions.
    b. rebellious provincial governors.
    c. the spread of Christianity.
    d. the barbarization of the Roman army.

53. The Diocletian reform that had the greatest impact was the
    a. division of the empire.
    b. reformation of the tax collection system.
    c. legalization of Christianity.
    d. abolition of slavery.

54. As a result of Constantine's reform of the tax system,
    a. tax collectors grew rich.
    b. the economy recovered despite the expense of constructing Constantinople.
    c. a whole class of moderately wealthy people was eliminated.
    d. the empire in the West was able to fend off the barbarians for another century.

55. All of the following were products of the economic turmoil of the third century *except*
    a. runaway inflation.
    b. a monetary system in ruins.
    c. destruction of latifundia agriculture.
    d. the reduction of free tenant farmers to serfdom.

48 / *The Pax Romana*

56. The reforms of Diocletian and Constantine included all of the following *except*
    a. administrative division of the empire.
    b. a freeze on wages, prices, and occupations.
    c. reform of the tax collection system.
    d. abolition of slavery.

57. Christianity was legalized by the emperor
    a. Theodosius.
    b. Constantine.
    c. Diocletian.
    d. Decius.

58. In general, the relationship between Christians and Rome was characterized by
    a. phases of toleration with sporadic outbursts of persecution.
    b. unrelenting persecution until the late fourth century.
    c. Christian efforts to overthrow the state and predictable Roman response.
    d. mutual respect and toleration during Caligula's time.

59. Pagans distrusted Christians for all of the following reasons *except* the belief that
    a. Christians were cannibals.
    b. Christians were monotheists.
    c. Christian rituals were immoral.
    d. the Christians refused to recognize traditional pagan gods.

60. The most important socio-economic feature of late antiquity was the
    a. rise of independent peasant farmers as the base unit of agriculture.
    b. disappearance of slavery.
    c. increasingly urban nature of the West.
    d. enormous wealth gap between rich and poor.

61. The characteristics of the Christian religion in late antiquity include all of the following *except*
    a. exclusivity and intolerance of other religions.
    b. egalitarianism and a sense of community among all believers.
    c. rejection of the urban environment and transformation to a rural religion.
    d. an increasing secular role for the leaders of Christian churches in the West.

62. In the intellectual sphere of late antiquity,
    a. Christian society rejected the intellectualism of classical antiquity.
    b. the dichotomy between urbane, tolerant aristocratic culture and "popular culture" of Christianity was maintained.
    c. the intellectual achievements of classical antiquity were highly valued.
    d. *otium*, the aristocratic ideal of leisure to pursue intellectual activities, emerged.

63. The life of the soldier Bithius, featured in "Individuals in Society," exemplified the
    a. Romanizing role of the army.
    b. brutality of military life.
    c. role of the army as emperor-maker.
    d. impact of third-century upheavals.

64. According to the evidence presented in "Listening to the Past," Emperor Claudius decided to allow Romanized Gauls to sit in the Senate because
    a. they had revolted against Roman control.
    b. Roman citizens were challenging Claudius for power.
    c. of their valiant if vain efforts to defeat Julius Caesar.
    d. they were loyal and capable individuals.

History and Geography

65. Describe the geographic basis of Diocletian's division of the empire.

66. Where did Constantine build his new capital city? What impact did its location have on its role for the future development of European civilization?

67. Describe the impact of Romanization along the frontiers of the empire: Europe, east and west of the Rhine; Asia Minor and north Africa; west Africa. How can we account for the differences?

CHAPTER 7

THE MAKING OF EUROPE

Key Terms

1. Justinian's *Code*
2. Petrine Doctrine
3. Bridget of Kildare
4. Nicene Creed
5. penitentials
6. *The City of God*
7. St. John Chrysostom
8. *Rule of Saint Benedict*
9. *gentes*
10. Clovis
11. comitatus
12. *Dooms of Ethelbert*
13. schism
14. *philanthropia*
15. *Piers Plowman*
16. *Qur'an*
17. jihad
18. Sunni
19. *Algebra*
20. Ibn-Sina

Essay Questions

21. One of the major concerns of early Christian leaders was the response to pre-Christian culture and civilization. How did the early Christian church view the pre-Christian world? How was the conflict resolved? How did the Christian church in the Byzantine Empire differ from that of the West in this regard?

    To begin there should be a brief discussion of the syncretic nature of Christianity. Next should be a discussion of the relationship between Christianity and the Roman state, being sure to indicate the changes in this relationship. A discussion of early attitudes toward pagans and civil authority in the first and second centuries after Christ's birth should follow. One should then describe the change in attitude that appeared after the third century. For the resolution of this antipathy with the Classical world, the role of Augustine must be discussed in some detail. The essay should also assess the difference between East and West; the role of the apologists and Byzantine efforts at preserving Classical thought is an example of the less antagonistic attitude in the East.

22. "Both Christians and Muslims developed a view of the state which maintained that the purpose of the state was to enable its people to lead a life based on the precepts of their respective religions." Assess the validity of this quotation, being sure to indicate the similarities and differences between the Islamic and Christian views on the state.

The essay should describe the relationship of secular to religious authority in both major religions. In Christian Europe, this can be done by examining papal, ecclesiastical, and monastic role in shaping the lives of Europeans. In the Muslim world, the impact of the *Qu'ran* and the *umma* in the reordering of society must be discussed. For both, the manner in which expansion occurred should also be discussed. Mention should be made of Europeans' stress on geographic boundaries for states, while for Muslims, such artificial lines were of little importance.

23. European civilization developed out of the Greco-Roman legacy, Germanic culture and tradition, and the Christian religion. What did each of these elements contribute? How did they interact to produce a distinctive European civilization? What impact did the Byzantine Empire and Islam have on European civilization?

For this question one should indicate the various contributions of each strand from which European civilization was woven; this should include (but is not limited to) such things as Roman law and political administrative divisions, Latin language, Greek philosophy, science, and art; German customary law, militaristic clans and social stratification; Christianity's spread to encompass most of Europe as a unifying force and common belief system. Areas of interaction would include Roman and German law, Christian assimilation of pagan beliefs, Christian and Germanic views of women and marriage. Finally, the discussion on the contributions of Byzantium and Islam should include the protective shield afforded by Constantinople and both cultures' role in the preservation and transmission of Classical culture.

24. The bishop of Rome acquired not only spiritual but also secular leadership in the early fifth century. How did this come about? What was the intellectual justification for this development?

This essay should include first a narrative of the collapse of authority experienced by the political authorities of Rome and the accompanying enhancement of power and prestige of the bishops of Rome during the era. Following the narrative, one should then discuss the intellectual justification for this, beginning with Ambrose's insistence on the independence of the church and the bishops' role as judges of emperors, including a thorough discussion of Augustine's views on the issue.

25. Describe Germanic society in this period. What impact did the traditions, beliefs, and laws of the Germanic peoples have on the subsequent development of European civilization? How were the Germans affected by Christianity?

For this question, one should describe fully early Germanic society, including customary laws, religion, daily life, and societal organization. Next one should indicate how these early aspects of Germanic society were incorporated into the synthesis that produced European civilization, including the interaction between Germanic society and both the Greco-Roman tradition and Christianity.

26. One aspect of the growth of the Christian church was monasticism. Trace the history of the monastic movement from its Eastern roots through *The Rule of Saint Benedict*. Why was *The Rule of Saint Benedict* so successful? What impact did the Benedictine monasteries have on the church and on society in general?

This essay should begin with a discussion of eremitical monasticism and the emergence and eventual dominance of coenobitic monasticism. One should also discuss the role of monasteries in the conversion process in pagan Europe. The role of church leadership in this development should be discussed. Next, there should be a description of the *Rule*, including why and how Saint Benedict created it. Following the description, one should discuss the features of the rule, such as its simplicity, adaptability, and universal acceptance, which explain its success. Finally, one should conclude with a discussion of the role played by the Benedictine order.

27. One of the most remarkable accomplishments of the early church was the conversion of pagan Europe. What tools and strategies were employed by the Christian missionaries in their efforts? How does the story of the conversion of Clovis, presented in "Listening to the Past," exemplify the strategy of early Christian missionary activity? How successful were these efforts?

This essay should include a complete discussion of the manner in which the conversion of the peoples of Europe was accomplished; this should include such aspects as focus on the rulers, role of royal women (Bridget of Kildare, for example) assimilation, confessions, penitentials. The essay should include a discussion of the inspired efforts of individual missionaries such as St. Martin of Tours and St. Patrick. The conversion of Clovis offers a strong example of both the role of women and the concentration on rulers; it also indicates the reason many converted to Christianity. Finally, there should be a discussion of not only the geographic spread of Christianity, but also a consideration of the thoroughness of conversion among the pagans of Europe.

28. Some scholars have argued that Christianity is a religion which continually evolves. What evidence does this chapter present to support this assertion? What were the most profound changes? What was the role of heresy in this evolution? How can one explain these changes in Christian doctrine and practices?

First, one should discuss the most important changes in the early years, including the relationship between church and state, the nature of God and Christ, views about women and marriage, the nature of sin and grace. Next, there should be a discussion of the role of heresy, including a brief description of Arianism and Donatism and how these heresies (and their resolution) affected the development of Christian doctrine. The conclusion should consider how modern scholars have explained the evolutionary nature of early Christianity: the interaction with Classical culture, attainment of secular authority, conversion of European pagans, and the changing socio-economic conditions are all factors which should be discussed.

29. What impact did Byzantine and Islamic civilizations have on western Europe?

To answer this question, one must first describe the most important aspects of both civilizations, including: church-state relations, societal organization, art, medicine and science, and law. Next describe and assess how the unique aspects of these two affected the West; for example, one should discuss the preservation, advancement, and spread of Classical science by the Muslims, Justinian's emphasis on jurisprudence, Byzantine art, and Byzantium's protection of the frontier.

Multiple-Choice Questions

30. The most important ingredient in the making of a distinct European civilization was the
    a. political legacy of Rome.
    b. philosophical legacy of Greece.
    c. synthesizing power of Christianity.
    d. traditions of the Germanic tribes.

31. St. Paul used the term *ekklesia* to refer to
    a. a parish church.
    b. the Mediterranean-wide assembly of Jesus' followers.
    c. the offices and officials of the Christian religion.
    d. the building in which Christians worshiped.

32. The Petrine Doctrine asserts the
    a. authority of the bishop of Rome over other bishops.
    b. rejection of Classical knowledge.
    c. falseness of the Donatist heresy.
    d. supremacy of the church over the state.

33. The Byzantine emperor Justinian is most famous for his
    a. reconquest of Italy.
    b. conversion of the Slavic peoples.
    c. contributions to Christian theology.
    d. code of law.

34. The value which Germanic tribes ascribed to the worth of individual members was known as the
    a. *doom*.
    b. *gentes*.
    c. *comitatus*.
    d. *wergeld*.

35. Bridget of Kildare is remembered for her
    a. efforts in support of St. Patrick's conversion of Ireland.
    b. life of ascetic monasticism in Egypt.
    c. rise to power and influence as the wife of Justinian.
    d. opposition to the misogyny of church leaders such as John Chrysostom.

36. Recent research stresses that the terms *German* and *Celt* can best be understood as
    a. racial terms of differentiation.
    b. linguistic terms of differentiation.
    c. tribalistic terms of differentiation.
    d. anachronistic terms used by Romans to describe non-Romans in Europe.

37. Assimilation was the process of
    a. integrating the Christian church into the Roman state.
    b. reconciling Christian theology with Classical philosophy.
    c. first converting the kings and chiefs of pagans.
    d. using the similarities between pagan and Christian customs to facilitate conversion.

38. According to Ambrose of Milan and Pope Gelasius I, a well-ordered Christian society depended upon the
    a. supremacy of the secular authority.
    b. supremacy of ecclesiastic authority.
    c. adoption of the Arian concept of the relationship between church and state.
    d. mutual responsibility of the secular and religious authorities.

39. The Arian heresy asserted the concept
    a. of the supremacy of the bishop of Rome.
    b. that Christ's nature lay between God and humanity.
    c. that God and Christ were co-equals.
    d. that the church was subordinate to the emperor.

40. The basic organizational structure of the early Christian church was based on the
    a. teachings of Paul of Tarsus.
    b. boundaries between the various Germanic tribes.
    c. administrative divisions of the Roman Empire.
    d. reforms of St. Augustine of Hippo.

41. All of the following factors influenced pagan rulers to convert to Christianity *except*
    a. the persuasion of a Christian wife.
    b. the warrior-nature of many of the early Christian missionaries.
    c. the possible acquisition of literate assistants.
    d. its use as an ideological basis for their rule.

42. Penitentials seemed to be most concerned with
    a. sexual transgressions.
    b. crimes of property.
    c. instilling the teachings of Jesus into the hearts of new Christians.
    d. suppressing heretical views.

43. The success of the Frankish kingdom was most likely the result of
    a. divine intervention.
    b. the Franks' alliance with the Byzantine Empire.
    c. the acquisition of Roman Gaul, with its administrative machinery intact.
    d. the diversion of Islamic invasions in Spain.

44. The success of Constantinople at resisting attacks resulted from all of the following *except*
    a. the weakness of its enemies.
    b. strong military leadership.
    c. its fortifications.
    d. its geographic location.

45. Under the influence of Christian writers such as Tertullian and St. John Chrysostom, Christianity became a/an
    a. egalitarian religion.
    b. amalgamation of Jesus' teachings and Greek philosophy.
    c. misogynist, sex-negative religion.
    d. a syncretic religion, incorporating pagan rituals and beliefs.

46. In *The City of God*, St. Augustine stated that
    a. the church was free from sin.
    b. tainted priests could not administer the sacraments.
    c. secular states were unnecessary.
    d. history is the account of God acting in time.

47. In *The Confessions*, St. Augustine of Hippo suggested that
    a. Christianity should adopt the Donatist view of priesthood.
    b. secular states were unnecessary.
    c. Greeks and Romans had nothing to offer Christians.
    d. humans have an innate tendency to sin.

48. The basic premise of the Donatist heresy was that
    a. Christ was a creation of God and therefore not divine.
    b. the church should be subservient to temporal authorities.
    c. the church consisted of a small spiritual elite.
    d. only Jews could become Christians.

49. The monasteries of the Byzantine East
    a. provided important social services.
    b. were often in conflict with the state.
    c. adopted the Benedictine rule.
    d. had little impact on the Greek church.

50. The separation between Germanic West and Byzantine East resulted from all of the following factors *except*
    a. religious tensions between East and West.
    b. differences in the way in which both Christianity and Classical culture were received.
    c. expansion of the Arabs into the Mediterranean.
    d. Byzantine refusal to defend the eastern frontier of Europe.

51. Penitentials were
    a. the prayers required of sinners.
    b. Celtic monks who Christianized Scotland.
    c. manuals that guided the assignment of penance.
    d. days on which sinners were supposed to fast.

52. The success of *The Rule of Saint Benedict* was the result of its
    a. emphasis on spirituality.
    b. allegiance to the bishop of Rome.
    c. moderation and adaptability.
    d. rejection of Classical ideals.

53. Military units composed of and led by free barbarians were called
    a. laeti.
    b. foederati.
    c. gentes.
    d. comitati.

54. According to the account of Gregory of Tours, in "Listening to the Past," Clovis converted to Christianity
    a. in order to win a battle.
    b. to ensure his eternal salvation.
    c. because his wife was a Christian.
    d. because his people demanded it.

55. In early Germanic villages, a man's wealth and social status was based on
    a. his relationship with the king.
    b. the amount of land he owned.
    c. how many wives he had.
    d. the number of cattle he possessed.

56. The basic Germanic social unit was the
    a. comitatus.
    b. folk.
    c. clan.
    d. village.

57. According to the text, the Arthurian legends reflect
    a. Anglo-Saxon history in England.
    b. the long years of Roman domination.
    c. Celtic resentment at the Anglo-Saxon invaders.
    d. Celtic society's early adherence to Christianity.

58. The *Dooms of Ethelbert* was
    a. an early Christian penitential.
    b. a collection of Germanic folk laws.
    c. moralistic literature sponsored by the Christian church.
    d. a gossipy history of Byzantium.

59. The Salic Law of the Franks indicates that German law was concerned primarily with
    a. abstract concepts of justice.
    b. relationship between Germans and Romans.
    c. avoiding or reducing violence.
    d. protecting landed property.

60. In general, Germanic law codes reveal that German society viewed women as
    a. relatively equal to men.
    b. completely valueless.
    c. revered and even dominant.
    d. family property.

61. The "Justinian plague"
    a. severely weakened the military resources of Byzantium.
    b. decimated the Muslim armies attacking Byzantium.
    c. refers to the oppressive nature of Justinian's *Code*.
    d. was the term Italians used to describe Justinian's attempt to reunify the Roman Empire.

62. The historic role of Byzantium included all of the following *except*
    a. as a protective buffer against invasions from the East.
    b. preserving Classical political and philosophical texts.
    c. as a contributor to new scientific and mathematical discoveries.
    d. preserving the scientific texts of the Classical world.

63. The biography of Justinian's wife Theodora, featured in "Individuals in Society," is an example of
    a. the feeble nature of imperial rule in Constantinople.
    b. a talented individual rising from humble origins to a position of authority.
    c. the relationship between church and state, known as caesaropapism.
    d. the decline of religious belief in Byzantium.

64. According to Mohammed
    a. salvation can be achieved by adherence to the rituals.
    b. Judaism and Christianity must be destroyed.
    c. religious warfare was required of all Muslims.
    d. salvation came only by the grace of Allah.

65. According to Islam, the term *dhimmis* refers to
    a. Muslims.
    b. peoples of the Book.
    c. pagans.
    d. Islamic warriors killed defending the faith.

66. After the assassination of Caliph Ali in 661, the Islamic religion split into two groups, the Shi'ites and the
    a. Ummas.
    b. Sunnis.
    c. Umayyads.
    d. Dhimmis.

67. Muslims typically viewed the state as a/an
    a. organized geographic entity, with specific policy aims.
    b. necessary evil, resulting from the sinful nature of humans.
    c. place where Muslims could lead life according to the mandates of the *Qur'an*.
    d. institution which was separate from the religious life of its citizens.

68. The *al-Qanun* of Ibn-Sina of Bukhara
    a. codified all Greco-Arabic medical thought.
    b. strongly denounced Christian civilization.
    c. justified the schism within Islam.
    d. was a learned treatise on Justinian's *Code*.

History and Geography

69. Where were the three main concentrations of Germanic settlers in Europe?

70. Trace the spread of Christianity in Europe. How did geographic factors affect this spread?

71. Why was Constantinople's location so critical both to the separation of East and West but also as a defensive bulwark against invasion?

72. After consulting Map 7.4, describe the extent of Muslin expansion by 733. What were the major Muslim cities and why were they important?

CHAPTER 8

THE CAROLINGIAN WORLD: EUROPE IN THE EARLY MIDDLE AGES

Key Terms

1. Charles Martel
2. *Rex et sacerdos*
3. *Dux*
4. Benet Biscop
5. *The Song of Roland*
6. *missi dominici*
7. Lindisfarne
8. missals
9. *The Ecclesiatical History of the English People*
10. St. Hilda
11. *Beowulf*
12. Alcuin
13. vassal
14. leeches
15. *Arrangement of the Empire*
16. counts
17. serfs
18. manorialism
19. Danelaw
20. Old Church Slavonic

Essay Questions

21. According to the text, historians have "been tyrannized by a [seventeenth-century] construct" when dealing with the medieval period, the construct of feudalism. Describe, in general terms, how this feudalism worked and why it developed. How have historians attempted to come to grips with feudalism?

    After a brief introduction to the problems of conceptualization, the essay should discuss the manner in which feudalism operated, on both levels (that of armed retainers and royal officials);

the evidence from "Listening to the Past" should be used as examples of oaths of fealty, investment, and homage; the differences between the first and second documents can be used to indicate the evolution of feudalism. The essay should then describe the factors, such as the collapse of centralized political power and the increase of the raiding activities of Vikings, Magyars, and Muslims as causes. Next, the essay should discuss Marc Bloch's interpretation, and the more delimited Marxist and political-legal interpretations. The good essay would then return to the introduction and attempt to reconcile the reality of ninth-century Europe with the conceptual framework of modern historians.

22. Despite the violence of the era, Merovingian and Carolingian rulers were able to govern their territories with a fair degree of success. Discuss the evolution of administration in the Frankish kingdom under the Merovingians and Carolingians. What was the role of the Frankish aristocracy? What role did ideology play? What were the weaknesses of the system?

The essay should begin with a description of the violence of the era, both domestic and international. Then the Merovingian administrative machinery should be described, including civitas, comites, dux, capitula. The role of the Carolingian major domos should then be described; finally Charlemagne's state should be described: *missi dominici*, the peripatetic nature of his court, counties, marches. For the aristocracy, it should be stressed that this class of people were indispensable to the kingdom, mentioning their role as local judicial power, representatives of the king, tax collectors, maintainers of roads and bridges, etc. The good essay will indicate that the emergence of inheritable counties strengthened great nobles at the expense of royal power. For ideology, the essay should mention the Merovingian exploitation of the cult of St. Denis; for early Carolingians, the concept of *rex et sacerdos* and Augustinian political theories. Weaknesses include unclear succession law, leading to civil war, and reliance on the personality of the monarch for viability of the state.

23. The Carolingian renaissance may have been the greatest accomplishment of Charlemagne's reign. What were the intellectual roots of this renaissance? What were its practical results? What part did Charlemagne play in the process?

Here again a brief, introductory description of the renaissance should be included. Next, there should be a thorough discussion of the Northumbrian intellectual climate, being sure to include the works of the Lindisfarne monastery and, of course, the Venerable Bede. Next, the work of Alcuin should also be discussed: the moral *exempla* and the standards they set for royal behavior and the impact on political theories of authority, power, and responsibility; carolingian miniscule should also be mentioned, as should the establishment of schools throughout Europe, the preservation of ancient texts, and the rebirth of interests in Classical Greece and Rome. Finally, one should assess Charlemagne's role in the renaissance; his letter to the bishop of Fulda and the "General Admonition" to leading clergy urging establishment of cathedral and monastic schools are necessary examples; having Alcuin as his confessor and adviser is also important. The essay should stress Charlemagne's insistence on the necessity of education: a Christian education.

24. Although European civilization in this period was male-dominated, some women made valuable contributions to society. What role did royal and aristocratic women play during this period? In what other areas of knowledge and/or activity did women play a significant role? How can we explain these roles for women?

This essay should begin with a description of the theoretical basis for the status of royal women: diplomacy, personal relationship with the king; role as guardian of minor-age princes, control of royal treasury. Then the essay should indicate that some royal women went beyond this threshold, using Queen Brunhilda as an example. Second, role of aristocratic women as leaders of convents with political and intellectual influence should be discussed; St. Hilda of Whitby is a good example. Next, the essay should discuss the role of aristocratic women as managers of the household economy in the feudal system, owning land, etc. The essay should describe women's monopoly on knowledge about the birth process. Finally, the student should offer her/his own interpretation of why women had these opportunities.

25. With the collapse of the Carolingian Empire after the Treaty of Verdun, Europe became an easy target for foreign invasions. Describe the various assaults on western Europe. What impact did the barbarian invasions have on medieval Europe?

First there should be a description of the raids of the Vikings, Magyars, and Muslims. Impact includes: establishment of Normandy in France and the appearance of Danelaw in England; acceleration of disintegration of Carolingian Empire and the emergence of feudalism and manorialism; economic impact (stimulation of production of food and wine); slavery; resentment against Muslim raiders.

26. This period saw the appearance of the Kievan state. What were the origins of this state? How did it differ from the West?

This essay should begin with a brief description of the Slavic people living in the area. Next, one should describe the appearance of the Vikings and their ultimate domination of the region and establishment of the Kievan state; there should be some mention of why the Vikings were present (international trade) and then their assimilation by the native Slavs. Following this, there should be a description of Kievan society, including conversion to Orthodoxy, lack of strong central power, freedom of both nobles and peasants; one should indicate the connection between fragmented princely power, private property, and personal freedom. This description provides the basis for the comparison to western Europe.

27. During the Middle Ages, monasticism continued to be an important factor in European society. What functions did the monks and nuns perform?

In this essay, one should be sure to consider the intellectual achievements of the Northumbrian monastic world, including its contribution to the Carolingian Renaissance; the role of monks and nuns in the work of evangelization and in the new Christian learning; and, finally, the role of monasteries and convents as dispensaries of health care.

Multiple-Choice Questions

28. In the Merovingians dynasty, royal succession was determined by
    a. primogeniture.
    b. papal appointment.
    c. violence and assassination.
    d. the dying king's designation.

29. According to the interpretation of Marc Bloch, feudalism was a/an
    a. system of values, including politics, economics, and culture.
    b. economic system of production.
    c. political and legal system, solely.
    d. myth.

30. Charlemagne's marriage decisions were influenced most by diplomatic pressures and
    a. his Christian beliefs.
    b. the need to secure the royal succession.
    c. his sexual passion.
    d. Salic law.

31. The phrase *rex et sacerdos* refers to the
    a. innovations in writing style during the Carolingian renaissance.
    b. brutal wars of Charlemagne.
    c. spiritual nature of the Christian kings.
    d. administrative machinery of the Merovingian kingdom.

32. Charlemagne's political power was based on
    a. the cooperation of the Frankish aristocracy.
    b. his alliance with the papacy.
    c. the efficiency of his bureaucracy.
    d. his elimination of petty violence.

33. The status of royal women, in theory, was based on all of the following *except*
    a. mother/guardianship of minor-age princes.
    b. control of the royal treasury.
    c. a personal relationship with the king.
    d. an individual level of ruthlessness.

34. The fortified areas on the edges of Charlemagne's empire were called
    a. Basques.
    b. marches.
    c. counties.
    d. frontiers.

35. The significance of *The Song of Roland* is
    a. as a record of Charlemagne's wars.
    b. as a record of Charlemagne's only defeat.
    c. as a portrayal of later views of Charlemagne.
    d. its use of French rather than Latin.

36. The rise of the Carolingian dynasty can be attributed to all of the following factors *except*
    a. alliance with the Byzantine Empire.
    b. profitable marriages.
    c. military successes.
    d. alliance with monastic leadership.

37. The complexity of Merovingian civil wars resulted from all of the following *except*
    a. lack of a succession law.
    b. the army's desire for warfare which would result in more "loot" for the soldiers.
    c. Viking and Magyar invasions.
    d. emergence and evolution of court cliques with the royal family.

38. Charlemagne's letter to the bishop of Fulda and other leading clergymen called for
    a. a crusade against the Muslims in Spain.
    b. their acceptance of the papal coronation.
    c. greater acceptance of classical texts.
    d. the establishment of cathedral and monastic schools.

39. Typically, peasants owed the landlord all of the following *except*
    a. labor.
    b. military service.
    c. a percentage of the annual harvest.
    d. various fees, such as inheritance fees.

40. Feudalism was important because it
    a. prevented the political centralization of Europe.
    b. created a hierarchical social system in Europe.
    c. protected the people.
    d. accelerated the growth of the monastic movement.

41. The term *missi dominici* refers to the
    a. spiritual nature of Christian kings.
    b. leaders of double monasteries.
    c. children given to monastic houses.
    d. royal agents of the Carolingian emperor.

42. The Merovingian administrative system included all of the following *except*
    a. *civitas*.
    b. *comites*.
    c. *sacerdos*.
    d. *dux*.

43. Besides Charlemagne, the group or individual that gained the most from his coronation in 800 was the
    a. pope.
    b. Byzantine emperor.
    c. Frankish aristocracy.
    d. *missi dominici*.

44. The career of Queen Brunhilda represents her fierce determination to exercise power and
    a. her remarkable beauty.
    b. the role of women in monastic and intellectual life.
    c. the dangers which accompanied childbirth.
    d. the domestic violence of the Merovingian royal family.

45. The Carolingian renaissance drew its greatest inspiration from the
    a. intellectual achievements of the Islamic world.
    b. preservation work of the Byzantine Empire.
    c. intellectual developments in Northumbria.
    d. Greco-Roman legacy.

46. The Venerable Bede was
    a. Charlemagne's confessor and adviser.
    b. the author of *Beowulf*.
    c. the best example of Northumbriam scholarship.
    d. the leader of the medical school at Salerno.

47. The administrative system of Charlemagne's empire featured all of the following officials *except*
    a. counts.
    b. missals.
    c. margraves.
    d. *missi dominici*.

48. Besides Charlemagne, the individual most responsible for the success of the Carolingian Renaissance was
    a. the Venerable Bede.
    b. Abbess Hildegard.
    c. St. Boniface.
    d. Alcuin.

49. The main purpose of the Carolingian renaissance was to
    a. promote an understanding of Scriptures and of Christian writers.
    b. revive interest in classical knowledge.
    c. rebuild the Roman Empire.
    d. combat the danger of Islam on the frontiers of the empire.

50. The dominant political ideology of the period derived from the writings of
    a. St. Augustine.
    b. Alcuin.
    c. Venerable Bede.
    d. Charlemagne.

51. The leading medical school in the Middle Ages was located in
    a. Salerno.
    b. Aachen.
    c. Venice.
    d. Rome.

52. Women found useful employment and personal fulfillment in all of the following *except*
    a. management of aristocratic households.
    b. government administration.
    c. leadership of monastic houses.
    d. midwifery.

53. In the sixth and seventh centuries, medical treatment was most commonly available in
    a. manor houses.
    b. Italy.
    c. state-operated hospitals.
    d. monasteries.

54. The level of medical science in the Middle Ages led people to
    a. adopt a stoical attitude toward illness.
    b. turn to pagan religions for relief.
    c. respect the medical profession.
    d. adopt an optimistic attitude toward illness.

55. Medical knowledge concerning procreation
    a. was surprisingly advanced.
    b. was held primarily by women.
    c. was rigidly controlled by the church.
    d. lowered the death rate of mothers and newborns.

56. In his *Arrangement of the Empire*, Charlemagne's son Louis
    a. stressed the importance of the unity of the empire.
    b. made his sons equal in inheritance of land, power, and title.
    c. described his ruthless execution of all rivals for his throne.
    d. named his oldest son as his only heir, depriving the others of any inheritance.

57. According to newer research, the disintegration of the Carolingian Empire was the result of
    a. the assassination of the rightful heir.
    b. fratricidal wars among Louis the Pious's sons.
    c. the revolts and conspiracies of the great nobles.
    d. the alliance between the pope and the Byzantine emperor.

58. Feudalism existed at two social levels: the level of royal officials and the level of
    a. enserfed peasants.
    b. free farmers.
    c. free townsmen.
    d. armed retainers.

59. The technological breakthrough that had a great impact on the development of feudal military institutions was
    a. the lance.
    b. the stirrup.
    c. the saddle.
    d. armor.

60. The position of aristocratic women in feudal society was
    a. one of responsibility.
    b. insignificant.
    c. degrading.
    d. limited to bearing children.

61. In feudal society, aristocratic women's rights and duties included all of the following *except*
    a. management of the manorial and household economy.
    b. ownership of land.
    c. receiving homage from military retainers.
    d. inheritance of feudal estates.

62. In return for the peasant's land and labor, the lord furnished
    a. very little.
    b. protection.
    c. food and shelter.
    d. justice and religion.

63. The Kievan state was created by the
    a. Magyars.
    b. Byzantines.
    c. Muslims.
    d. Vikings.

64. One of the commodities most prized by the raiders of the ninth and tenth centuries was
    a. art.
    b. grain.
    c. spices.
    d. slaves.

65. As a result of the invasions of the ninth and tenth centuries
    a. manorialism disappeared.
    b. the development of feudalism was accelerated.
    c. many Germans reconverted to pagan religions.
    d. Europe developed several centralized kingdoms.

History and Geography

66. What was the extent of Charlemagne's empire? How was it divided by his grandsons?

67. Where did the Vikings come from and what areas of Europe did they affect most?

68. After having consulted Map 8.3, describe the invasion routes of the Vikings, Magyars, and Muslims.

CHAPTER 9

REVIVAL, RECOVERY, AND REFORM

Key Terms

1. Rollo
2. Edward the Confessor
3. *The Deeds of Otto*
4. Nicolaites
5. Cluny
6. water mills
7. Citeaux
8. Pope Gregory VII
9. lay investiture
10. *militia Christi*
11. *reconquista*
12. Albert the Bear
13. curia
14. Pope Innocent III
15. Manzikert
16. Albigensians
17. Ashkenaz
18. Bernard of Clairvaux
19. simony
20. indulgence

Essay Questions

21. During the High Middle Ages, the church underwent reform on two fronts: spiritual and secular. Trace and discuss these two reform movements. What were the immediate and long-range effects of the reforms?

    For this question, one should discuss the reforming efforts found in the monastic movement, notably those efforts associated with Citeaux, Gorze, and Cluny. The essay should include the monastic efforts aimed at such practices as simony and strict observance of *The Rule of Saint Benedict*. Next, the essay must address thoroughly the reform efforts which can be considered more secular, especially the reforms of Gregory VII in his efforts to improve the church and to control it more effectively. As for the consequences of the monastic reform movement, the

68 / Revival, Recovery, and Reform

Cistercian movement's land reclamation efforts should be mentioned as both immediate and long-range consequences; the Clunaic movement would result in the enhancement of the beauty of the liturgy but more importantly in the fact that many subsequent reformers such as Gregory VII came from this movement. The consequences of the papal reform efforts would include the short-term improvement of the spiritual aspect of the papacy and the church, the burgeoning of the papal bureaucracy, the very negative impact on emergence of centralized government in Germany, and the Crusades.

22. The lay investiture controversy had its greatest impact on the German empire. Briefly trace the narrative of the controversy. What was the main issue? Why did lay investiture cause greater concern in Germany than in France and England? Who were the ultimate winners and losers in this battle?

    Following the narrative of the significant events in the contest of wills between Henry IV and Gregory VII, the essay must identify the issue, that is, who would control ecclesiastical appointments, the secular rulers or the pope. Then the essay should explain why lay investiture was more critical for the German emperor than for the English and French kings; in essence this calls for the student to indicate the reliance of the German emperor on loyal, educated officials who could only be recruited from the clergy. Finally, the essay should identify winners and losers. Losers would include the German emperors, German peasants and landless knights, and, in the long run, the papacy, while the winners would include the German feudal aristocracy.

23. The Crusades are probably the greatest symbol of the religious enthusiasm of the age. What were the goals of the Crusades? Targets? What motivated people to go on crusade besides religious zeal? How do we account for the Crusades' general failure? How were the Crusades viewed by the Muslims, as indicated by the evidence from "Listening to the Past"? What lasting impact did they have?

    To begin, the essay should certainly indicate the desire to liberate the Holy Land from Muslim control; the good essay should also mention papal desire to exert influence over Christian Europe, find a place for young knights to work off some aggression, desire to reunite the eastern and western branches of the church; the danger posed to Christian pilgrims by the Turkish conquests in the region was also a factor; better essays will also address the goals of Crusades against internal enemies, such as Jews and Albigensians, and the effort at societal homogenization, using the evidence presented in the "Individuals in Society" feature. While religious zeal should be mentioned as a motivating factor, one should also include the desire for adventure and material profit; the desire of centralizing monarchs to rid themselves of troublesome knights might also be mentioned; a thoughtful essay might mention the fact that warfare was a distinctive aspect of the noble lifestyle. Next, the ultimate failure of the Crusades must be assessed; poor planning, strategic problems and the like should be considered. The essay should then describe the Muslim view of the Crusades; this should mention the Muslim estimation of Christian motives and explanation of early success. Finally, the lasting impact would include increased contact with the East, in terms of trade, the deterioration of Latin-Byzantine relations, and the legacy of resentment felt by Muslims for the Europeans.

24. The High Middle Ages saw "the expansion of Latin Christendom." Describe this expansion. How was cultural unity imposed on the frontiers of Europe?

COPYRIGHT © HOUGHTON MIFFLIN COMPANY. ALL RIGHTS RESERVED.

This essay should begin with a brief introduction which includes the economic recovery and the Crusades as precursors to expansion. Next, the essay should describe the expansion process in northern and eastern Europe, being sure to indicate tactics of Europeanization, especially the establishment of ecclesiastical organization in Scandinavia, Baltic, Poland, Bohemia, etc., the ruthless crusading activity exemplified by Albert the Bear, and the migration of thousands of Germans settlers into eastern Europe, adoptions of German law in many towns and cities. For Spain, the essay should describe the *reconquista*, including civil wars among Muslims, military successes of various Spanish rulers, desecration of Muslim holy sites, use of French knights, ecclesiastical and monastic organization, and the immigration of businesspeople. While many of the practices outlined in the expansion process would help with Europeanization, the essay should stress that the most important component was the papal insistence on uniformity of religious worship and loyalty to the institution of the Roman papacy.

25. What led to the eleventh-century revival and recovery? Who enjoyed the benefits of prosperity?

Factors influencing this recovery included political stability, steady population growth, decline of foreign invasions, no major plagues, and moderate weather patterns; in addition one should also mention increased used of mechanized devices, such as water mills and then wind mills which greatly enhanced agricultural efficiency. Increased agricultural yields benefited most everyone, in terms of diet; women especially were more healthy and thus could successfully deliver more children, resulting in population growth. Commerce and industry were also enhanced by political stability, population growth, and expansion of agriculture. The northern Italian cities such as Venice and Genoa enjoyed the benefits of prosperity brought on by increased trade.

26. How did the return of prosperity and the Crusades affect women? Was this effect felt across societal divisions?

The general prosperity enjoyed by Europe at the time improved the diet and life expectancy of women. With the improvement in diet, women were able to deliver more children successfully. The impact of the Crusades on women varied, according to social status, with little known about the impact on peasant women. The essay should mention the fact that some women did go on crusade. More importantly, the essay should stress the role of women who did not go; the assumption of the responsibilities of running a manor, for upper-class women, brought a degree of power; for women who operated businesses such as inns, the Crusades increased profits. Prostitutes were also afforded more business opportunities.

27. The relationship between church and state in Europe throughout the Middle Ages was a very complicated issue. In what ways did the political revival of secular monarchies affect the church and how church reform efforts affected the secular monarchies? Which benefited most, the church or the secular rulers?

This essay should begin with a discussion of the emergence of strong monarchies in England, France, and Germany. Second, the essay should then consider the role of church officials in governmental positions in these new monarchies and how this sparked conflict between the papacy and the secular rulers. The good essay would then mention the role of Cluny and its independence from secular rulers as an introduction to the reformist efforts which culminated in the lay investiture controversy. There should be a discussion of church reform efforts. In the assessment of who benefited most, the student should consider both immediate and long-term consequences; thus, in Germany, chronic civil war did not really benefit anyone except the feudal aristocracy; England and France, although not as negatively affected as Germany, would not challenge papal authority for two centuries; in the short-term, the papacy achieved phenomenal success, but this success would lead to abuse of power and decline of the papacy's spiritual prestige.

MULTIPLE-CHOICE QUESTIONS

28. Pope John XII
    a. led the papal effort during the lay investiture controversy.
    b. was the epitome of corruption in the Christian church.
    c. founded the monastery at Cluny.
    d. instigated the First Crusade.

29. The practice of selling church offices was known as
    a. simony.
    b. indulgence.
    c. investiture.
    d. usury.

30. The two principal actors in the lay investiture controversy were Emperor Henry IV and
    a. William the Conqueror.
    b. Leo IX, the Byzantine emperor.
    c. Gregory VII.
    d. Philip I of France.

31. The most important factor in the revival of Europe was
    a. the reforming spirit of the church.
    b. a decline in foreign invasion and domestic violence.
    c. the moderate climate.
    d. the introduction of the water-powered mill.

32. The famous Bernard of Clairvaux was a product of the monastery at
    a. Cluny.
    b. Citeaux.
    c. Gorze.
    d. Bury St. Edmunds.

33. Duke William I of Normandy made feudalism work by
    a. bribing his vassals.
    b. strictly controlling the distribution of lands.
    c. cooperating with the Capetian king.
    d. establishing a strong bureaucracy.

34. The assimilation of Anglo-Saxons and Vikings is best personified by
    a. Alfred.
    b. Canute.
    c. Edward the Confessor.
    d. the Venerable Bede.

35. The basis of Otto I's power was
    a. his alliance with and control of the church.
    b. the support of the feudal nobility.
    c. his alliance with the northern Italian cities.
    d. his strict control over lands distributed to the nobles.

36. Hrotswitha of Gandersheim was
    a. the founder of the Cluny monastery.
    b. the influential wife of Otto I.
    c. a nun who had a remarkable literary career.
    d. a woman who led a Crusade.

37. The new religious orders, such as the Knights Templars, were
    a. very disruptive in western Europe.
    b. vigorously opposed by the Cistercians.
    c. a minor consequence of the Crusades.
    d. crucial in extending the presence of Christianity on the frontiers of Europe.

38. Of the five dominant counties of northern France, the one which emerged as the strongest was
    a. Normandy.
    b. Aquitaine.
    c. Anjou.
    d. Île-de-France.

39. The development that had the greatest impact in terms of the number of people personally affected in the era of revival, recovery, and reform was the
    a. reform of the papacy.
    b. *reconquista*.
    c. use of natural energy.
    d. monastic revival.

40. John de Courcy, a Norman nobleman with estates in southwestern England,
    a. led the First Crusade.
    b. began the Anglo-Norman conquest of Ireland.
    c. founded the monastery at Citeaux.
    d. organized the anti-Jewish crusade in the Rhineland.

41. The monastery at Cluny gradually came to stand for clerical celibacy and the suppression of
    a. simony.
    b. usury.
    c. lay investiture.
    d. indulgences.

42. The greatest threat faced by the Europeans during the High Middle Ages was
    a. foreign invasion.
    b. major plagues.
    c. harsh winters and summer droughts.
    d. crop failure and starvation.

43. Cultural unity on the fringes of Europe resulted primarily from
    a. military conquest by western European kings.
    b. the establishment of crusader kingdoms.
    c. the religious policies of the papacy.
    d. maintenance of dualistic legal systems on the frontiers.

44. In the High Middle Ages
    a. women's diet allowed for greater fertility.
    b. women suffered from a higher incidence of anemia.
    c. women had shorter life spans than men.
    d. there was a sharp decline in the fertility rate.

45. The greatest contribution the Cistercians made to twelfth-century society was their
    a. role in ministering to the needs of urban dwellers.
    b. pioneering work in reclaiming land.
    c. introduction of the windmill to Europe.
    d. intellectual contributions in the fields of philosophy and theology.

46. The term *Nicolaites* refers to
    a. the monks who left the monastery of St. Nicolas to found the first Cistercian monastery.
    b. church officials who practiced simony.
    c. parish priests who had taken a wife.
    d. the supporters of Gregory VII in his reform efforts.

47. In the High Middle Ages, the papacy and the German empire struggled over control of
    a. Aquitaine.
    b. Scandinavia.
    c. eastern Poland.
    d. northern Italy.

48. The efforts by various Spanish leaders to expel the Muslims was known as the
    a. *reconquista.*
    b. *militia Christi.*
    c. *expulsiona*
    d. *dismoorisma.*

49. In the tenth and eleventh centuries, the church
    a. grudgingly accepted private marriage.
    b. recognized conciliar authority over the papacy.
    c. allowed divorce, but only for a wife's adultery.
    d. gained exclusive jurisdiction over marriage.

50. According to Gregory VII, the punishment for laymen who invested clerics was
    a. decapitation.
    b. imprisonment.
    c. excommunication.
    d. expropriation.

51. The real winners in the conflict over lay investiture were the
    a. Gregorian reformers.
    b. German nobility.
    c. German peasantry.
    d. German burghers.

52. The curia was the
    a. college of cardinals who elected the pope.
    b. parish clergy.
    c. clerics who served as royal officials.
    d. papal bureaucracy and court of law.

53. According to the Muslim chronicle of the siege of Antioch, presented in "Listening to the Past," the Christians won because
    a. they had superior siege weaponry.
    b. of the betrayal by an inhabitant of Antioch, who opened the gates for the Christians.
    c. the ruler of Antioch and his advisers were craven cowards who sold out to the Christians.
    d. of the greater bravery of the Christian knights.

54. The popes supported the Crusades for all of the following reasons *except* to
    a. get rid of violent young knights
    b. strengthen their claim to leadership of Christian society.
    c. improve relations with Byzantium.
    d. influence areas controlled by the Greek Orthodox Church.

55. The Crusade launched against the Jewish communities living in Rhineland cities
    a. was the work of foreign crusaders.
    b. was resisted by local townspeople.
    c. was ordered by the bishop of Speyer.
    d. included foreign crusaders and local townspeople.

56. The main reason for the success of the First Crusade was the
    a. religious zeal of the Crusaders.
    b. superior technology of the Christians.
    c. Christians' superior leadership.
    d. crusaders' meticulous planning and preparation

57. The permanent legacy of the Crusades include the deep bitterness between Christians and Muslims and the
    a. establishment of European states in the Middle East.
    b. extension of European control of the Holy Land until the twentieth century.
    c. continued and flourishing commercial contact between Europeans and Muslims.
    d. establishment of cultural ties between Europe and the Islamic world.

74 / *Revival, Recovery, and Reform*

58. As a consequence of the Fourth Crusade,
    a. thousands of European children were enslaved.
    b. Jerusalem was captured.
    c. the political fragmentation of Germany was assured.
    d. the Byzantine Empire was mortally wounded.

59. Some of the Crusades were directed at "social enemies" within Europe, among them the
    a. Albigensians.
    b. Vikings.
    c. Albanians.
    d. Cistercians.

60. For women, the Crusades generally meant
    a. early widowhood.
    b. increased responsibility.
    c. a rare chance for adventure.
    d. an erosion of their position.

61. According to the analysis presented in the "Individuals in Society" feature, the underlying animosity felt against Jews resulted from all of the following *except*
    a. their rejection of Christianity.
    b. economic competition.
    c. Jewish support for the Muslims in the early Crusades.
    d. the perception of Jews as aliens.

62. The Europeanization of the frontier areas of eastern Europe resulted from all of the following *except*
    a. the establishment of bishoprics and dioceses.
    b. the collapse of the Byzantine Empire.
    c. ruthless crusading activities against the Slavic peoples.
    d. the aristocratic diaspora.

63. The efforts of Spanish leaders to expel the Muslims included all of the following *except* the
    a. establishment of ecclesiastical organization.
    b. establishment of Cistercian monasteries.
    c. immigration of foreign businesspeople.
    d. invitation to Rhineland Jews to immigrate to Spain.

History and Geography

64. In addition to the conflict over lay investiture, the popes and the German emperors were also involved in a struggle with each other over a particular region in Europe. What was this region and why was it worth fighting over?

65. Which European cities profited most from the Crusades? Why?

66. What were the frontier regions of Europe which were brought into the European sphere? What were the significant differences between the regions? Did these differences affect the manner in which the different regions were Europeanized?

CHAPTER 10

LIFE IN CHRISTIAN EUROPE IN THE HIGH MIDDLE AGES

Key Terms

1. villeins
2. manor
3. fallow
4. indulgences
5. chivalry
6. ministerials
7. oblate
8. Guibert of Nogent
9. primogeniture
10. *Salve Regina*
11. inner economy
12. Hildegard of Bingen
13. choir monks
14. *The Leech Book of Bald*
15. widwifery
16. hagiography
17. open-field system
18. marriage portion
19. *popolani*
20. manumission

Essay Questions

21. "In the society of the High Middle Ages, function determined social classification." Discuss this statement in terms of those who worked, those who prayed, and those who fought. Does it adequately describe the reality of society at that time? Why or why not?

    In this essay, one should describe the three estates - nobles, clergy, peasants - in terms of duties, rights, and ways of life. After a thorough description of these main societal subdivisions, the essay should then discuss those who did not fit into this functional social structure, specifically, townspeople and parish priests. The thoughtful essay would also discuss the fact that the people

specifically, townspeople and parish priests. The thoughtful essay would also discuss the fact that the people in the towns did not fit into the traditional functional structures and that this indicates the changing nature of European society; the discussion of parish priests, including the social origins and functions of these individuals, will reveal the limited nature of the traditional view of society as well as the role of the village and parish church in the lives of most Europeans and their interaction with the outside world of monarchs and popes.

22. Describe popular religion in this period. How did church authorities respond to these popular beliefs and practices? What do these popular beliefs and practices reveal about medieval society?

First, one must describe the nature of popular religion: the importance of the village church and the pervasiveness of Christian practices in everyday life must be discussed. Cults of the saints, (several examples can be found in the text), the symbolism of the Mass, the cult of the Virgin Mother, afterlife, and indulgences should also be discussed. For church response, one could discuss the friction between papacy and local populations over cults of local saints, with some churchmen denouncing these cults as idolatry; one could also discuss the emergence of the sacramental system. As a reflection of society, one should reaffirm the central importance of the village church and Christian practices; the hard, short life of many people gave rise to pessimism, but prayers, pilgrimages, and indulgences offered hope.

23. In medieval times, the nobles were "those who fought." Is this an adequate description of the European nobility of the period? How did the code of chivalry reinforce this function? Did the family arrangements of the nobles reinforce this function? What other roles did nobles perform?

For this question, the student is asked to discuss the role of the noble class in medieval society. The military function must be considered. A discussion of the chivalric code should include not only the code as a reinforcement of the traditional function but should also consider the code as a justification for and definition of the noble class. The role of family, children (especially oblation), and women should also be discussed, with Guibert of Nogent's evidence from the "Listening to the Past" feature cited. Next, the nobility's various other roles, as landlords, judges, and government officials, must be discussed.

24. The medieval view of society stressed the stable, even static nature of that society, including the rural world of the peasants. What was the lifestyle of the European peasants? How did the lives of "those who worked" reflect this stability?

The essay should begin with a description of peasant life which should include life on the manor: agricultural practices; technology, including changes and improvements in this area; households and role of women; health care; and popular religion. In the second section, the essay should discuss the degree and nature of urban immigration, opening of new lands, and social mobility. The evidence for social mobility from the "Individuals in Society" feature should be used to support the possibility of upward mobility.

25. Most people believed that the role of the clergy was to pray for the rest of society. Is this an accurate description of what the members of the clergy did? Why or why not? What contributions did the monastic orders make to medieval society? How did monastic organization reflect and reinforce these functions? What did other members of the clergy contribute to society?

First, the essay should address the primary social function, praying, of the monastery and how the organization and daily rhythm of monastic life was geared to this aspect. Next, the essay should discuss the other functions of monasteries, including such things as educational centers, healthcare providers, and landowners; the organization of the monasteries and how such organization enhanced or detracted from these functions should also be addressed. The role of monasteries (and convents) as havens for children of the noble class should also be discussed. The role of monasteries in medieval politics, as both active participant and as adviser, is yet another function that should be mentioned. Finally, the role of parish priest must be examined.

26. Medieval agriculture was based on the manor. Describe a typical manor. What changes had European agriculture undergone and with what consequences? How effective was manor-based agriculture in supplying the needs of Europeans at the time?

To begin, the essay must include a thorough description of a manor, including physical layout, crops cultivated, tools and machinery employed, duties and obligations of lords and peasants; the varied nature of manor agriculture should be indicated. Next, changes must be described: new tools, increased reliance on horses. The impact of these changes, such as improved efficiency and crop yields, leading to surplus agricultural output which enabled growth of towns, should be discussed. The role of improved weather should also be mentioned, as should the tentative nature of this interpretation.

27. The family life of European nobles contrasted sharply with that of the peasants. Compare the two. What were the role and place of women and children in each? How does the life of Guibert''s mother, presented in "Listening to the Past," help explain both family life and women's choices?

This comparative question requires first a brief description of the family life of the noble and peasant classes, in order to compare the two. Such a comparison could include such things as diet, education, marriage choices, life expectancy, employment. The student should not be completely blind to the similarities, despite the paucity of them: most important would be the role of wives, noble and peasant, in the inner economy of the family. The role of wives and children in each class should then be addressed; for the nobility, the importance of maintaining the family holdings should certainly be stressed while for the peasantry, the importance of every individual, especially the wife, to the family economy must be emphasized.

MULTIPLE-CHOICE QUESTIONS

28. In the High Middle Ages, peasants
    a. often supplemented agricultural labor with work in other trades.
    b. were legally constrained to perform only agricultural work.
    c. supported only themselves and their families.
    d. became increasingly irreligious.

29. The living and working conditions for European peasants
    a. were generally uniform across the Continent.
    b. differed only between England and the Continent.
    c. varied widely across Europe.
    d. featured increasingly harsh obligations.

30. Typically the parish priest in the rural areas of Europe
    a. used the power of the church to control local landlords.
    b. was a poor peasant.
    c. had little concern for his parishioners, as he pursued career advancement.
    d. rejected the local cults of the saints.

31. The conditions and obligations of European serfs during the High Middle Ages included all of the following *except*
    a. performance of labor services.
    b. payment of various fees.
    c. military service.
    d. hereditary non-free status.

32. The parish priest was appointed and financed by
    a. his bishop.
    b. the king.
    c. his manorial lord.
    d. the pope.

33. Birth by caesarian section
    a. had not yet been developed.
    b. was performed to save the life of the mother.
    c. was performed in order to baptize the child.
    d. indicated that the child's life was more important than the mother's.

34. The primary obligation of the serf was to
    a. work on the lord's land.
    b. serve in the lord's army.
    c. pay taxes.
    d. pay rent on his land.

35. The prosperity of individual peasant families was usually dependent on the
    a. number of male children.
    b. education level of the father.
    c. amount of land held.
    d. wife's dowry.

36. A serf, in order to gain freedom through a cash payment to his/her lord, had to
    a. also bribe the parish priest.
    b. use a third party to make the payment.
    c. agree to leave the area.
    d. petition the papal curia to accept the case.

37. The demesne was the
    a. monk in charge of providing charity for the poor.
    b. "inner economy" of noble households.
    c. boundary line between individual peasants' land holdings.
    d. part of the manor which was cultivated for the lord.

38. Agricultural productivity was greatly enhanced by the use of all of the following *except*
    a. iron implements.
    b. animal power.
    c. new disease-resistant crops from the east.
    d. reclaimed lands.

39. The large number of accidental deaths in the thirteenth century has been attributed to
    a. drunkenness.
    b. suicide.
    c. new mechanical devices used in agriculture.
    d. violence at the hands of bachelor-knights.

40. The typical peasant family
    a. was an extended family of moderate size.
    b. was a nuclear family, with five members on average.
    c. featured parents who got married in their thirties.
    d. restricted women's work to household tasks.

41. All of the following apply to peasant women *except* that they
    a. were forbidden to work as agricultural day laborers.
    b. shared with their men the labors of the fields.
    c. managed the family household.
    d. brought in extra money by working outside the home.

42. The training of midwives
    a. usually took place in monasteries.
    b. was controlled by the medical faculties of the universities.
    c. was done through practical apprenticeship.
    d. was nonexistent.

43. The production of beer and ale was dominated by
    a. monasteries.
    b. burghers.
    c. convents.
    d. women.

44. In the popular cults of the local saints, a saint's status, according to the lay people who created these cults, was purely a function of the
    a. heroic nature of his or her life.
    b. miracles performed by the saint.
    c. social origins of the saint.
    d. pious devotion of the saint.

45. The typical peasant diet included all of the following *except*
    a. bread.
    b. cheese.
    c. beer and ale.
    d. meat.

46. Hospital care in this period
    a. was available in urban environments.
    b. had declined from earlier periods.
    c. was equally available in rural and urban areas.
    d. relied heavily on female practitioners.

47. The hagiographic cults of local saints
    a. originated with local believers.
    b. were created by the church leadership.
    c. indicates the weakness of religious feelings.
    d. were endorsed by the papacy.

48. The center of community life in the village was the
    a. manor house.
    b. tavern.
    c. church.
    d. mill.

49. According to medieval theology, the most powerful intercessor with Christ was
    a. St. Elmo.
    b. the Virgin Mary.
    c. the pope.
    d. the Holy Spirit.

50. The popular belief in ghosts led to
    a. the church's discovery of purgatory.
    b. a great witch hunt.
    c. an internal crusade againt heresy.
    d. the rise of the cult of the Virgin Mother.

51. The popular religion of medieval Christians included all of the following *except*
    a. cults of local saints.
    b. daily rituals.
    c. centrality of the parish church.
    d. the practice of oblation.

52. In the higher ranks of the social structure of the High Middle Ages,
    a. all knights were nobles.
    b. wealth was the greatest determinant of power and influence.
    c. non-noble women could enter the nobility through marriage.
    d. the nobility enjoyed a special legal status, based on birth.

53. The term *ministerials* refers to
    a. a large class of servile knights in Germany.
    b. the parish clergy in the Holy Roman Empire.
    c. the expanded papal bureaucracy.
    d. church officials who also served lay rulers.

54. The most prevalent means of limiting family size during the High Middle Ages was
    a. infanticide.
    b. abandonment.
    c. abstinence.
    d. abortion.

55. Strategies to control nobles' family size included all of the following *except*
    a. oblation.
    b. late marriage.
    c. infanticide.
    d. birth control.

56. One source of tension in noble families was the
    a. generation gap between father and son.
    b. mother's dominance of family affairs.
    c. increasing value of women's marriage portions.
    d. abolition of oblation.

57. The cuckolded husband as a theme in many works of this period is probably a result of the
    a. lavish lifestyle of the nobility.
    b. practice of oblation among the nobility.
    c. age difference between husbands and wives.
    d. decline of religious fervor.

58. The practice of oblation seems to have
    a. declined drastically by the High Middle Ages.
    b. had little impact on the composition of monastic populations.
    c. been denounced by the church leadership.
    d. provided the nobility with a humane option for superfluous children.

59. Nobles' responsibilities included all of the following *except*
    a. military service to their liege-lord.
    b. management of their estates.
    c. maintenance of order and dispensation of justice on their estates.
    d. maintenance of a monastery or convent on their estates.

60. Noble women in this period
    a. managed the manor's "inner economy" and the estate in the husband's absence.
    b. found their role limited to bearing and rearing children.
    c. saw their role greatly reduced by the use of professional estate managers.
    d. were able to travel extensively.

61. Aristocratic widows
    a. usually returned to their parents' home.
    b. often controlled family properties and exercised great authority.
    c. were forced to enter convents.
    d. had no legal rights.

82 / *Life in Christian Europe in the High Middle Ages*

62. Noble violence was most often a consequence of
    a. foreign invasion.
    b. economic depression.
    c. late inheritance.
    d. oblation.

63. The primary source of recruitment for monasteries and convents was
    a. adults who joined for personal and religious reasons.
    b. noble children given as child-oblates.
    c. serfs seeking to escape the unfree system of serfdom.
    d. parish priests who yearned for the contemplative life.

64. For noble women who did not wish to marry or live at home,
    a. convent life was the only available option.
    b. apprenticeship in select trades was acceptable.
    c. there were no options.
    d. endless pilgrimages to religious sites was their only option.

65. The career of Hildegard of Bingen was
    a. relatively typical for religious women of her class.
    b. remarkable for its intellectual creativity and political influence.
    c. limited to administrative achievements in her convent.
    d. representative of the influence of the friar orders.

66. The career of the nun Isabella of Lancaster is typical for women of her class because of her
    a. literary success.
    b. devout religious feelings.
    c. sexual promiscuity.
    d. administrative skills.

67. Daily life in monasteries centered on
    a. intellectual pursuits.
    b. the liturgy.
    c. the oblates.
    d. estate management and operations.

68. In medieval monasteries, manual labor was performed by the
    a. lay brothers.
    b. choir monks.
    c. almoners.
    d. sacristan monks.

69. Jean Mouflet of Sens, whose story is featured in "Individuals in Society," was able to secure his manumission from serfdom by
    a. running away to an unsettled region of Brittany.
    b. living in the city of Sens for one year.
    c. making an annual payment to his lord, Abbot Gregory.
    d. participating in a land reclamation project.

70. The typical response of monasteries to their financial problems was to
    a. improve the management of their estates.
    b. exhaust their cash reserves and credit.
    c. appeal to Rome for subsidies.
    d. sell off treasures accumulated in better times.

71. In "Listening to the Past," the kinsmen of Guibert of Noyon attempted to get his father to join a monastery because
    a. of his poor health.
    b. his religious nature was so overwhelming.
    c. the family was indebted to a local monastery.
    d. they wanted to possess his property.

History and Geography

72. How many fields was the typical manor likely to be divided into? What factors influenced which crops were planted and the method of crop rotation in these fields? Besides the arable fields where the crops were planted, what were the other features of a typical manor?

73. In what ways did geographic conditions affect the institution of serfdom in various regions of Europe?

# CHAPTER 11

THE CREATIVITY AND VITALITY OF THE HIGH MIDDLE AGES

Key Terms

1. sheriffs
2. *Domesday Book*
3. Frederick II Hohenstaufen
4. Philip Augustus
5. Frederick Barbarossa
6. territorial lordship
7. Magna Carta
8. common law
9. Thomas Becket
10. Chretien de Troyes
11. bill of exchange
12. faubourgs
13. Lübeck
14. Latin Quarter
15. flying buttress
16. Thomas Aquinas
17. *universitas*
18. merchant guilds
19. Albigensians
20. Franciscans
21. troubadours
22. "road revolution"

Essay Questions

23. The emergence of towns during the High Middle Ages had a profound impact on Europe. Describe and assess the impact of the growth of towns on European society and the economy. What impact did the emergence of the towns have on the church and the state in this period?

    The essay should briefly describe the emergence of towns in this period. Second, the essay should consider the impact on societal structure, discussing the rise and growth of the middle classes and the urban working classes, and the appeal to peasants of Europe and how this affected relations between landlords and peasants. Next, the changes in the economy, such as the burgeoning of long-distance trade and manufacturing, must be described; the interrelationship between society and economy should also be mentioned. The impact on the church should include such things as urban dissatisfaction with the clergy, and the message of medieval Christianity and the poor response of the church. The role of towns in the emergence of strong, centralized governments, both by providing greater sources of revenues through taxation and as political allies against independent aristocrats must also be described. The thoughtful essay would conclude by stressing the rise of towns in all these areas and how the changes would lead to the modern world.

24. The economic changes of the twelfth and thirteenth centuries are often referred to as revolutionary, even capitalistic. Why? What were the roots of this commercial revolution? How did the business community respond to the new economic situation? How were commerce and trade organized and facilitated? What were the roles of the merchants' and artisans' guilds?

This essay should begin with a description of the origins of the commercial revolution: especially the rise of towns; the resumption and expansion of long-distance trade and the growth of the wool trade; new silver mines in Germany, Bohemia, northern Italy, etc., and the impact of increased coinage on international trade (with a wide array of commodities). One should include peace and stability, rising agricultural output, and growing population. Next, one should describe the various innovations which appeared at the time: banks with European-wide branch offices; regular business correspondence; business registers; group investments and ventures; and the evolution of complex, international trading companies. The role of "road revolution" should also be mentioned. The Hanseatic League and northern Italian city-states should certainly be discussed. The regulatory and social roles of merchant and artisanal guilds should be described. Finally, the essay should include a conclusion in which one considers the degree to which these changes should be considered capitalistic.

25. A word associated with late medieval towns is *liberty*. What did this mean for individuals? For the towns? How did individuals and towns gain their liberty?

This essay should begin with a definition of the term, as it was used in the High Middle Ages. Next, one should describe the nature of personal liberty for townspeople in this era; a juxtaposition to the status of peasants could be used to indicate the urban situation. Third, the political status of towns needs to be addressed; specifically, one should discuss the somewhat independent nature of the towns and the political alliance with the centralizing monarchs. Finally, the manner in which liberty was attained must be described for both individuals and the towns. In this section, one could discuss the importance of tax revenues and political and military support which the monarchs received from the towns. The impact on serfdom should also be mentioned.

26. What impact did the economic changes and emergence of urban life have on the role of women and their life choices?

This essay should focus on the opportunities available to women in the urban environment; the role of women in both merchant and artisanal guilds must be discussed. Employment of women in textiles manufacturing should also be addressed. Women as independent businesspeople should be included. The thoughtful essay may consider the unsettled nature of urban life at the time and the fact that women represented a majority of the urban population as enabling factors.

27. One of the most critical aspects of the emergence of the new monarchies was the development of

royal justice. How did the kings of France and England establish the primacy of royal justice over local justice? In what ways were they similar? Different? What was the impact of the expansion of systems of royal justice?

Initially, the essay should indicate why the development of royal justice was critical. Next, the student should describe the manner in which royal justice was established in England and France, including such things as *baillis, senechals,* and sheriffs. This section should indicate the similarities (royal officials in charge of justice) and differences (the use of local notables in England as opposed to reliance on non-locals in France, for example). Finally, one should assess the overall impact of the emergence of royal justice, not only on the struggle between monarchs and nobilities, but also on governmental bureaucracy, intrusion of the state in local affairs, social relations, and jurisprudence in each state.

28. The High Middle Ages saw the emergence of two new art forms: Gothic architecture and troubadour poetry. Since art is often considered a mirror of life, how do these two art forms reflect their age?

In order to address this question fully, the essay should begin with a brief description of both art forms. Next, one should discuss the ways in which Gothic architecture, especially the cathedrals, reflect society; for instance civic pride and piety, urban wealth, and increasingly sophisticated abilities and tastes (indicated by increasingly sophisticated construction techniques and decorative arts) are all reflected. Troubadour poetry should then be considered for what it reveals about society. (A strong essay should note the regional nature of troubadour poetry and indicate the difference between northern and southern traditions.) The usual themes of this literary style should be indicated; the social class (the nobility) for whom much of the troubadour poetry was produced will help to illuminate the themes. One should mention the influence of troubadour poetry on the development of vernacular languages. Finally, the essay should provide a conclusion on the more worldly nature of both art forms; a good essay would close by indicating the role of art as medium of social communication.

29. During the High Middle Ages, the medieval monarchs of England, France, and Germany had common goals and faced similar problems. The solutions to the problems laid the foundations for their modern states. What were these solutions and how did these lay the foundation for modern states.

The essay should begin by outlining the common goals: extension of royal authority, improved means of communication, public order, increase of tax revenues, and establishment of efficient bureaucracies. Then the essay should describe the changes instituted: the manner by which the monarchs increased unity and improved communications; how revenues were raised and the relationship between the army, the bureaucracy, and taxpayers; the medieval concept of just war and the resultant constrictions on taxation and how the monarchs dealt with this problem: the blending of the old (feudal taxes such as scutage) with the new (the Norman inquest) is a good example of this. Finally, the essay should define what a modern state is and then compare the attributes of a modern state with those created by the medieval monarchs of the High Middle Ages.

30. In this era of state-building, Germany was less successful than England or France. Why? How does the career of Frederick Barbarossa illustrate the problems of centralization?

This essay should begin discussing the concept of "territorial lordship." Then the essay should discuss the inherent problems of the size of the empire and the impact of the lay investiture controversy on German political and social evolution. The economic growth of the twelfth and thirteenth centuries greatly enriched territorial lords, allowing them to maintain and even increase their power and independence. The essay should also point out that the German emperor lacked the strong, central, royal domain (like the Île de France), and the elective nature of the office of emperor. Next, the essay should provide a brief narrative of the career of Emperor Frederick Barbarossa, including: his efforts at establishing royal justice, with the unfortunate consequence of strengthening power of local nobles, through the institution of the peace associations (*landfrieden*); misguided attempt to annex the wealthy, northern Italian cities rather than focusing his efforts on unifying the empire.

31. Perhaps the most remarkable event of the High Middle Ages was the emergence of towns. What was urban life like? What does William fitz-Stephen's description of London reveal about everyday life and the people who lived such lives? Who lived in the towns and what did they do? What was the role of the guilds? What was the primary function of the towns?

This should be a descriptive essay of urban life. The descriptions in the text and "Listening to the Past" provide excellent material to support one's descriptions. In addition to everyday life, the social structure must be discussed thoroughly, including not only the relationship between one''s employment status and one's social status, but also the participation of women in the urban economy and their position in the social structure. Next, one should describe the economic, political, and social functions of both merchant and artisanal guilds. Finally, the essay should attempt to indicate the role of towns and cities in European civilization, such as commercial centers and administrative headquarters; the thoughtful essay should extend this discussion to consider the role of towns and cities in the emergence of the modern world more generally.

32. Heresy, a serious problem in the High Middle Ages, was closely linked with the emergence of the towns. Why? How did it manifest itself? How did the church and the state combat this behavior? With what degree of success? Why did the authorities react so strongly against heretical movements?

This essay should begin with a consideration of the factors that encouraged the explosion of heresy in the towns, such as the inadequacy of church leadership in regard to urban culture, the rural basis of Christian theology, and desires of urban populations for a pious, capable clergy. Second, the essay should include examples of heretical movements. Third, church and state response, including the concept of medieval unity as justification, should be discussed; this must include both the internal crusades against the Albigensians, the establishment of the mendicant orders, and the Inquisition.

33. "The birth of the university is another example of the creativity and vitality of the High Middle Ages." Assess this quotation critically, being sure to indicate the roots of the university, its methods of scholarly and pedagogical practices, composition and size of faculty (teachers and students), and impact on European civilization. How accurate is the quotation?

This essay should begin with a discussion of the roots: cathedral and monastic schools, using the example of Chartres; *studium generale*; universities in Bologna and Salerno. Next should be a thorough description of the curriculum and the Scholastic method; a discussion of the impact of

Islamic transmission of Greek texts on European philosophy would be a valuable addition. Composition and size should indicate some of the more famous scholars, but must also include a discussion of the broad appeal and influx of students to Paris, Oxford, Cambridge; the Latin Quarter serves as a good example of this growth. The impact includes the contributions of Abelard, Aquinas, John of Salisbury, and foundations for future scientific discoveries, and the role of university graduates in the expanding bureaucracies of the new monarchies of Europe.

MULTIPLE-CHOICE QUESTIONS

34. Women with access to cash money
    a. did not exist.
    b. often made small, short-term loans, often to other women.
    c. almost always donated it to the parish church.
    d. were excluded from the guilds.

35. The term *territorial lordship* refers to the
    a. decentralized nature of political power in Germany.
    b. pope's claim of infallibility.
    c. local officials of England.
    d. emergence of centralized monarchies in England and France.

36. Perhaps the most significant difference between the administration of justice in the early Middle Ages and that of the High Middle Ages was the
    a. use of trained legal experts.
    b. change in perception, from crimes against an individual to that of crimes against the public interest.
    c. adoption of the trial by ordeal as an evidentiary tool.
    d. codification of laws, judicial procedure, and penal practices.

37. St. Thomas Aquinas argued that
    a. reason undermines faith.
    b. Scripture contradicts reason.
    c. reason can demonstrate some but not all Christian principles.
    d. Scripture must be accepted on faith.

38. Gothic cathedrals were
    a. dark, gloomy buildings.
    b. used strictly for religious ceremonies.
    c. the cause of much social tension.
    d. symbols of civic pride and urban wealth.

39. The Fourth Lateran Council forbade priests from attending trials by ordeal, thus effectively abolishing the practice, for all of the following reasons *except* that
    a. King Henry II did not approve of trial by ordeal.
    b. there was no basis for trial by ordeal in the Scriptures.
    c. it did not exist in Roman law.
    d. the practice seemed to "force" God to perform a miracle to serve human interests.

40. In England local administration was
    a. exercised by royal army officers.
    b. in the hands of unpaid, well-to-do local residents.
    c. exercised by professional bureaucrats from London.
    d. controlled by the local clergy.

41. Frederick Barbarossa's sworn peace associations (*landfrieden*)
    a. paved the way for the establishment of centralized monarchy in Germany.
    b. enhanced the independence and power of the German nobility.
    c. indicated the contempt with which the emperor regarded noble rights.
    d. greatly reduced the power of the seigneurial and manorial courts.

42. William the Conqueror had the *Domesday Book* compiled in order to
    a. codify English law.
    b. commemorate the Norman conquest of England.
    c. engender a feeling of national unity.
    d. tax accurately and set feudal obligations.

43. New developments in music included all of the following *except*
    a. atonal composition.
    b. counterpoint harmony.
    c. musical notation.
    d. the organum style of singing.

44. The fundamental principle of French administration was the idea that
    a. local and royal interests should be balanced.
    b. the French king was not superior to the pope.
    c. the French people's interests should be protected.
    d. royal interests superseded local interests.

45. The mendicant orders were formed
    a. to minister to the spiritual needs of townspeople.
    b. as a response to reform of the papacy.
    c. as a rejection of the urban lifestyle.
    d. to revitalize the monastic movement.

46. The most significant barrier to the centralization of Germany was
    a. the incomplete nature of the German people's conversion to Christianity.
    b. the resistance of the Hanseatic League.
    c. the power of the German nobility.
    d. the constant interference by France.

47. The greatest expense a city government had to meet was that of
    a. upkeep of its walls.
    b. payment of the tax liability to the lord.
    c. payment of its dues to the powerful Hanseatic League.
    d. street cleaning and charity works.

48. The explosive growth of international trade resulted in the evolution of new business arrangements of individual firms which included all of the following operations *except*
    a. a sedentary merchant running the home office, organizing the firm's international trade.
    b. carriers who transported the goods.
    c. mercenary military units to protect the firm's investments.
    d. company agents living in foreign cities.

49. According to medieval practice, kings could levy taxes only to
    a. provide basic social services.
    b. build and furnish cathedrals.
    c. fight just wars.
    d. pay the salaries of royal officials and the clergy.

50. Frederick II Hohenstaufen was able to create a strong state in Sicily by
    a. striking a bargain with the feudal nobility.
    b. consolidating economic and political power in the hands of the royal government.
    c. using the resources of the Holy Roman Empire.
    d. allying himself with the papacy in the struggle with Frederick Barbarossa.

51. Perhaps the most important element in the growth of royal power was the
    a. support of the great nobles.
    b. support of the papacy.
    c. economic collapse of manorial agriculture.
    d. establishment of royal judicial systems.

52. Archbishop Thomas Becket was murdered because he
    a. challenged the belief that faith and reason are in constant opposition.
    b. supported Philip the Fair's attempts to tax the French clergy.
    c. opposed Henry II's attempt to make the English clergy subject to royal justice.
    d. preached against the growing tide of anti-Semitism in Europe.

53. In the German empire, the regional magistracies, *landgericht*,
    a. dealt with civil, petty matters.
    b. were presided over by imperial magistrates.
    c. had wide jurisdiction over serious criminal cases.
    d. replaced seigneurial and manorial courts.

54. The constant reissuing of the Magna Carta from 1215 to 1485 resulted in the document acquiring an enduring importance, signifying that
    a. all Englishmen were created equal.
    b. all Englishmen, including the king and government, must obey the law.
    c. local interests would always prevail against increasing royal power.
    d. English common law would only apply to English men and women.

55. Themes in the troubadour poetry of southern France included
    a. courtly love and carnal desire.
    b. the problems of urban life.
    c. theological disputes.
    d. Greek and Roman legends.

56. Prejudice against Jews and homosexuals was most likely a product of
    a. increasing wealth.
    b. contact with the Muslim world.
    c. the desire for social conformity.
    d. the increasing visibility of both groups.

57. The primary function of towns and cities was
    a. to pay taxes to the monarch.
    b. as a market center.
    c. as an administrative center.
    d. to provide an escape valve for rural overpopulation.

58. The economic opportunities available to women in the towns were
    a. limited to prostitution.
    b. little different from that of the rural economy.
    c. limited to domestic service.
    d. concentrated in the craft guilds.

59. Towns and cities in the Low Countries and Italy usually were governed by
    a. the leaders of the merchant guilds.
    b. royal governors.
    c. elected popular assemblies.
    d. the clergy.

60. Roman law was based on
    a. legal precedents.
    b. common traditions.
    c. fixed maxims of the Justinian Code.
    d. trial by ordeal.

61. The Hanseatic League was
    a. a coalition of the northern Italian cities.
    b. formed to combat heresy in northern Europe.
    c. created to challenge Venice for control of trade with the east.
    d. a trading union of northern European cities.

62. The major gift which Arabic thinkers gave to western Europe was the
    a. transmission of Greek texts.
    b. Islamic philosophical tradition of tension between faith and reason.
    c. concept of zero.
    d. troubadour tradition of music and poetry.

63. Beguines were
    a. heretics who believed sexual activity was evil.
    b. religious women who worked, prayed, and taught in the towns.
    c. female troubadours.
    d. imperial officials who allied with Frederick Barbarossa.

64. According to the Scholastic philosophers, one achieved salvation through
    a. God's grace alone.
    b. faith and God's grace.
    c. God's grace and the use of reason.
    d. the use of reason.

65. English common law featured all of the following *except*
    a. reliance on precedence.
    b. judicial interference.
    c. access to evidence.
    d. no torture to secure evidence.

66. The individual whose work was most critical in the building of Gothic cathedrals was the
    a. bishop or archbishop.
    b. architect.
    c. banker.
    d. master mason.

67. Secular authorities joined the church in the efforts to combat heresy primarily because
    a. religious uniformity was deemed vital for a society to survive.
    b. they feared for the immortal souls of their subjects.
    c. kings did not want the church leaders to exercise any power in their states.
    d. most heretical movements refused to pay taxes.

68. The Albigensians believed that
    a. salvation came from the sacraments.
    b. God had created spiritual things and the Devil had created material things.
    c. sacraments given by immoral priests were tainted.
    d. women were the scourge of God.

69. In general, troubadour poetry
    a. reflected the ideals of the aristocracy.
    b. reflected the ideals of the merchant class.
    c. retarded the development of vernacular languages.
    d. found expression only in France.

70. Enrico Dandolo, doge of Venice whose role in the Fourth Crusade is presented in the "Individuals in Society," is representative of the
    a. religious intensity of the age.
    b. decline of Venice as an economic power in the Mediterranean.
    c. secular and bourgeois interests of many in this era.
    d. desire to return the Holy Land to Christian control.

71. All of the following were characteristics of the new Dominican and Franciscan orders *except*
    a. an urban orientation.
    b. apostolic poverty.
    c. education.
    d. a strict hierarchy.

72. The Inquisition was an attempt to
    a. root out and destroy heresy.
    b. inventory the wealth of England.
    c. regulate university curricula.
    d. counteract the influence of the mendicant orders.

73. The most significant outcome of the war between Edward I of England and Philip the Fair of France in 1294 was the
    a. redefinition of "just war."
    b. development of standing professional armies in both states.
    c. loss of power and prestige experienced by the papacy.
    d. centralization of Germany while France was occupied elsewhere.

74. According to William fitz-Stephen's description of London, presented in "Listening to the Past," the most troublesome problems were
    a. business stagnation and unemployment.
    b. overcrowding and lack of educational facilities.
    c. immoderate drinking and frequency of fires.
    d. the poor quality of available agricultural produce and the decline of religious activities.

History and Geography

75. In general, one could argue that all of the changes discussed in this chapter resulted from the rebirth and great expansion of international trade. Describe the trade routes and products which were critical to the revival of long-distance trade.

76. What were the major cities of the Hanseatic League? Describe the trade routes of the Hanseatic traders.

77. According to William fitz-Stephen, London was a bustling commercial center. Why?

CHAPTER 12

THE CRISIS OF THE LATER MIDDLE AGES

Key Terms

1. "seven lean years"
2. Christine de Pisan
3. Statute of Laborers
4. *atra mors*
5. Tana
6. Joan of Arc
7. Crécy
8. vernacular
9. François Villon
10. Charles University
11. Babylonian Captivity
12. Mudejars
13. House of Commons
14. John Wyclif
15. Margaret Paston
16. conciliar movement
17. Hot Street
18. Statute of Kilkenny
19. Jacquerie
20. fur-collar crime
21. *natio*
22. *Deutschtum paragraph*
23. banns

Essay Questions

24. Despite the obvious disastrous impact of the Black Death, European society seemed to recover and actually emerge stronger after the worst ravages of the plague had passed. How can one account for this development?

    This essay should describe fully the consequences of the Black Death: the social consequences must include a discussion of the mortality rate, indicating both the higher incidence of death among the lower classes and the fact that the upper classes were affected as well; mortality among the clergy, especially in Germany, should be included. The discussion of the economic consequences should consider both the traditional and newer views: the traditional view of the Black Death as an economic disaster compared to the newer view which emphasizes economic resilience, rising per capita wealth, higher wages, more equitable distribution of wealth, and labor mobility. This should be connected to social consequences in that the laboring classes gained advantages. Mention should be made of the increased use of slaves imported in the Mediterranean. Then the psychological consequences must be discussed, with the emphasis on the profound pessimism exemplified certain works of art and the extreme behavior of groups like the flagellants. Finally, the essay should include a discussion of the torn fabric of European society, increased slavery, new national institutions of higher education (Clare College in Cambridge, Charles University in Prague) to respond to shortages of priests but which indicated the decline of the international nature of medieval culture.

25. During the later Middle Ages vernacular literature rose to prominence. What was unique about this new literature? Who were its main practitioners? How did the new national literature reflect the political and social development of the times?

In this essay, the student should first provide a definition of vernacular literature, stressing the usage of vernacular languages such as English and French; this section should also include a discussion of the more worldly themes of vernacular literature. The essay should include several examples of vernacular writers (Dante, Chaucer, Villon, Pisan) and their works. The essay then should discuss vernacular literature as it related to the development of national consciousness and national pride; works on national history exemplify this, including the works of writers on the frontiers of Europe such as the Bohemian *Dalimil Chronicle*. Growing literacy among lay people should also be discussed and thus the increased audience for writers, which can also be tied to the discussion of new, worldly, modern themes. In general, a discussion of the growth of literacy and literature to meet the needs of an increasingly complex society should conclude the essay.

26. In addition to all the other crises of the later Middle Ages, and in large part resulting from these crises and adding to them, there was an outbreak of popular uprisings all across Europe. What caused these uprisings? Against whom were they directed? What tactics did each side use? What were the goals of the rebels? How successful were they?

This question refers to the general unrest in the lower classes; a thoughtful essay will consider not just peasant uprisings, but also urban riots (the Peasants' Revolt in England and *ciompi* in Florence are good examples) either connected with or isolated from rural uprisings. The general socio-economic conditions should be discussed as causative factors: feudal obligations, rising money rents on lands, decreasing opportunity to become artisanal masters, fur-collar crime, plague, famine, and taxation. The brutality of each side must be described. The goals, usually limited to alleviation of economic problems and relaxation of manorial obligations, should be considered, along with aristocratic failure to respond. The essay must assess the overall success of the uprisings: in France, lack of effort to alleviate problems led to further revolts; in England, despite noble resistance, serfdom disappeared by 1550. A good conclusion connects the success of the Peasants' Revolt in England to general trends of late medieval society.

27. The Hundred Years' War had serious consequences for both England and France. What were the immediate political, social, and economic results of the war on both sides of the English Channel? What were the long-term implications? Which side seems to have won?

In this comparative essay, the student must explain the impact of the war on both states. For France, immediate consequences would include population loss, decreased agricultural productivity, loss of trade, decline of international status, and a disaffected peasantry; for England, this would include loss of manpower for local government, breakdown of order at local level, increased number of beggars and criminals ("Listening to the Past" offers several examples to support this,) and a slump in the wool industry. The discussion of long-term consequences should focus on the emergence of national consciousness, the connection of royal and national interests which were linked to military success in both states, and on the growing power of the English parliament and the lack of such a development in France.

28. The problems of the papacy, exemplified by the Babylonian Captivity, gave rise to the conciliar movement and led to schism in the church. What were the underlying causes of this development? What were the consequences - religious, social, and political - of this crisis in the Christian church?

In this essay, the student must address the problems of the church at the time, including such things as decline of papal prestige, identification with French policies, lack of spiritual objectives, and the extravagance of the papal court, using Pope John XII as an exemplar. Next, the political aspects of the Great Schism must be discussed fully. The subsequent calls for reform and the confusion of the common people should be discussed. The conciliar movement should then be considered, including its roots and supporters (such as Marsiglio, Wyclif, and Conrad), what these individuals argued for, and the impact of the Council of Constance. The discussion should include John Hus, his ideas and his followers, and his fate. Finally, one should conclude by addressing the impact of the movement on Europe; for the people, pre-Reformation movements offered spiritual support, for the states, increased control over their clergies, and finally, the continued decline of papal prestige.

29. The later Middle Ages saw a transformation on the frontiers of Europe, a transformation which was caused by the great surge in migration and colonization from England, Germany, and France. Describe the changes resulting from this colonization of frontier regions. What was the primary cause of these changes and what were the consequences?

This essay must describe the influx of colonists into the various frontier regions of Europe: English into Ireland and Scotland, Germans, French and others into eastern Europe, French into Spain; one should stress the surge of Germans into eastern Europe occasioned by plague. The essay should then juxtapose the previous dualistic practices, exemplified by the policies of Spanish monarchs toward the Mudejars, and the imposition of uniform, and typically discriminatory, legal systems, with the Statute of Kilkenny being one of many which could be used as an exemplar. Next, the essay should identify the general trends of discrimination (for instance in the appointment of ecclesiastical offices,) ghettoization, and racism based on blood descent, and the corresponding nativist reaction, especially prevalent in eastern Europe; the examples of Bishop John of Cracow, Jakob Swinka of Gniezno, John of Drazic, the *Deutschtum paragraph*, and the *Dalimil Chronicle* are all useful inclusions. Finally, the essay should emphasize the role of racism, a socially constructed category, with the emphasis on blood descent, as the root cause of these new arrangements; a good essay would include economic competition and the competition for ecclesiastical appointments as supplemental causes of the racial strains on the frontiers of Europe.

Multiple-Choice Questions

30. All of the following were typical of the legal codes imposed in eastern Europe *except*
    a. a ban on intermarriage between Germans and Slavs.
    b. children of mixed marriages would be considered the race of the mother.
    c. membership in guilds would berestricted to those of German blood.
    d. holders of public office had to be of "pure" German descent.

31. The *Dalimil Chronicle* traces the history of the
    a. Bohemian people.
    b. Black Death in eastern Europe.
    c. English conquest of Ireland.
    d. Great Schism.

32. To cope with the agrarian crises, monarchs resorted to all of the following policies *except*
    a. condemnation of speculation.
    b. strict regulation of the grain trade.
    c. importation of grain from abroad.
    d. abolition of slavery.

33. All of the following are true about vernacular literature in eastern Europe *except* that it
    a. featured translations of the knightly sagas of the West in native languages.
    b. featured translations of religious literature from Latin into native languages.
    c. rejected everything from the West.
    d. arose as a response to German immigration and its impact on native culture.

34. In general, the clergy during the plague
    a. cared for the sick and buried the dead.
    b. fled to monasteries in the countryside.
    c. were relatively untouched by the epidemic.
    d. refused to administer sacraments to plague victims.

35. The highly infectious nature of the plague was enhanced by
    a. the imposition of quarantine measures.
    b. an influx of peasants seeking medical care.
    c. urban congestion and lack of sanitation.
    d. the total absence of health-care facilities.

36. Economically, the Black Death resulted in a
    a. complete economic collapse.
    b. sharp drop in per capita wealth.
    c. sharp increase in per capita wealth.
    d. sharp increase in unemployment.

37. The social consequences of the agrarian crises included all of the following *except*
    a. abandonment of homesteads.
    b. urban migration by young males.
    c. rise in vagabondage.
    d. overpopulation in rural areas.

COPYRIGHT © HOUGHTON MIFFLIN COMPANY. ALL RIGHTS RESERVED.

38. The establishment of new colleges and universities in the years following the Black Death
    a. greatly weakened the international nature of medieval culture.
    b. were generally similar to the internationally oriented earlier universities.
    c. enhanced the role of the papacy in European affairs.
    d. had no apparent connection to the previous crises.

39. During the Hundred Years' War, the English kings were supported by French barons because they
    a. disapproved of the Babylonian Captivity.
    b. were promised estates in England.
    c. wanted to stop the French monarchy's centralizing efforts.
    d. were economically dependent on the English wool trade.

40. The English victory at the Battle of Crécy resulted from
    a. the chivalric superiority of the English knights.
    b. their alliance with the Germans.
    c. the cowardice of the French knights.
    d. the effective use of longbows.

41. The Hundred Years' War saw the
    a. English acquire substantial French territory.
    b. widespread use of government propaganda.
    c. first use of naval blockades.
    d. weakening of the House of Commons.

42. Conciliarists, such as the theologians Pierre d'Ailly and Conrad Gelnhausen, maintained all of the following *except* that
    a. reform could best be accomplished by general assemblies representing all Christians.
    b. the pope's authority derived from the Christian community he was to serve.
    c. the pope was not the head of the Christian church.
    d. a constitutional form of church government was preferable to the monarchical form.

43. The spread of literacy
    a. was a response to needs of commerce and government.
    b. was hampered by the crises of the era.
    c. did not affect women.
    d. occurred only among the nobility and the clergy.

44. The young woman who saved France during the Hundred Years' War was
    a. Catherine of Siena.
    b. Joan of Arc.
    c. Christine de Pisan.
    d. Françoise of Florence.

45. The Great Schism resulted in all of the following consequences *except*
    a. a weakening of the faith of many Christians.
    b. a transformation in the governance of the Christian church.
    c. the emergence of the conciliar movement.
    d. a decline in the prestige of and respect for church leaders.

46. All of the following were consequences of the Hundred Years' War *except*
    a. the development of a French national assembly.
    b. the emergence of the English Commons as a political force.
    c. a rise of nationalistic feeling in England and France.
    d. economic and social dislocation.

47. The most significant aspect of vernacular literature was that
    a. it usually was written in prose rather than verse.
    b. it reintroduced Greek and Roman styles of literature.
    c. it was written in the national languages.
    d. its themes were those of a modern society.

48. Villon's *Grand Testament* is distinguished from the works of Dante and Chaucer by its
    a. use of the female voice.
    b. use of prose rather than verse.
    c. use of the language of the poor and the criminal.
    d. spiritual themes.

49. In the wake of the Black Death, guilds established regulations which set entry qualifications based on all of the following criteria *except*
    a. gender.
    b. ethnicity.
    c. family relations.
    d. age.

50. In the absence of the papacy during the Babylonian Captivity, Rome
    a. experienced an economic rebirth.
    b. was racked by heretical uprisings.
    c. was left poverty-stricken.
    d. was ruled by the College of Cardinals.

51. In the struggle for power between the competing popes during the Great Schism,
    a. the Council of Constance was able to seize power.
    b. most ordinary Christians supported the antipope.
    c. secular rulers made their choice of allegiance on religious grounds.
    d. secular rulers aligned themselves along political lines.

52. John Hus, featured in "Individuals in Society," and his memory have been used to serve all of the following movements *except*
    a. the Protestant Reformation.
    b. Enlightenment and its defense of freedom of expression.
    c. nineteenth-century Czech nationalists agitating for independence.
    d. Marxist socialism.

53. Theologian John Wyclif argued that
    a. the conciliar movement was heretical.
    b. Scripture alone should determine church belief and practice.
    c. salvation came from grace and reason.
    d. popes should be elected by all members of the clergy.

54. The great council that met at Constance from 1414 to 1418
    a. implemented a series of important reforms.
    b. did little more than elect a pope.
    c. abolished the Inquisition.
    d. reformed the monastic and mendicant orders.

55. In the Middle Ages, who and when a person married were determined by
    a. economic considerations.
    b. romantic love.
    c. accidental pregnancies.
    d. physical attraction.

56. The correspondence between John and Margaret Paston indicates that
    a. Margaret was an important partner in the marriage.
    b. their marriage was purely a financial arrangement.
    c. some peasants were literate.
    d. their children received all the couple's affection.

57. In the later Middle Ages, relations on the frontiers of Europe were conditioned most by
    a. the proximity of non-European invaders.
    b. the emphasis on blood descent.
    c. legal dualism.
    d. the high incidence of intermarriage between colonists and natives.

58. The age at which people married was
    a. different for peasants and journeymen artisans.
    b. determined by church sanctions against early marriages.
    c. based on their ability to provide for a family.
    d. regulated by the secular authorities.

59. In the High Middle Ages, prostitution was
    a. ruthlessly prosecuted by authorities.
    b. found only in the bustling seaports of the Mediterranean.
    c. both a rural and urban phenomenon.
    d. regulated by state authorities.

60. The actions of Catherine of Siena
    a. were representative of many vernacular writers.
    b. exemplified the desire of many Christians for the pope to return to Rome.
    c. were instrumental in the French victory in the Hundred Years' War.
    d. exemplified the extremist response to the plague.

61. The history of *Mudejars* in Spain before the fourteenth century is representative of the
    a. emphasis on blood descent in legal and political affairs.
    b. legal dualism between natives and colonists prior to the fourteenth century.
    c. ruthlessness with which the Spanish monarchs eliminated all Spanish Muslims.
    d. spread of religious fanaticism during the Black Death.

62. In the fourteenth century, the fundamental objective of the craft guilds had changed in order to
    a. provide employment for female artisans.
    b. maintain a monopoly on their products.
    c. ensure the economic security of their members.
    d. provide their members with a sense of satisfaction and brotherhood.

63. In addition to the cultural division between town and country, the most contested arena between natives and newcomers on the frontiers of Europe was the competition
    a. to control the colleges and universities.
    b. to control entry into the guilds.
    c. for ecclesiastical offices.
    d. for access to new lands being opened for settlement.

64. For recreation, commoners enjoyed all of the following *except*
    a. bearbaiting.
    b. alcoholic consumption.
    c. executions.
    d. tournaments.

65. Fur-collar crime was usually
    a. committed by peasants.
    b. limited to robbery and extortion.
    c. limited to fraud and embezzlement.
    d. an urban problem.

66. English oppression in Ireland was exemplified by the
    a. Dalimil Chronicle.
    b. Council of Constance.
    c. Statute of Kilkenny.
    d. Statute of Laborers.

67. All of the following clergymen are representative of the racial tensions in eastern Europe *except*
    a. John of Spoleto.
    b. Jakub Swinka.
    c. John of Crakow.
    d. John of Drazic.

68. The rebellions that swept across Europe in the late fourteenth and early fifteenth centuries
    a. were primarily political movements.
    b. resulted in important reforms.
    c. sparked efforts to reform the church.
    d. involved both rural and urban laboring people.

69. According to the description of the general eyre presented in "Listening to the Past," the apprehension of criminals was the responsibility of
    a. the army.
    b. the royal police force.
    c. local sheriffs and ordinary citizens.
    d. regional militia and the royal army.

History and Geography

70. Where was the main area of the Peasants' Revolt in England? Explain briefly this geographic concentration.

71. After examining Map 12.1, describe the spread of the Black Death in the fourteenth century. How can we account for this spread?

72. Describe the extension of colonization on the frontiers of Europe. Why did colonists from England, Germany, and elsewhere move to these frontier regions?

CHAPTER 13

EUROPEAN SOCIETY IN THE AGE OF THE RENAISSANCE

Key Terms

1. international style
2. Medici dynasty
3. Laura Cereta
4. balance of power
5. Francesco Petrarch
6. Gentile Bellini
7. humanism
8. *The Courtier*
9. movable type
10. Office of the Night
11. *Utopia*
12. Niccolò Machiavelli
13. François Rabelais
14. Jerome Bosch
15. Sofonisba Anguissola
16. Concordat of Bologna
17. Michelangelo
18. Star Chamber
19. "new Christians"
20. new monarchs

Essay Questions

21. While the Renaissance began in Italy, there was also a renaissance in northern Europe. Compare the Italian Renaissance with the Northern Renaissance. How can we account for the similarities and differences?

    For this essay, one should consider the exterior manifestations, such as the art produced in both regions and the spread of the international style. One should be sure to discuss the themes and subjects of works of art and literature, audiences and patrons in both regions, religiosity of each region. One should be sure to stress the greater role of Christianity and the social reformist nature of the Northern Renaissance. The lesser degree of classical influence on the north should also be noted and assessed as a factor explaining the differences between the two Renaissances.

22. Renaissance Europe saw the development of the so-called new monarchies. What were the guiding principles and basic tactics of the rulers of England, France, and Spain in their efforts to centralize their states? To what extent did these rulers rely on new policies and practices? How successful were the new monarchs?

This essay should first indicate the Renaissance political ideals which seemed to guide the new monarchs; referring to Machiavelli would be in order here. Emphasis should be placed on the efforts to control the nobles and establish domestic order. The discussion should include both innovative and traditional tactics of these rulers; this should include connection of royal authority with national identity, gaining of sovereignty, respect and loyalty of all peoples within the borders, ruthless suppression of opposition, Justinian legal code, middle-class officials, taxes, and armies. A brief narrative on each of the three states, emphasizing unique features, should then follow, for example the Spanish *reconquista* and the use of the Inquisition against the "new Christians." The essay should conclude with an assessment of the success of these centralizing monarchs.

23. The Italian city-states developed a theory and practical forms of international politics which would eventually be adopted by the great powers of Europe: the balance of power. Describe the basic tenets of this system of international relations and assess why that system was able to preserve the independence of the Italian city-states. What were the major deficiencies of the system and what was the impact on the Italian city-states?

The student should begin by defining balance-of-power diplomacy; this description should include discussion of equilibrium, compensation, and shifting alliances. The practices of permanent ambassadorships to conduct the foreign relations should also be described. Next, the essay should address how this system worked, with a brief narrative of the shifting alliances among the five major Italian powers outlined in the text. This description should lead, then, to a consideration of the weaknesses of the system such as its instability and, concomitantly, the virtual power vacuum resulting from instability, treachery, and lack of cooperation. Foreign invasions and domination were the impact of these deficiencies.

24. In what ways do Machiavelli's *The Prince*, Castiglione's *The Courtier*, and Alberti's "Self-Portrait of a Universal Man" (presented in "Listening to the Past") echo the fundamental principles of the Italian Renaissance? Choose one of the three and explain how that work would have been used by a Renaissance person to provide guidance.

First the student should state the fundamental principles (humanism, individualism, secularism) and then analyze each of the three works on this basis. This analysis calls for a degree of description for each work, to support or detract from the essay's arguments. The essay should then consider how effectively these works could be used by contemporaries; obviously, for princes, Machiavelli is most germane, while for courtiers, Castiglione is most germane; Alberti's autobiography seems best suited for artists. The astute essay writer should also address the general aspects of all three, using Alberti to emphasize the belief in personal genius.

25. In many ways the Renaissance was primarily an artistic movement. Describe Renaissance art. What were its themes and techniques? (Be sure to include relevant examples.) How were artists trained? What was their status in society? Who was their audience? How did Renaissance art reflect the changing attitudes and interests of Europeans?

In this question on the artistic aspect of the Renaissance, the student should begin with a discussion of the themes, religious and classical, of the movement; second, the techniques, such as realism, perspective, and balance, should be described. Examples should be cited; the text provides many such examples. Next, one should turn to the artists themselves, considering their training and status; the better essays could connect artistic genius (exemplified by Alberti's autobiographical sketch) with increasingly humanistic and realistic works of art. The system of patronage should also be discussed. Finally, the essay should attempt to assess to what extent Italian Renaissance art, with its increasingly secular styles, represented changing attitudes.

26. The issue of gender and status for both women and men underwent modification during the Renaissance. What was the status of women, both upper class and common, in this era? What does this reveal about Renaissance society in general?

This essay should certainly indicate the declining status of women from one the Middle Ages to the Renaissance, in terms of political power, property rights, and work. Better education for women should be mentioned; careers of female artists and writers should be included. The essay must also indicate that the world of upper-class women, described above, differed sharply with that of lower-class women. The evidence of the legal code's treatment of rape should be mentioned. The great divide between the upper and lower class should definitely be emphasized, with wealth and education defining the great social divide. The separate spheres of male and female activity, among the upper classes, and behavior should also be discussed. The essay should emphasize that women were considered part of a husband's household - a decoration, a possession.

27. The textbook maintains that, during the Renaissance, homosexual relations were an integral component in the shaping of masculine gender identity. Why?

This essay should discuss the evidence of homosexual activity: legislative acts, court records and especially the evidence of the Florentine Office of the Night. This discussion needs to indicate the age and status of the partners in order to demonstrate the cultural values implicit in the homosexual relations. Then the essay needs to indicate the various reasons offered for the incidence of homosexual activities, such as lack of "respectable" women and the notion that a homosexual act did not preclude sexual relations with women, and the fact that for many men, such acts were forms of male sociability.

28. The formation of the modern Spanish state by Ferdinand and Isabella resembled, in some ways, the examples of England and France; in other ways, the Spanish experience was profoundly different. How did the Spanish experience resemble yet differ from the other two? What are the implications of this historical development?

This essay should first indicate the Renaissance political ideals which seemed to guide the new monarchs, particularly Machiavelli. Emphasis should be placed on the efforts to control the nobles and establish domestic order, using innovative and traditional tactics. The essay should include reform of royal council, control of church, *hermandades*, etc. The essay should stress the lack of homogeneity of the Iberian peninsula and its continued confederated state. Most significantly, the essay must discuss the issue of the "new Christians" and the ultimate use of the Inquisition against them. The essay should conclude with an assessment of this racially motivated and justified policy to create ethnic homogeneity, as opposed to cultural homogeneity.

MULTIPLE-CHOICE QUESTIONS

29. Typically, the punishment for sexual crimes in Florence was based on the idea that
    a. women were not really human.
    b. women were too sexually oriented.
    c. women were the property of men.
    d. the body parts involved had to be punished or removed.

30. Florentine economic vitality rested primarily on banking and
    a. the wine industry.
    b. overseas trade.
    c. the wool industry.
    d. mining and agriculture.

31. The Italian urban nobility were united by all of the following *except*
    a. kinship.
    b. antagonism with the rural nobility.
    c. economic interests.
    d. social connections.

32. All of the following were among the Italian powers that dominated the peninsula *except*
    a. the Papal States.
    b. Florence.
    c. Paris.
    d. Venice.

33. The first artistic and literary manifestation of the Italian Renaissance appeared in
    a. Florence.
    b. Rome.
    c. Venice.
    d. Naples.

34. The Italian *popolo*
    a. established democracies in the Italian city-states.
    b. desired government offices and equality of taxation.
    c. were never able to influence Italian politics.
    d. controlled the wool industry.

35. By 1300, most of the Italian city-states were ruled by either signori or
    a. kings.
    b. oligarchies.
    c. elected assemblies.
    d. ecclesiastical princes.

36. As consumer habits changed, an aristocrat's greatest expense was usually his
    a. urban palace.
    b. military hardware and training.
    c. daughter's dowry.
    d. entertainments.

37. The appearance of clocks was closely connected with all of the following *except*
    a. urban life.
    b. the urge to control.
    c. a conceptualization of the universe in visual and quantitative terms.
    d. the social reformism of the northern Renaissance.

38. The official attitude toward rape indicates that
    a. the status of women had improved.
    b. it was a serious crime against the victim and society.
    c. it was not a serious crime against either victim or society.
    d. prostitution was designed to eradicate the crime.

39. Italian balance-of-power diplomacy
    a. was designed to prevent a single Italian state from dominating the peninsula.
    b. successfully prevented foreign domination of Italy.
    c. was primarily concerned with controlling the papacy.
    d. was critical to the economic success of Italy.

40. The Florentine Office of the Night was created to control
    a. homosexual activities.
    b. prostitution.
    c. radical elements in the *popolo*.
    d. the outbreak of heresy during the Renaissance.

41. The subjugation of the Italian peninsula by outside invaders was
    a. the product of the invaders' overwhelming superiority.
    b. the result of the economic collapse of Italy.
    c. inevitable.
    d. the result of the Italians' failure to coordinate a common defense.

42. Gentile Bellini's *Procession in the Piazza San Marcos*, described in "Individuals in Society," represents the
    a. decline of civic pride in Venice.
    b. role of confraternities in artistic patronage.
    c. social composition of the population of Constantinople.
    d. reformist traits of the Italian Renaissance.

43. The Italian Renaissance had as one of its central components
    a. Christian humility.
    b. a concern for the improvement of society in general.
    c. a glorification of individual genius.
    d. the attempt to use art to educate the urban masses.

44. Italian humanists stressed the
    a. study of the classics for what they could reveal about human nature.
    b. study of the classics in order to understand the divine nature of God.
    c. absolute authority of classical texts.
    d. role of the church in the reform of society.

45. The most important factor in the emergence of the Italian Renaissance was the
    a. decline of religious feeling.
    b. political disunity of Italy.
    c. rise of a wealthy, urban business elite.
    d. creation of powerful, centralized monarchies.

46. Alberti's autobiography, excerpted in "Listening to the Past," reveals all of the following *except*
    a. Renaissance individuals' quest for knowledge.
    b. the role of women in Renaissance society.
    c. the various skills expected of Renaissance individuals.
    d. the Renaissance belief in the individual.

47. The leaders of the Catholic church
    a. ignored the Renaissance.
    b. attempted to crush the secularism of the Renaissance.
    c. readily adopted the Renaissance spirit.
    d. used Renaissance ideals to promote moral reform.

48. According to Castiglione's Renaissance manual on courtesy and good behavior,
    a. the man was expected to cultivate skills to please the woman.
    b. the woman was to make herself pleasing to the man.
    c. men and women were virtually equals in love and romance.
    d. love and sexuality were interdependent.

49. According to Laura Cereta, the inferiority of women was a consequence of their
    a. biologic reproductive function.
    b. own failure to pursue personal fulfillment.
    c. lack of economic rights.
    d. overzealous commitment to religion.

50. Rich individuals sponsored artists and works of art
    a. because it was good for business.
    b. in order to please God.
    c. to glorify themselves and their families.
    d. to control unemployment.

51. Renaissance culture was
    a. enjoyed by most Europeans.
    b. rejected by the church for its secularism.
    c. that of a small, urban, business elite.
    d. limited to the Italian peninsula.

52. All of the following observations about homosexual activities are accurate *except* that
    a. all social classes were involved.
    b. such activities were completely rejected by society.
    c. boys were the passive objects of desire.
    d. such acts were part of the construction of masculine gender identity.

53. According to Machiavelli, the sole test of "good" government was whether it
    a. provided the necessary public services.
    b. was based on Christian morality.
    c. protected the liberty of its citizens.
    d. was effective.

54. The ultimate significance of Machiavelli''s work rests on two concepts: that politics is a science and
    a. the inevitability of the establishment of one permanent social order.
    b. government should provide justice for its citizens.
    c. that one permanent social order, reflecting God's will, cannot be established.
    d. that all politics must be amoral.

55. The invention of movable type led to all of the following *except*
    a. increased literacy.
    b. the use of government propaganda.
    c. the inculcation of national loyalties.
    d. the use of French as the language of polite society.

56. In terms of gender relations, Renaissance humanists argued that
    a. men and women were equals in intellectual pursuits.
    b. the status of women had improved since the Middle Ages.
    c. men and men alone should act in the public sphere.
    d. women should have equal opportunity in marital and extra-marital sexual relations.

57. For ordinary women, the Renaissance
    a. had very little impact.
    b. improved the material conditions of their life.
    c. worsened their status.
    d. allowed them access to education for the first time.

58. During the Renaissance, black slaves were
    a. used only as entertainers.
    b. highly prized for their exotic rarity.
    c. never used for manual labor.
    d. expelled from most of Europe.

59. The emergence of the private chapel as a component of the urban palace of Renaissance elites signified the
    a. passing of religious power into private hands.
    b. increased piety of the Renaissance.
    c. need for reform in the Christian church.
    d. siege mentality of many of these people.

60. The northern humanists believed that human nature
    a. was fundamentally corrupt.
    b. was fundamentally good.
    c. was incapable of improvement.
    d. had been changed forever by Adam's fall.

61. Thomas More's *Utopia* placed the blame for society's problems on
    a. human nature.
    b. God's will.
    c. society itself.
    d. the individual.

62. According to the Dutch humanist Erasmus, the key to reform was
    a. education.
    b. control of the papacy.
    c. a pious life.
    d. the concerted effort which only a strong state could afford.

63. *Gargantua and Pantagruel* indicates all of the following about Rabelais *except* that he
    a. disliked hypocritical clergy, pedantic academics, and pompous lawyers.
    b. believed institutions molded individuals.
    c. believed in educational reform.
    d. preferred sophisticated wit and intellectual cleverness.

64. The term "international style" refers to
    a. Italian balance-of-power diplomacy.
    b. the use of movable-type printing in Europe.
    c. the spread of artistic techniques and ideals.
    d. the tactics of the centralizing monarchs.

65. The social group that most often resisted the centralizing efforts of the "new monarchs" was the
    a. peasantry.
    b. nobility.
    c. bourgeoisie.
    d. urban workers.

66. The policies of the "new monarchs" of the fifteenth century were usually
    a. copied from Machiavelli.
    b. innovations.
    c. a combination of traditional and innovative practices.
    d. based on Augustinian political theory.

67. All of the following were aspects of the centralizing efforts of Charles VII of France *except*
    a. reform of the royal council.
    b. redistribution of feudal lands.
    c. reform of the judiciary.
    d. a permanent royal army.

68. The Concordat of Bologna
    a. asserted the superiority of a general council over the pope.
    b. ended the Habsburg-Valois wars.
    c. institutionalized the French king's control of the French church.
    d. established the French Estates General.

69. In order to undercut the power that the aristocracy exercised through its control of Parliament, English kings
    a. used their own financial resources.
    b. appealed directly to their subjects for tax monies.
    c. borrowed heavily from Italian bankers to meet their needs.
    d. augmented the ranks of the aristocracy with loyal henchmen.

70. The Star Chamber
    a. dealt with noble threats to royal power in England.
    b. was dominated by the great nobles of England.
    c. was the English equivalent of the Spanish Inquisition.
    d. dealt with the finances of the English government.

71. The Tudors won the support of the upper middle class by
    a. reforming the church.
    b. promoting peace and social order.
    c. restricting the wages of the working classes.
    d. lowering taxes and subsidizing the wool industry.

72. The "new Christians" of Spain were deeply resented for all of the following reasons *except*
    a. their role as tax collectors and money lenders.
    b. their excessive influence in government and administration.
    c. their prominence in commerce, medicine, and law.
    d. their control of the Inquisition.

73. Royal authority in Spain was enhanced by all of the following *except*
    a. the revival of the *hermandades*.
    b. the retention of the confederation structure among the kingdoms.
    c. the restructuring of the royal council.
    d. control of the church hierarchy.

74. Justification for the attacks on the "new Christians" in Spain was based on
    a. the insincerity of the Jews who converted to Christianity.
    b. Scriptural teachings that Jews could not become Christians.
    c. racial arguments that maintained Jews could be nothing but Jews.
    d. the belief that the "new Christians" had not renounced Islam.

History and Geography

75. What were the five major powers on the Italian peninsula? How did this affect the development of diplomatic relations in Italy?

76. After studying the text and Map 13.2, estimate the extent of Muslim territory on the Iberian peninsula in 1200 and in 1492.

77. What was the principal battlefield for the Habsburg-Valois wars? What impact did this have on the Italian city-states?

CHAPTER 14

REFORM AND RENEWAL IN THE CHRISTIAN CHURCH

Key Terms

1. Diet of Speyer
2. Twelve Articles
3. Brethren of the Common Life
4. Pilgrimage of Grace
5. Ninety-Five Theses
6. indulgence
7. predestination
8. priesthood of all believers
9. *Against the Murderous, Thieving Hordes of the Peasants*
10. *The Institutes of Religion*
11. Peace of Augsburg
12. Anabaptists
13. Catherine of Aragon
14. Supremacy Act (1534)
15. Puritans
16. John Knox
17. Gustavus Vasa
18. Council of Trent
19. Ursuline Order
20. Ignatius Loyola

Essay Questions

21. The Christian church had experienced periodic calls for reform prior to Luther's rebellion. How can we explain why Luther's challenge to the sale of indulgences sparked such startling revolution in European history?

    In this essay, one should describe the intellectual, moral, economic, and political situation in Europe on the eve of the Reformation. The discussion of intellectual roots should include the reformist trends of the northern humanists, the piety of most people, the increased literacy among urban populations and their resultant dissatisfaction with ignorant and immoral priests. The problems within the church, such as pluralism, absenteeism, and general lack of spiritual prestige should also be considered. The discussion of the social roots should include both a discussion of peasant unhappiness with the manorial system as well as urban dissatisfaction with both the clergy and the message of Christianity; the peasant grievances presented in "Listening to the Past" should be cited as supporting evidence as should the Twelve Articles. The state of political affairs in Germany (lack of political unity, role of papacy in German diplomacy, extensive outflow of gold from Germany to Rome) should next be discussed. Finally, one should discuss economic roots, which is of course related to social roots, changes in manorial obligations which harshened the existence for the peasantry (citing evidence from the text and "Listening to the Past"), rising taxes and clerical immunity from taxation, and in general the growth of the urban economy. Finally, the essay should certainly mention the indispensable role of Luther as a theologian and writer (coupled with the technological breakthroughs in printing).

22. Although the Protestant Reformation usually is interpreted as a religious movement, it did have a profound impact on European civilization in general. Discuss the political, social, and economic consequences of the Reformation. How did the Reformation affect women?

    The discussion of the political impact should include: the destruction of the concept of European unity; the idea of religious homogeneity within a state, decided by the prince; declining influence of the church in political affairs; churches' increasing identification with the state. One should also provide a brief narrative of the political history of the era, including the military confrontations. In the discussion on the social consequences, the Peasants' War should be considered carefully, with special attention to both the role of Luther and the results of that conflict; this discussion could indicate not only the limited impact on the social status of peasants but also the close and supportive relationship between Lutheranism and the state. The impact on urban society should certainly include a discussion of the Protestant tenet that all vocations have merit in God's eyes, thus providing religious justification for the business classes; a brief discussion of the Weberian concept of the Protestant work ethic can be included, but such a discussion should indicate the weaknesses of this argument. The impact on women should include Luther's exaltation of marriage and procreation as well as his denunciation of monastic lifestyle; within this framework, the loss of a career opportunity for upper-class women in Protestant states should be considered. The shared responsibility of husband and wife in the family should also be discussed, being sure to indicate that the husband was the ruler of the household. The role of women as leaders in the domestic religious arena and the increased role of upper-class women in charity work should be included.

23. How did the established Christian church, headquartered in Rome, respond to the challenge presented by Luther and subsequent Protestant reformers? How successful was this response?

    Initially, the essay should define both the Catholic and the Counter Reformations, indicating the spiritual renewal emphasized by the Catholic Reformation and the fear of infection emphasized by the Counter-Reformation. Following this, the essay should consider the attempts and slow pace of the conciliar reform movement, the new religious orders (Ursulines and Jesuits) and their effort both at spiritual renewal and missionary and reconversion activities, which is indicative of the blurring between the two components of the Catholic response. The role of the Inquistion, including mention of the Sacred Congregation and the Index, must also be included; the role of the Jesuits in this endeavor is further evidence of the intertwined nature of the Catholic Reformation and Counter-Reformation. The Council of Trent must be thoroughly discussed, both in relationship to the reforms that were produced as well as the attempt to incorporate the Protestant leadership. Finally, an assessment must be made; this should include the checking of the spread of

Protestantism (and even retrenchment) and the limited effectiveness of the Inquisition, citing the thriving publishing industry of Venice which ignored the Index. The essay must also indicate that the religious unity of Europe was shattered and impossible to reimpose.

24. Discuss the attempts—religious and secular—to reassert the unity of a Catholic Europe. Was this two-pronged offensive effective? Why or why not? In what ways did religion and politics work against each other?

   In this essay one should first describe the Counter-Reformation and its efforts at reconversion, including the effort of the Inquisition and the limited effectiveness of this attempt. Second, the political and military efforts of Charles V to reimpose unity on Europe should be fully discussed. The limited effectiveness of both efforts should next be described and explanations offered; such explanations should include not only religious convictions of Protestants and Catholics, but also political reasons (such as princely independence in Germany, for example) and economic factors (which could include not only the businesspeople's identification with Protestant theology but also the more avaricious aspect of the allure of rich monastic lands and control of church tithes). The slow pace of reform within the Catholic church could also be cited. Finally, the ongoing rivalry between the rulers of France and Habsburg should be considered, stressing the support given by the Catholic king of France to Protestant princes fighting against Charles V. One should also mention the far-flung empire of Charles and the distractions that this created; the threat of the Ottoman Turks should also be discussed.

25. According to the text, Luther did not ask new questions but offered new answers to old questions. What were these questions and what were Luther's answers?

   First, the essay should ask the questions: How is salvation achieved? What is the nature of the church? What is the source of religious authority? One should then move to a discussion of Luther's theology, being sure to stress salvation by faith alone, biblical authority, church as a community of believers, the merit of all vocations, differing number of sacraments, and the concept of consubstantiation. These should be juxtaposed to the Catholic positions: faith and works; Bible and church tradition; church equals the clergy; the primacy of clerical life; sacraments; and transsubstantiation.

26. How can we explain the success of Calvinism?

   To begin, a brief description of the spread of Calvinism should be provided. Next should be an assessment of its success; this assessment should include a description of the existing conditions in the areas affected by Calvinism, the appealing aspects of Calvin's theology, and Calvin's skill as a writer.

27. According to the text, the English Reformation was an act of state, initiated by the king's emotional life, as well as dynastic and political concerns. How accurate is this assessment? What were the long-term consequences of the English Reformation?

   This essay should include a thorough narrative of the English Reformation, including the emotional and political causes and the course of Henry VIII's efforts. Mention must be made of the Lollard tradition in England, but the recent scholarship indicating the vitality of the church must also be included, thus underscoring the political and personal nature of Henry's attack on the Roman church. Consequences should include a discussion of the impact of the confiscation of monastic properties on both the upper classes, tying them to the Tudor dynasty, and on the growth of bureaucracy to manage, temporarily, the confiscated lands which prompted a thorough reform of royal government. The limited spiritual nature of the Reformation and its impact on ongoing conflict among Puritans, Anglicans, and Catholics should also be discussed. The good essay will also mention the impact of Henry's reformation on Scottish and Irish religious reformations.

28. How do the actions of both Protestant and Catholic leaders exemplify the basic political creed of uniformity prevalent in Europe in the sixteenth century?

    Initially, the essay should provide an explanation of this concept, with perhaps pre-Reformation indications of this concept at work (expulsion of the Jews from Spain and internal crusades against heretics, for example). The essay should next consider the actions of religious and secular leaders in relation to this concept; this should include the efforts of Charles V, the Inquisition, John Calvin's condemnation of Michael Servetus, the Peace of Augsburg, and the seemingly European-wide antipathy toward the Anabaptists.

MULTIPLE-CHOICE QUESTIONS

29. In the early sixteenth century, critics of the church attacked all of the following *except*
    a. religious doctrine.
    b. clerical immorality.
    c. the ignorance of the parish clergy.
    d. the problems of pluralism and absenteeism.

30. The Brethren of the Common Life represent
    a. the extent of Protestant conversions in Italy.
    b. the power and appeal of John Calvin's message.
    c. an example of pre-Reformation popular piety.
    d. a typical response of the papacy to the Reformation.

31. Martin Luther wrote his letter entitled "Ninety-Five Theses" to Archbishop Albert in response to
    a. Luther's personal struggle with the question of salvation.
    b. the election of Charles V.
    c. the draining of Germany's wealth by the papacy.
    d. a new campaign to sell indulgences.

32. According to Luther, salvation
    a. comes from good works and faith.
    b. can be earned.
    c. comes from God's free gift of grace.
    d. is predestined.

33. Luther believed that he was justified in his reforming efforts because he
    a. was a Christian.
    b. was divinely inspired.
    c. had earned a professorship.
    d. had undergone a conversion experience similar to Paul of Tarsus.

34. In his Ninety-Five Theses, Luther criticized the selling of indulgences for all of the following reasons *except* that it
    a. failed to release any souls from purgatory.
    b. undermined the sacrament of penance.
    c. competed with preaching the Gospel.
    d. downplayed the importance of charity.

35. The Twelve Articles were
    a. the charter of the Lutheran church.
    b. grievances of the Swabian peasants.
    c. part of the political settlement of Augsburg.
    d. the pope's rebuttal to the Ninety-Five Theses.

36. In his *On Christian Liberty*, Luther used the term *freedom* to mean
    a. freedom from poverty.
    b. political liberty.
    c. freedom from the Roman church.
    d. freedom from any type of servile situation.

37. The Reformation affected women in all of the following ways *except*
    a. by exalting marriage.
    b. that husband and wife were to be equal partners in marriage.
    c. that women assumed control of the domestic religious arena.
    d. that women played a greater role in organizing public charity.

38. Luther believed that women should
    a. manage the household economy.
    b. be equal in all things.
    c. rule the household.
    d. pursue careers outside the home.

39. Luther's ideas about Roman exploitation of Germany
    a. appealed to political aspirations of German princes.
    b. were met with dismay by the ruling elite.
    c. led to administrative reform in the empire.
    d. found an audience only among the peasantry.

40. The Colloquy of Marburg was a
    a. negative response to Henry VIII's religious reforms in England.
    b. meeting of the electors of the empire at which Luther was found guilty of heresy.
    c. Catholic religious order formed to combat the Reformation.
    d. failed attempt to unify Protestant theology.

41. Charles V believed it was his duty to
    a. enable his subjects to lead their life in peace and prosperity.
    b. destroy Protestantism.
    c. maintain both the political and religious unity of Europe.
    d. reform the Catholic church.

42. John Knox was influential in the Reformation in
    a. Ireland.
    b. Scotland.
    c. Switzerland.
    d. Sweden.

43. As a result of the Peace of Augsburg, the people of Germany
    a. remained Catholics.
    b. were able to practice the religion of their choice.
    c. converted to Lutheranism.
    d. became either Lutheran or Catholic depending on the preference of their prince.

44. The majority of the German princes who adopted Lutheranism did so
    a. for economic and political reasons.
    b. for religious reasons.
    c. to appease their subjects.
    d. only with great reluctance.

45. The Protestant Reformation in Germany
    a. weakened the power of secular states.
    b. contributed to its continued fragmentation.
    c. destroyed Habsburg influence in the empire.
    d. helped pave the way for a unified nation.

46. In its relationship to secular power, Lutheranism can best be described as
    a. antagonistic.
    b. indifferent.
    c. supportive.
    d. rebellious.

47. Calvin's reform movement was
    a. suppressed by the civil authorities in Geneva.
    b. restricted to Switzerland and France.
    c. thoroughly integrated into the civil government of Geneva.
    d. rejected any role in the secular government of Geneva.

48. Ulrich Zwingli attacked all of the following *except*
    a. indulgences.
    b. monasticism and the Mass.
    c. cooperation between religious and civil authorities.
    d. clerical celibacy.

49. Central to Calvin's theology is the principle of
    a. free will.
    b. predestination.
    c. Christian liberty.
    d. justification by faith and good works.

50. According to Calvin, the elect were
    a. the leaders of the Genevan Consistory.
    b. the intellectual leaders of the Reformation.
    c. those individuals chosen for salvation.
    d. all Protestants.

51. The Genevan Consistory
    a. regulated the behavior of Genevans in a manner consistent with other European cities.
    b. severely regulated the conduct of Genevans.
    c. routinely harbored religious dissenters from around Europe.
    d. attempted to suppress Calvinism.

52. The decision to burn Michael Servetus at the stake indicates
    a. Calvin's hatred of Roman Catholicism.
    b. the religious intolerance of the Catholic Inquisition.
    c. Luther's rejection of other Protestant theologians.
    d. Calvin's harsh view of religious dissent.

53. The other Europeans oppressed the Anabaptists for all of the following reasons *except* their
    a. practice of adult baptism.
    b. pacifism.
    c. religious toleration.
    d. belief in the separation of church and state.

54. Calvinism became the driving force in international Protestantism because
    a. it preached predestination.
    b. Luther was embroiled in the conflict with the papacy.
    c. of the social and economic applications of Calvin's ideas.
    d. of Calvin's linguistic and legal skills.

55. The dissolution of the English monasteries
    a. resulted from Henry VIII's desire to confiscate their wealth.
    b. resulted in a more equitable distribution of land.
    c. deeply disturbed the English upper classes.
    d. was the result of rebellious activities by the monks.

56. Recent research on the English church before Henry VIII's break with Rome indicates that
    a. a vast gap existed between the clergy and the English people.
    b. the church was in a very healthy condition.
    c. conditions in England mirrored those on the Continent.
    d. clerical abuse and ignorance was worse in England than on the Continent.

57. The Reformation in England was primarily the result of
    a. dynastic and romantic concerns of Henry VIII.
    b. the missionary activity of the Lollards.
    c. the terrible conditions then existing in the English churches.
    d. efforts by Luther and his followers.

58. The pope refused to annul Henry VIII's first marriage for all of the following reasons *except* that
    a. he was distracted by the Lutheran revolt and the Habsburg-Valois wars.
    b. he would have had to concede that the previous pope had erred, adding fuel to Luther's fire.
    c. Henry's wife was the aunt of Charles V, who had just captured Rome.
    d. Henry's case for annulment had no justifiable basis in canon law.

59. The Pilgrimage of Grace attested to
    a. the continued strength of Catholicism in southern Europe.
    b. the popularity of John Calvin.
    c. popular opposition in northern England to Henry VIII's Reformation.
    d. popular support of Luther in his conflict with the pope.

60. The parliamentary acts that removed the English church from papal jurisdiction
    a. were probably misunderstood by most members of Parliament.
    b. were passed unanimously.
    c. made the archbishop of Canterbury the leader of the church.
    d. also forbade all Catholic ritual and doctrine in the new Anglican church.

61. The Catholic Reformation sought to
    a. reform the liturgy of the Catholic church.
    b. restore the conciliar movement.
    c. initiate institutional reform.
    d. stimulate a new spiritualism.

62. In religious affairs, Elizabeth I of England followed a policy that
    a. supported the efforts of the Puritans.
    b. emphasized personal and public religious conformity.
    c. was a middle course between Catholic and Protestant extremes.
    d. favored Catholics over Protestants.

63. The efforts of the Catholic and Counter Reformations were generally
    a. a great failure, allowing Protestantism to continue to grow.
    b. effective only in Italy and Spain.
    c. successful in halting the spread of Protestantism.
    d. hampered by the harshness of their methods.

64. In the wars that accompanied the Protestant Reformation in Germany, the German princes were supported by
    a. the Habsburg dynasty.
    b. the Ottoman Turks.
    c. France.
    d. Charles V.

65. The Tridentine decree *Tametsi* stipulated that
    a. for a marriage to be valid, it had to be witnessed by a priest.
    b. each diocese had to establish a seminary.
    c. bishops had to live in their own dioceses.
    d. the sale of indulgences was illegal.

66. In the sixteenth century, French foreign policy was based on the
    a. defense of Burgundy and acquisition of the Low Countries.
    b. territorial expansion of the French state.
    c. continuation of political fragmentation of Germany.
    d. desire to crush the Protestant movement.

67. Teresa of Avila, featured in "Individuals in Society," organized new convents in Spain
    a. at the request of the king.
    b. after voices and visions chastised her for frivolity.
    c. to support the educational work of Loyola's Jesuits.
    d. as part of the papacy's efforts against Protestantism in Spain.

68. The overriding goal of the Catholic religious orders established in the sixteenth century was
    a. institutional reform.
    b. reconciliation with Protestantism.
    c. to combat heresy and Protestantism.
    d. to uplift the spiritual condition of both clergy and laity.

69. The new religious order for women that emerged in the sixteenth century was the
    a. Ursuline Order.
    b. Society of Jesus.
    c. Sacred Congregation of the Holy Office.
    d. Colloquy of Marburg.

70. The Index was
    a. a list of official doctrines of the Catholic church.
    b. a list of individuals condemned by the Roman Inquisition.
    c. the cardinals who directed the Roman Inquisition.
    d. a catalog of forbidden reading.

71. The grievances of the peasants of Stuhlingen, presented in "Listening to the Past," included all of the following *except*
    a. a denunciation of hunting practices of the nobility.
    b. unhappiness with the immorality of their local priests.
    c. a protest against their enserfment.
    d. a plea for the cessation of onerous fees and obligations exacted by the lords.

History and Geography

72. Religion played a very important role in defining the political geography of Europe. Which areas of Europe remained predominantly Catholic? Lutheran? Calvinist? Were there any regions in which religious diversity existed and, if so, where?

73. Emperor Charles V ruled vast territories. What was the extent of the lands ruled by Charles V? What impact did this have on the attempt to maintain the religious unity of Europe?

73. How did geography affect the Reformation?

CHAPTER 15

THE AGE OF EUROPEAN EXPANSION AND RELIGIOUS WARS

Key Terms

1. Michel de Montaigne
2. Dutch East India Company
3. witch hunt
4. Elizabeth Hardwick
5. Peter Paul Rubens
6. United Provinces
7. caravel
8. Spanish Armada
9. War of the Three Henrys
10. Henry II the Navigator
11. Gustavus Adolphus
12. William Shakespeare
13. Huguenots
14. Hernando Cortez
15. Hispaniola
16. nobility of the robe
17. Peace of Westphalia
18. sugar cultivation
19. Defenestration of Prague
20. Edict of Nantes

Essay Questions

21. The period from 1450 to 1650 witnessed a profound extension of European society beyond the borders of the Continent. What were the factors that facilitated this expansion? What was the motivation, both for the individual European explorers and the states which supported them?

    This essay should begin with a consideration of the general factors that influenced the exploration and expansion of Europe; this should include such aspects as political centralization, Renaissance curiosity, increasing trade contacts, crusading zeal, religious fervor, technological innovation which enabled the exploration, and the impact of the Ottoman Empire and Ming Dynasty on overland trade routes. For individual explorers, the discussion should set their motives within the general framework mentioned above, and then include an indication of the limited nature of economic and political opportunities in Europe; thus one should emphasize material profit as the primary motive. To conclude, the essay should assess the role of mercantilistic economic theory and the more general nature of states to attempt to increase their power.

22. The sixteenth and seventeenth centuries were characterized by long, violent wars, including the revolt of the Netherlands, the War of the Three Henrys, and the Thirty Years' War. What were the common characteristics—of causes, tactics, ideologies, diplomacy, and results—of these three conflicts? What was distinctive?

    A brief narrative of these major conflicts would help put the similarities and differences into the historical context. Similarities of causation would include the role of religious differences and persecution, often cloaking desires for independence or political power; a distinction should be made between the international nature of the conflicts in the Netherlands and Germany and the comparative lack of foreign involvement in France. The tactics, including the brutality directed against enemies and the attacks on clergy and churches (Notre Dame of Antwerp is a good example), should be discussed next; such a discussion should also mention the role of mercenary armies (Wallenstein) and the impact on civilians. The siege tactics of Farnese should be mentioned. The concept of societal homogeneity should be considered in the discussion on ideology. The diplomatic moves made both by the principal protagonists and the other powers at the time should next be considered; in particular one should assess why states choose to enter a conflict and whom to support. For example, the English decision to intervene in the Netherlands should be compared to the Swedish and French decisions to intervene in the Thirty Years' War; in this comparison, the role of religious affiliation should be juxtaposed to considerations of economic and political factors.

23. In the last third of the sixteenth and early seventeenth centuries, European diplomacy revolved around the situation in the Low Countries. Why? What was the impact of the revolt of the Netherlands on the Low Countries, Spain, and England? How did the Dutch revolt affect European politics in general?

    In general this essay calls for a thorough discussion of the Dutch revolt. One should include the factors which made the revolt an affair of continental importance: economic situation in the Low Countries, Philip II's role, English anxieties. For the Netherlands, one should certainly discuss the acquisition of independence by the northern provinces (the United Provinces). The political disunion of the northern and southern regions of the Netherlands should also be considered; the social, economic, religious, and geographical differences between the two should be described as well. For Spain, the discussion should center on the disastrous impact of the revolt, including the huge financial drain, loss of territory, the Armada, and international prestige. Perhaps most importantly was the resultant malaise of defeatism that infected Spain. For England, one should include a discussion of not only the defeat of the Spanish Armada and the subsequent impact on national pride, but also a consideration of the religious implications of Elizabeth's policy on the struggle between Puritans and Roman Catholics in England. Finally, the essay should include mention of the fact that Spain and the Habsburgs would not be able to reimpose religious unity on Europe; the rise of English power and the decline of Spanish power should be reemphasized.

24. The Thirty Years' War marked a major turning point in European history. What were the political, social, economic, and religious consequences of the conflict?

Although the question is about the consequences of the war, the international nature of the conflict must be mentioned. The discussion of the political consequences should include a discussion of the Peace of Westphalia and its impact: independent sovereignty of German princes, effective destruction of the Holy Roman Empire, recognition of the United Provinces, increased prestige of France and Sweden, reduced influence of the papacy. (Brief mention of territorial arrangements could be included.) Next, the economic and social consequences should be considered; these two are of course closely connected. The destructive nature of the war should be stressed; this should include: demographic impact; damage to trade, especially for southern German cities, while northern cities prospered. Agriculture must be thoroughly discussed, specifically the destruction of small farmers and the rise of noble-owned large estates which led to a new serfdom. Finally, the religious aspect of the settlement, in essence a widening of the Treaty of Augsburg to include Calvinism, should conclude the essay.

25. The status of women changed dramatically as a result of the Reformation. In what ways were women affected? How can we explain these changes?

This discussion should focus on the changes resulting from the Reformation, especially the contractual nature of marriage and thus availability of divorce for Protestants. One should also discuss the increased emphasis on the household as first priority, the decline of the double standard of morality, continued deference to husbands and fathers. The continued existence of licensed houses of prostitution should be included. The loss of convents in Protestant countries should be considered for the impact on upper-class women. The example of Elizabeth Hardwick should be included to indicate the possibility of success for individual women in this era. Finally, the role of women from the popular classes, working in many professions or working with their husbands in the family business, must be discussed. To explain these changes, the essay should reemphasize the Protestant contractual view of marriage; one could also attempt to explain the declining status of women by discussing the witch hunt phenomenon.

26. The European witch hunt is one of the more bizarre phenomena of Western history. How do historians explain the witch hunt? How did this phenomenon reflect European civilization in the sixteenth and seventeenth centuries?

A brief narrative of the witch hunt should be presented. Following the narrative, the student should then describe the various theories presented by historians: explaining the unexplainable; elimination of nonconformists; fear of evil power; witches' sexuality. In general, the misogynistic tradition in Europe and the belief in the concept of women as "weaker vessels" must be discussed.

27. The year 1992 marked the quincentenary of Christopher Columbus's first voyage to the Americas, an event which has caused much debate about the impact of Columbus. What are the facts about the role of Columbus in the European incursion into the Americas? How do historians interpret his role? Was Columbus a typical European explorer? In what ways do his own words, presented in "Listening to the Past," help us to understand Columbus?

This question asks students to participate in the continuing debate about Columbus and the voyages of discovery. First, the raw facts should be described. Next, the student should indicate the sources, such as the sea logs, upon which historians have relied. Next the poles of the debate, Columbus as great man and Columbus as mass murderer, should be discussed. In the next section of the essay, the student should place Columbus and his actions within his historical milieu by comparing him to other explorers and by analyzing what he wrote.

28. What was the impact of European expansion on the indigenous peoples of the Americas, European society, and the new American civilization?

In this essay, the student must certainly stress the very negative demographic impact on indigenous peoples, as well as their enslavement. The impact on Europe would include: a draining of key elements of the population in Spain; reliance on bullion and impact on Spanish and European economy, especially inflation from which the middle class prospered while most everyone else suffered; expansion of world economy, increasingly controlled by Europe. Finally, one should discuss the evolution of a unique culture in the Americas, including a thorough discussion of European racial attitudes and the establishment of race-based slavery in the Americas.

MULTIPLE-CHOICE QUESTIONS

29. Fifteenth-century Europeans were forced to look westward because of the territorial expansion by the
    a. Byzantines.
    b. Magyars.
    c. Ottoman Turks.
    d. Russians.

30. European overseas expansion was facilitated by all of the following innovations *except* the
    a. use of sail power.
    b. caravel.
    c. mounting of cannon on naval vessels.
    d. astrolabe.

31. Prince Henry II of Portugal is significant for his
    a. role in subduing the Dutch revolt.
    b. support of exploration.
    c. support of the Protestants in the Thirty Years' War.
    d. opposition to slavery.

32. The Europeans were assisted in the creation of the transatlantic slave trade by
    a. Arabic slave traders in northern Africa.
    b. Venetian slave traders in the Black Sea.
    c. native Americans who joined European slavers on expeditions to Africa.
    d. Africans who sold people from other African societies.

33. Before the Portuguese gained control of the spice trade in the Indian Ocean, the trade had been controlled by the
    a. Muslims.
    b. Venetians.
    c. Spanish.
    d. Byzantines.

34. The primary factor determining the direction of Spanish exploration in the Americas was
    a. missionary zeal.
    b. the search for a shorter route to Asia.
    c. the lure of precious metals.
    d. prevailing winds and tides.

35. The European kingdom which took the lead in overseas exploration was
    a. Portugal.
    b. Spain.
    c. France.
    d. England.

36. In the mid-sixteenth century, the commercial capital of the European world was
    a. Lisbon.
    b. Madrid.
    c. London.
    d. Antwerp.

37. The Dutch East India Company represents the
    a. role of Spanish silver in the economic vitality of the Low Countries.
    b. commercial imperialism of the Dutch.
    c. peaceful introduction of Christianity into India.
    d. Calvinist missionary activity supported by the United Provinces.

38. The primary motivation for European explorers was
    a. material profit.
    b. population pressure.
    c. crusading zeal.
    d. Renaissance curiosity.

39. The influx of silver from the New World into Spain resulted in all of the following *except*
    a. economic prosperity in Spain.
    b. no direct correlation to the inflationary spiral.
    c. increased influence of Spanish power in the early sixteenth century.
    d. severe strains on Spanish governmental budgets.

40. The group of people who benefited the most from large price increases in the sixteenth century was the
    a. Spanish bureaucracy.
    b. nobility.
    c. urban working class.
    d. middle class.

41. The critical reinterpretation of Columbus focuses primarily on
    a. the greatness of his discoveries.
    b. the role of the Spanish monarchy in his voyages.
    c. his deeply held religious convictions as his primary motivation.
    d. his role in the destruction of indigenous American societies.

42. The Peace of Westphalia resulted in all of the following *except*
    a. enhanced prestige and power for France.
    b. an increased role for the papacy in German affairs.
    c. a powerful Swedish presence in northern Germany.
    d. recognition of the independence of the United Provinces.

43. The *quinto* was
    a. the general term for the Spanish colonial administration.
    b. a Spanish tax on all precious metals mined in its colonies.
    c. the term for African slaves in Portugal.
    d. the term used to describe the decimation of the natives of Hispaniola.

44. The central feature of Columbus's character was his
    a. racism.
    b. deep religious convictions.
    c. rapacious greed.
    d. Renaissance curiosity.

45. The population losses caused by the plague and the Hundred Years' War
    a. greatly benefited the French nobility.
    b. resulted in the virtual disappearance of serfdom in France.
    c. led to foreign invasion of France.
    d. led to the introduction of serfdom in France.

46. The French royal budget in the first half of the sixteenth century was strained by both the Hapsburg-Valois wars and
    a. loss of feudal dues and rents.
    b. overseas exploration.
    c. extravagant promotion of the arts by the monarchs.
    d. the military defeats of the Thirty Years' War.

47. In order to pay for the Habsburg-Valois wars, the French monarchs
    a. instituted taxes on the nobility.
    b. sold many Renaissance masterpieces.
    c. sold public offices.
    d. confiscated monastic lands.

48. The wars of the sixteenth and seventeenth centuries differed from those of earlier centuries in that
    a. dynastic concerns were the primary motivations.
    b. religion ceased to be a major motivation.
    c. warfare did not often affect the lives of civilians.
    d. the armies were much larger and more expensive.

49. Philip II shared with Luther and Calvin the belief that
    a. salvation comes by God's gift of grace.
    b. church and civil authorities should destroy heresy.
    c. the state should impose morality on its subjects.
    d. the pope was not infallible.

50. In France, Calvinism
    a. often served as a cloak for noble independence.
    b. became the majority religion.
    c. had little impact on the nobility.
    d. was rejected by the middle class and artisans.

51. The Saint Bartholomew's Day massacre
    a. was the event that sparked the Dutch Revolt.
    b. resulted in the Concordat of Bologna.
    c. was caused by the Edict of Nantes.
    d. exemplified the hatred between French Catholics and Protestants.

52. The Edict of Nantes
    a. expelled the Huguenots from France.
    b. expelled the Jews from France.
    c. established Catholicism as the state religion of France.
    d. granted the Huguenots the right to public worship.

53. The primary causes of the revolt of the Netherlands were the repression of the Calvinists and
    a. the weakness of Spain.
    b. high taxes.
    c. English influence and support for the independence movement.
    d. the assassination of William the Silent.

54. Alexander Farnese's strategy against the rebellious Low Countries cities was
    a. patient siege.
    b. political terrorism.
    c. diplomatic negotiation.
    d. pitched battles.

55. The fate of Johan van Oldenbarnevelt, featured in "Individuals in Society," was sealed by his
    a. religious intolerance.
    b. his support of religious toleration and federalism.
    c. treasonous relations with Alexander Farnese.
    d. conversion to Catholicism.

56. All of the following were factors in Elizabeth I's decision to intervene in the Dutch revolt *except*
    a. damage to the English wool industry.
    b. the assassination of William the Silent.
    c. the fall of Antwerp to the Spanish.
    d. the impact of inflation on the Spanish economy.

57. The defeat of the Spanish Armada in 1588
    a. prevented Philip II from reuniting western Europe.
    b. impeded the flow of silver from the New World to Spain.
    c. ended Spanish attempts to subdue the revolt in the Netherlands.
    d. prevented Spain from protecting its possessions in the New World.

58. The Bohemian phase of the Thirty Years' War ended with the
    a. intervention of Gustavus Adolphus of Sweden.
    b. Battle of the White Mountain.
    c. Defenestration of Prague.
    d. Peace of Westphalia.

59. French policy during the French (international) phase of the Thirty Years' War was motivated by
    a. the desire to maintain the political fragmentation of the empire.
    b. the necessity to support its ally, Spain.
    c. religious beliefs.
    d. Richelieu's hatred of the Protestants.

60. In the aftermath of the Thirty Years' War,
    a. French influence in German affairs declined.
    b. Sweden lost substantial territories to the empire.
    c. papal authority in Germany increased significantly.
    d. the peasantry in eastern Germany was enserfed.

61. The "winner" of the Thirty Years' War seems to have been
    a. France.
    b. the empire.
    c. the papacy.
    d. Bohemia.

62. In the sixteenth and seventeenth centuries, Protestants
    a. believed marriage should be based on love.
    b. saw marriage as a contract between husband and wife.
    c. and Catholics viewed marriage as a permanent union.
    d. encouraged marriages arranged by parents.

63. Peter Paul Rubens is best remembered as
    a. a painter whose work exemplifies the sensuality of baroque painting.
    b. the leader of the Dutch revolt against the Spanish.
    c. a Huguenot leader in France.
    d. the writer who developed the essay as a literary genre.

64. During the sixteenth and seventeenth centuries, prostitution
    a. declined dramatically.
    b. was common.
    c. catered to men and women.
    d. was outlawed in Protestant cities.

65. The great witch hunt reflects the
    a. increased role of witchcraft among Europeans of the era.
    b. impact of tolerant attitudes produced by the Reformation.
    c. changing status of women.
    d. anxiety created by the European discovery of the Americas.

66. The introduction of slavery into the Americas was conditioned most by the production of
    a. cotton.
    b. spices.
    c. rice.
    d. sugar.

67. The European attitude toward blacks derived from Christian theological speculation and
    a. African attacks on European traders and missionaries.
    b. Arab ideas about Africans.
    c. Renaissance racism.
    d. Greco-Roman attitudes about Africans.

68. The dominant characteristic of Michel de Montaigne''s writings was his
    a. piety.
    b. French nationalism.
    c. dogmatic Catholicism.
    d. tolerant sensitivity.

69. Shakespeare's history plays, such as *Richard II*,
    a. exalt the English nation.
    b. glorify the Classical ideal.
    c. were usually set in Italy.
    d. were very unpopular at the time.

70. The Authorized Version of the Bible reflected the efforts of the Anglicans and Puritans to
    a. stamp out Catholicism.
    b. unite their churches.
    c. encourage the laity to read the Bible.
    d. identify themselves with the English throne.

71. Baroque art was
    a. reserved for rich patrons and the educated elite.
    b. intended to kindle the faith of the common people.
    c. banned in Protestant countries.
    d. simple and austere, lacking in emotion.

72. According to the evidence presented in "Listening to the Past," Christopher Columbus considered the native Americans to be
    a. unintelligent and uncooperative.
    b. fierce warriors.
    c. unfit for conversion to Christianity.
    d. timid, intelligent, and generous.

History and Geography

73. On the blank outline map, identify both the primary sources from which African slaves were acquired and the main areas of importation of these slaves. What does the latter reveal about the economic factors of plantation slavery?

74. After examining Map 15.3, explain the geopolitical reasons behind French support of the Protestants in the Thirty Years' War.

75. How did geography affect the economic conditions in the Low Countries? How did geography affect the course of the revolt in the Netherlands, and the ultimate political resolution of the revolt?

CHAPTER 16

ABSOLUTISM AND CONSTITUTIONALISM IN WESTERN EUROPE (CA. 1589-1715)

Key Terms

1. La Rochelle
2. *généralités*
3. Jean-Baptiste Colbert
4. Versailles
5. Molière
6. War of the Spanish Succession
7. Canal des Deux Mers
8. Protectorate
9. Navigation Act
10. administrative monarchy
11. Fronde
12. Bill of Rights
13. Battle of Rocroi
14. *stadholder*
15. "ship money"
16. *Second Treatise on Civil Government*
17. Francois le Tellier, Marquis de Louvois
18. French Academy
19. Miguel de Cervantes
20. joint-stock company

Essay Questions

21. During the reign of Louis XIV, France attempted to upset the equilibrium of the balance of power in Europe. How did the European concept of balance of power work? What impact did the wars of Louis XIV have on the European international system?

    This essay should begin with a brief narrative of the wars. Then one should describe the coalitions which Louis faced, especially the League of Augsburg and the Grand Alliance. A good essay would indicate the perceived necessity to copy the military and administrative reforms of the

French. The consequences for the European system include: control of French expansion; decline of the Dutch Republic (including the role of England in that decline); rise of England; final demise of Spain as a great power. The balance of power concept, exemplified by the War of the Spanish Succession and the Treaty of Utrecht, should be fully discussed.

22. In the seventeenth century, the Spanish monarchy crumbled. Why?

The discussion of the collapse of absolutist Spain should include broad social, economic, and political trends as well as specific historical events. The essay should cover the lack of a middle class (resulting from expulsion of the Jews and Muslims), agrarian crisis, population decline, lack of investment, intellectual isolation, and psychological malaise. Philip II's efforts to re-Catholicize Europe and its impact, especially the economic and psychological aspects, should be fully discussed. Cultural antipathy to commerce must also be considered. The agrarian crisis, resulting from the nobles' exploitation of the peasantry, should also be considered. The genetic degeneracy of the ruling dynasty must also be discussed. The essay should then turn to a consideration of specific events, including the wars against the Dutch and the French, the Thirty Years' War, and revolts in Catalonia and Portugal, as both causative factors in the decline and as symptoms of decline. Finally, the good essay would discuss Cervantes's *Don Quixote* as the ultimate symbol of Spain in decline.

23. Despite the evolution of a strong, centralized, monarchical system of government, France still experienced periods of civil unrest and war. Describe these periods. How can we explain the discrete occurrences? Is there an overarching reason for why France continued to experience civil unrest?

The essay should first present a brief narrative, including government response, of the various cases of civil upheaval: Huguenot uprising of 1625; the various incidences of serious urban protests; and the Fronde. Next, specific causation should be discussed (or such discussion could be included in the above section of the essay): for the Huguenot uprising, religious factors, coupled with Louis XIII's uneasiness over the "state within a state" created by the Edict of Nantes and the Huguenots' oppression of Catholics; for the various urban protests, the issues of unemployment, bread prices and availability, taxes; for the more complicated Fronde, its provincial beginnings, political and social pretensions of the nobility, unhappiness of the royal bureaucracy, taxation policies. Finally, the essay should assert a general interpretation for the persistence of civil disorder and protest in France; the concept of expanding administrative monarchy evoking a culture of retribution is the obvious response to this aspect of the question.

24. "Louis XIV is the greatest example of royal absolutism." Assess the validity of this statement.

This essay calls for the student to make an estimation of just how absolute Louis XIV really was. Such an analysis should begin with an explanation of the basis for the quotation, a brief consideration of his reign, relations with the nobility, military encounters, and the European-wide emulation of at least the style if not the substance of his court and government; this section should describe the manner in which Louis portrayed himself and allowed himself to be portrayed: art and architecture, especially Versailles, must be discussed fully in this context. Saint-Simon's memoirs are an excellent source for Louis's cultivation of awe and veneration. The discussion of limitations should include the technological limitations on his power to gather information and impose his orders. More importantly, one must consider the limits to royal power in certain aspects and regions; tax farming is one such area while the issue of the Canal des Deux Mers and the compromise with the Languedoc nobles and the revocation of the Edict of Nantes must be considered. The evidence of Saint-Simon's memoirs and the collaborative relationship revealed by the Canal episode are indicative of the rather complex relationship between Louis XIV and his nobility, which should be indicated in the essay.

25. The seventeenth century is often called "the Golden Age of the Netherlands." What was the basis of Dutch success in this century? What caused the decline of the Netherlands?

First, the essay should include a brief justification for the sobriquet. Second, the political development of the Dutch Republic should be discussed. The commercial prosperity should be described and strongly emphasized; along with this emphasis, the student should attempt to assess the reasons for this prosperity, including such things as religious toleration, strong industries, commercial instruments, and imperial expansion. The discussion of decline must include the military conflicts with France and England in the 1670s and the involvement in the War of the Spanish Succession; weakness of the confederation form of government should also be mentioned in helping to explain the decline.

26. Seventeenth-century France has been called the model of royal absolutism. How did the French crown create an absolutist state out of the anarchy of the civil-religious wars of the last half of the sixteenth century? How absolutist was the French monarchy?

This essay essentially asks the student to describe and discuss the French model of absolutism. The roles of Henry IV, Richelieu, and Louis XIV must be described, with an emphasis not just on their actions and policies but also on the underlying premise, supremacy of the monarch, of their political beliefs. The French bureaucracy, administrative divisions, Academy, royal army, corporations (guilds) should all be mentioned as they relate to absolutist government. The selling of offices, outlawing of dueling, and daily life at Versailles, should all be used to enhance the essay; one could also indicate the deleterious long-term impact of such things as selling of offices, courtly extravagance, and tax farming. The use of the middle class and nobles of the robe in the bureaucracy must be emphasized. The opposition of nobles and Huguenots should next be mentioned; the suppression of both groups by Richelieu and Louis XIV should be included. Finally, the ongoing urban protests and the necessity to collaborate with certain elements in France, illustrated by the Languedoc compromise over the Canal des Deux Mers, indicates the limits of monarchical power. The good essay should then include a discussion of the concept of administrative monarchy as an alternative interpretation of the French case.

27. In the seventeenth century England displayed little political stability, yet by the end of the century England had laid the foundations for constitutional monarchy. What were the political, social, economic, and religious factors and events that led ultimately to the Glorious Revolution?

This essay calls for thorough discussion of the history of England in the seventeenth century. A brief narrative could be included to set the analytical sections into the historical context. The student should then examine the political balance between crown, Commons, and Lords prior to the civil war; the economic changes, especially the emergence of rural gentry and urban business class in the political, social, and economic life of the country should be discussed. This discussion would then tie together the major political, social, and economic developments of the era. This should be buttressed with a discussion of the Puritan leanings of many new men, the perception of Catholic leanings of James I and Charles I, Archbishop Laud, the Scottish rebellion and the troubles in Ireland. These broader developments then provide the backdrop for the confrontation between Charles I and Parliament. Finally, one should consider the general situation at the time of the Glorious Revolution; that is, the essay should consider the maturation of the upper middle classes and the political ascension of Parliament and how factors such as these obviated the need for civil war.

MULTIPLE-CHOICE QUESTIONS

28. The French military reforms included all of the following *except*
    a. a supply system.
    b. standardization of weapons and uniforms.
    c. exclusion of noble participation in the army.
    d. a rational system of training and promotion.

29. All of the following are characteristics of "administrative monarchy" *except*
    a. unlimited royal power.
    b. centralization of power.
    c. an expanded bureaucracy.
    d. the ability to achieve more goals.

30. The enemy of the Grand Alliance during the War of the Spanish Succession was
    a. Spain.
    b. France.
    c. the Holy Roman Empire.
    d. the United Provinces.

31. The most important lesson Louis XIV learned from the Fronde was that the
    a. Edict of Nantes needed to be revoked.
    b. French bureaucracy needed massive reform.
    c. lower classes were dangerous and had to be suppressed.
    d. sole alternative to anarchy was absolute monarchy.

32. The relationship between Louis XIV and the Languedoc nobles indicates
    a. that the king often compromised and collaborated with the nobles.
    b. that the revocation of the Edict of Nantes was not very popular.
    c. the thorough subjugation of the nobility by the king.
    d. that the king could not trust the nobility.

33. Political power in the Dutch Republic was
    a. held by the central government.
    b. controlled by an oligarchy of wealthy merchants.
    c. held by the *stadholder* and his royal courtiers.
    d. exercised by a democratically elected States-General.

34. The term "ship money" refers to
    a. bribes paid by English Catholics fleeing England.
    b. a coastal defense tax that Charles I levied illegally on inland counties.
    c. the tax Colbert created to finance the French merchant marine.
    d. money invested in the stock of overseas trading companies.

35. The decline of Spain in the seventeenth century can be attributed to all of the following causes *except*
    a. conflict between the church and the state.
    b. lack of investment in productive enterprise.
    c. the expense and failure of the effort to repress the Dutch Revolt.
    d. intellectual isolation and psychological malaise.

36. The policies of Henry IV can be characterized by all of the following *except*
    a. aggressive foreign policy.
    b. reconciliation and pacification of religious conflict.
    c. support for economic growth.
    d. short-sighted taxation policies.

37. French intendants were almost always recruited from the
    a. nobles of the sword.
    b. new, judicial nobility.
    c. commercial elite.
    d. university professors.

38. The Dutch "golden age" was based on all of the following *except*
    a. fishing and overseas transport.
    b. religious toleration.
    c. strong, monarchical government.
    d. the moral and ethical precepts of Calvinism.

39. The guiding force behind Cardinal Richelieu's domestic policies was
    a. reform of the church.
    b. a belief in decentralization.
    c. the subordination of all groups and institutions to the monarchy.
    d. the sovereignty of the people.

40. The endemic urban protests that plagued France were triggered by all of the following *except*
    a. high unemployment.
    b. price and availability of grain.
    c. taxation policies.
    d. foreign invasions.

41. Louis XIII's decision to destroy Huguenot independence was based on
    a. the Huguenots' close relationship with England.
    b. Huguenot attempts to resume the religious wars of the previous century.
    c. the king's desire to confiscate Huguenot property.
    d. the Huguenot's refusal to allow Catholics freedom of worship in Huguenot cities.

42. To solve their increasingly disastrous financial difficulties, Spanish monarchs often resorted to
    a. printing paper money.
    b. canceling the national debt.
    c. increased imports of New World bullion.
    d. the confiscation and sale of church property.

43. In general the wars of Louis XIV
    a. had a disastrous impact on the French economy.
    b. added vast new territories to France.
    c. had little impact beyond the glorification of the Sun King.
    d. destroyed the European balance of power.

44. The decline of the Dutch economy was caused by
    a. an inflationary spiral created by Spanish gold.
    b. the wars of the seventeenth century.
    c. labor unrest and rebellion.
    d. the collapse of the wool industry.

45. The center of the struggle between the French crown and the Huguenots' in 1627 was
    a. Paris.
    b. La Rochelle.
    c. Nantes.
    d. Languedoc.

46. The causes of the Fronde include all of the following factors *except*
    a. resentment of influential elements in the nobility of the sword.
    b. anger of the French bureaucracy, who felt manipulated.
    c. peasants' and urban workers' resentment of higher taxes and government interference.
    d. religious conflict between Catholics and Huguenots.

47. Mercantilistic theory postulated that
    a. government should not interfere in the economy.
    b. imports and exports should be equally balanced.
    c. government should intervene to secure the largest share of limited resources.
    d. overseas colonies were an unwanted drain of valuable gold bullion.

48. The spark that caused the English Glorious Revolution was the
    a. conflict over taxation between Charles II and Parliament.
    b. fear of a Catholic dynasty being established by James II.
    c. economic dislocation that had resulted from the civil war.
    d. defeat suffered in the War of the Spanish Succession.

49. Colbert's contributions to the economy of France included all of the following *except*
    a. creating a national bank.
    b. establishing new industries and colonial ventures.
    c. improving the transportation system within France.
    d. creating a powerful merchant marine to transport French goods.

50. The memoirs of Glückel of Hameln attest to all of the following *except* her
    a. upper-middle-class status in Jewish society.
    b. success as leader of the family after her husband's death.
    c. narrow and provincial view of the world.
    d. deep immersion in Jewish religious culture.

51. The most important legislation enacted during Cromwell's Protectorate was the
    a. Instrument of Government.
    b. Bill of Rights.
    c. Test Act.
    d. Navigation Act.

52. The primary instrument of Dutch overseas imperialism was the
    a. Royal Navy.
    b. Dutch East India Company.
    c. Bank of Amsterdam.
    d. Company for Trade and Exploitation of the East.

53. The state that gained the most from the War of the Spanish Succession was
    a. Spain.
    b. France.
    c. the United Provinces.
    d. England.

54. Typically, French classicism
    a. challenged existing concepts concerning art.
    b. presented subject matter associated with the Greco-Roman past.
    c. had little support from the royal government.
    d. emphasized individualistic renderings of society.

55. According to the English Test Act of 1673,
    a. political participation was based upon adherence to the Church of England.
    b. only Parliament could initiate legislation.
    c. the cabinet was to be the official executive body of the English government.
    d. English people had inalienable rights of property and political participation.

56. A significant feature of English society in the sixteenth and seventeenth centuries was the
    a. growing wealth of the country gentry and middle-class businessmen.
    b. resurgence of Roman Catholicism.
    c. declining popularity of "reformed" religions.
    d. economic decline of the business classes.

57. Perhaps the most striking characteristic of the Dutch Republic was its
    a. large standing army.
    b. universally democratic form of government.
    c. religious toleration.
    d. rejection of imperial exploitation.

58. The *paulette*, introduced by Henry IV, was a(n)
    a. annual fee paid by royal officials to guarantee heredity in their offices.
    b. tax paid on salt.
    c. guarantee of religious freedom for Huguenots.
    d. property tax paid by all landowners in France.

59. In his political theories, John Locke
    a.   stressed the importance of universal manhood suffrage.
    b.   argued that sovereignty had been freely surrendered to the monarch.
    c.   linked economic liberty and private property with political freedom.
    d.   argued that sovereignty should be vested in the executive branch of government.

60. The final collapse of Spain as a great military power was symbolized by the defeat at the Battle of
    a.   Utrecht.
    b.   White Mountain.
    c.   the Pyrenees.
    d.   Rocroi.

61. The historical antecedent of the English cabinet system of government was the
    a.   Long Parliament.
    b.   "Kitchen" Cabinet.
    c.   Bill of Rights.
    d.   Cabal.

62. The European system of balance of power is best illustrated by the
    a.   Anglo-Dutch competition for overseas empire.
    b.   War of the Spanish Succession.
    c.   Spanish attempts to conquer the rebellious Netherlands.
    d.   Anglo-French efforts to reduce the power of the United Provinces.

63. French foreign policy under Richelieu focused primarily on the
    a.   prevention of the Habsburgs from unifying the territories surrounding France.
    b.   destruction of English naval power.
    c.   destruction of the economic power of the Low Countries.
    d.   protection of Burgundy.

64. Oliver Cromwell's Protectorate is best described as a
    a.   popular democracy.
    b.   cabinet-style parliamentary government.
    c.   constitutional monarchy.
    d.   Puritan, military dictatorship.

65. The plays of Molière
    a.   criticized the attitudes of the bourgeoisie.
    b.   analyzed the power of love.
    c.   castigated the French nobility.
    d.   rejected the official style of classicism.

66. According to *The Memoirs of the Duke of Saint-Simon*, Louis XIV moved the royal court from Paris to Versailles for all of the following reasons *except*
    a.   his fear of Paris.
    b.   the greater ability to detect the movements of the court.
    c.   to lower the expenses of the court.
    d.   to enhance the people's awe and veneration of the king.

History and Geography

67. On the blank outline map of Europe, mark the territories added to France by the wars of Louis XIV. Based solely on this geographic evidence, how would you assess the military aspect of Louis's reign?

68. In what ways did geography affect the balance of power in Europe in the seventeenth century?

69. Based on Map 16.3, what was the extent of Dutch commerce? What goods did the Netherlands import from South America, China, Indonesia, and Africa, respectively?

CHAPTER 17

ABSOLUTISM IN EASTERN EUROPE TO 1740

Key Terms

1. *robot*
2. Charles VI
3. Siege of Vienna
4. Junkers
5. Michael Romanov
6. "Prussian spirit"
7. *tsar*
8. Janissary corps
9. Mongol Yoke
10. Ivan III
11. service nobility
12. soul tax
13. Battle of Navra
14. Third Rome
15. Upper Belvedere
16. Stenka Razin
17. Frederick William the Great Elector
18. St. Petersburg
19. Cossacks
20. White Mountain

Essay Questions

21. While the monarchs of central and eastern Europe tried to imitate Louis XIV's absolutism, they were forced to modify the French model. How and why did this modification take place? How successful was this modification?

    In this essay, the student should examine the primary differences between the French model of absolutism and the eastern copies, most notably the composition of the bureaucracy and the role of the nobility in local administration and justice. The social structure of eastern Europe should then be considered, emphasizing the lack of an urbanized population and especially a middle class. The importance of large-scale agriculture based on serfdom should also be mentioned, as both the source of noble power as well as a severe brake on economic and social development. In the consideration of similarities, the essay should stress the obvious aping of Louis XIV (in terms of palaces, mistresses, war, art) as well as the industrious and ambitious nature of the eastern absolute monarchs; the primacy of the state should be considered in this section as well. Finally, the overall analysis of the success of eastern absolute monarchs should include mention of the effectiveness and necessity of strong government at the time as well as the flexibility of absolutism.

22. Trace the development of absolutism in Austria and Prussia. What factors influenced the development of each state? What were the similarities and differences in the development of absolutism in these two states? Which state created stronger and more efficient absolutism and why?

Initially, there should be a narrative of the development of absolutism in both states. Stress should be placed on the political, social, and economic impact of the Thirty Years' War; the social structure of eastern Europe, foreign threats, religion, and church-state relations should also be fully discussed. The discussion of the influencing factors should reveal some similarities and differences; the ethnic diversity of the Habsburg lands, the Ottoman threat and the resultant impact must be discussed and compared to the more homogenous Prussian state. The differences in size, militarism, and religion should be considered. The role of able monarchs should also be discussed. Finally, the student should assess which was the most effective absolutist system, based upon such things as honesty and efficiency of the bureaucracy, judicial system, taxation, standard of living of the subjects.

23. Absolutism in eastern Europe was built in large part on the social and economic structures which had emerged by the seventeenth century. What were these structures and how did their evolution affect the development of absolutism in eastern Europe?

This essay should begin with a description of the reimposition of serfdom in eastern Europe. The shortage of labor and the political weakness of rulers which enabled the nobles to enserf the peasants must be thoroughly discussed; the nobles' political power should be considered a very important factor as was the relative lack of urbanization in the east, depriving the monarchs of middle-class allies utilized by the western kings and peasants of haven from exploitative lords. The commercial relations between lords and foreign traders should be used to indicate the lack of a middle class. Next, the impact on absolutism must be considered, focusing on the necessity to use nobles at all levels of government, which reinforced their power over the peasants and further entrenched serfdom. In general, serfdom's negative impact on economic and social development should be discussed, emphasizing the continuing bipolar nature of the social structure and the monopolization of political, social, and economic power by the nobility.

24. "Art was used by the monarchs of eastern Europe to support absolutism." How accurate is this assertion?

In this essay the student should consider baroque art and its use by absolute monarchs to inspire and overawe both subjects and rivals. Its roots can be traced to the influence of Louis XIV and the need to emulate and compete with him. The essay should stress the architectural accomplishments, such as Schönbrunn, that aped Versailles and were the physical manifestation of the power of great and minor princes. One should then consider the palace-building mania as leading to the ultimate representation of the relationship between absolutism and art, the building of entire cities, such as St. Petersburg and Karlsruhe, to showcase a monarch's power.

25. "War - whether civil, international, or both - or the threat of war is critical to the emergence and development of absolutism." Assess the validity of this quotation in relationship to the history of absolutism in Austria, Prussia, and Russia.

In this essay, the student should use pertinent examples to illustrate the impact of war on absolutism. On the one hand the role of invasion by hostile forces (such as the Ottoman Turks), which was a factor in the cession of legislative power to the monarch (in return for protection from invaders), should be considered as should the governmental reforms necessary to support large standing armies (exemplified by the Russian experience under Peter the Great). In addition to foreign invasion, civil war as a destabilizing factor should also be considered; Thirty Years' War, Time of Troubles, and Stenka Razin's uprising are all good examples.

26. How "western" was Russia?

The essay should include the similarity to western Europe during the Middle Ages, but with the conquest by the Mongols and the subsequent Mongol Yoke marking a serious break; the rise of Muscovy, Time of Troubles, and the Romanov era up to Peter I should be traced to provide a framework for the unique features of Russian society: lack of private property, service nobility, nature of the tsar, sequestration of women, and the role of the Mongol Yoke in this development

27. "In many ways the construction of St. Petersburg exemplifies both the absolutist nature of Peter the Great's reign and the specifically Russian nature of his society." Assess the validity of this statement. How did this new city exemplify absolutism in general, the reforming efforts of Peter I, and the unique nature of Russian society?

After a brief description of the city and its construction, the essay should then discuss the building of the city as an artistic statement on the power of the absolute monarch; the role of baroque art in general might be included. Next, one should consider the building of St. Petersburg as a seemingly logical result of his efforts to secure a "Window on the West" and his attempts to reform and recast Russian government and society. In the draconian manner by which labor to build the city was recruited (the harshness of conditions and the death rate of the workers would provide a good example of the necessity to dragoon labor) and inhabitants secured, a glimpse of the all-powerful nature of the tsar is revealed.

MULTIPLE-CHOICE QUESTIONS

28. The most striking feature of the social system in eastern Europe was
    a. a vigorous middle class.
    b. a free peasantry.
    c. a peasantry reduced to serfdom.
    d. equal status enjoyed by men and women.

29. In response to the problems of the fourteenth and fifteenth centuries, the landlords of eastern Europe
    a. offered better economic terms to their peasants.
    b. used political power to gain control of the peasants.
    c. renounced their traditional control of local justice.
    d. imported labor from western Europe.

30. The first tactic employed by the landlords to cope with labor shortages was to
    a. destroy town liberties.
    b. employ women and children.
    c. encourage the emergence of small-scale farming.
    d. restrict peasant freedom of movement.

31. The administration of justice in eastern Europe generally was
    a. in the hands of trained jurists working for the monarch.
    b. controlled by local landlords.
    c. the basis of the monarch's reforms.
    d. relegated to the local clergy.

32. The importance and liberty of eastern European towns were undermined, in large part, by
    a. nobles selling agricultural commodities directly to foreign capitalists.
    b. the enserfment of the peasants.
    c. the creation of royal monopolies on trade.
    d. the depopulation resulting from the Black Death.

33. As a result of the revolt by the Bohemian nobility in 1618,
    a. Bohemia gained independence from the Habsburgs.
    b. the Habsburgs allowed Protestants to worship.
    c. the native Bohemian nobility was wiped out.
    d. the Bohemian parliament gained power over taxation.

34. Absolute monarchs in eastern Europe monopolized power in all of the following areas *except*
    a. taxation.
    b. the military.
    c. foreign policy.
    d. justice.

35. In the aftermath of the siege of Vienna in 1683, the Habsburgs
    a. were forced to relinquish Bohemia.
    b. reestablished the parliaments of Bohemia and Styria.
    c. pursued a peaceful relationship with the Ottoman Empire.
    d. conquered most of Hungary and Transylvania.

36. The Thirty Years' War served as a catalyst for the development of absolutism in
    a. Spain.
    b. Prussia.
    c. the Ottoman Empire.
    d. France.

37. Peter the Great of Russia incorporated all of the following in his effort to modernize his states *except*
    a. a standing professional army.
    b. new taxation policies.
    c. a bureaucracy based on merit.
    d. effective local government and judiciary.

38. Following the defeat of the rebellious Bohemian nobility at White Mountain, the Habsburgs
    a. replaced the native nobility with loyal servitors.
    b. suspended the Inquisition in Bohemia.
    c. introduced economic and legal reforms.
    d. recognized both Catholicism and Lutheranism.

39. Critical to the smooth functioning of the Ottoman social and political organization was
    a. the subjugation and conversion of Christian peasants.
    b. control of the trade routes between Asia and Europe.
    c. peace and prosperity.
    d. continuous territorial expansion.

40. In the Ottoman Empire,
    a. the hereditary nobility monopolized political and social power.
    b. Christians were systematically converted to Islam.
    c. there was virtually no such thing as private property.
    d. there was strict separation of church and state.

41. The hereditary provinces of the Habsburg state included all of the following *except*
    a. Brandenburg.
    b. Austria.
    c. Hungary.
    d. Bohemia.

42. The Pragmatic Sanction issued by Charles VI in 1713
    a. granted religious rights to non-Catholics.
    b. undermined papal influence in the Habsburg lands.
    c. stated that Habsburg lands were never to be divided.
    d. revoked the feudal rights of the Austrian nobility.

43. All of the following were factors in the Hungarians' fight against Habsburg absolutism *except*
    a. the strength of the Protestant faith in Hungary.
    b. an alliance with the Turks.
    c. the commercial and industrial strength of Hungary.
    d. early adherence to a national ideal.

44. The accomplishments of Frederick William the Great Elector include all of the following *except*
    a. abolition of serfdom.
    b. establishment of a standing army.
    c. introduction of permanent taxation without consent
    d. reduction of the power and independence of towns and cities.

45. Charles XII of Sweden scored a major victory over Peter the Great at the Battle of
    a. Poltava.
    b. Navra.
    c. St. Petersburg.
    d. Karlsruhe.

46. During the constitutional struggle between Frederick William the Great Elector and the Prussian nobility,
    a. the nobles allied with the towns.
    b. the nobles put national interest above personal interests.
    c. war and invasion strengthened Frederick William's hand.
    d. the estates gained control of taxation.

47. Frederick I the Ostentatious is remembered for his
    a. administrative reforms.
    b. creation of Prussian militarism.
    c. efforts to control the exploitation of the Prussian peasants.
    d. slavish imitation of Louis XIV and acquisition of the royal title of king.

48. The accomplishments of Frederick William I included all of the following *except* the
    a. inculcation of militaristic values into the entire society.
    b. establishment of an honest bureaucracy.
    c. conquest of new territories.
    d. recruitment of the Prussian nobility to serve in his army.

49. The policies and actions of Frederick William I were based on his belief that the welfare of the king and state depended on the
    a. army.
    b. agrarian economy.
    c. bureaucracy.
    d. nobility.

50. The most enduring legacy of Frederick William I was
    a. the establishment of a first-rate bureaucracy.
    b. his foundation for the most militaristic country of modern times.
    c. his decision to transform the peasants into serfs.
    d. the acquisition of the royal title.

51. The Cossack leader Stenka Razin claimed that
    a. the tsar was responsible for the suffering of the peasants.
    b. evil officials and nobles, not the tsar, were responsible for the conditions of the peasants.
    c. he was the true tsar.
    d. the reforms of Peter the Great were destroying the peasants.

52. Many scholars argue that Russia's fundamental differences from the West are the result of
    a. the Mongol Yoke.
    b. Peter the Great's reforms.
    c. early adherence to Eastern Orthodoxy.
    d. a non-European language group from which the Russians are descended.

53. The main reason the princes of Moscow were able to become the rulers of Russia was their
    a. great wealth.
    b. military prowess.
    c. cooperation with the Mongols.
    d. conversion to Orthodox Christianity.

54. Many scholars believe that the Russian concept of kingship was derived from
    a. the Mongols.
    b. imperial Rome.
    c. France.
    d. Byzantium.

55. The Cossacks were originally
    a. a Turkish tribe that settled in the Ukraine.
    b. runaway peasants from central Russia.
    c. religious dissenters.
    d. special military units of the tsars.

56. During the reigns of Ivan III and Ivan IV, Muscovite society
    a. was dominated by the landed nobility, the boyars.
    b. saw the rise of the service nobility.
    c. featured relative equality between men and women.
    d. converted to Orthodox Christianity.

57. After the Time of Troubles, the Romanov tsars
    a. increased the obligations of the nobility.
    b. relaxed the obligations of the serfs.
    c. relaxed the obligations of the nobility.
    d. fostered the growth of an urban middle class.

58. The reforms of Patriarch Nikon led to
    a. an independent church hierarchy.
    b. a split between the church hierarchy and the common people.
    c. more uniform practice of Orthodox Christianity.
    d. a closer relationship with the Catholic church.

59. Peter's involvement in the Great Northern War was a consequence of
    a. the aggression of the Swedes.
    b. his adherence to an aggressive alliance against Sweden.
    c. Russia's losses in the previous war with the Ottoman Empire.
    d. his attempt to westernize Russia.

60. The reign of Peter the Great was characterized by
    a. noble rebellion.
    b. relative peace.
    c. incessant warfare.
    d. economic and social transformation.

61. Peter's new tax, on "souls,"
    a. was levied on all clergy, church lands, church serfs, and monastic holdings.
    b. attempted to make the wealth of the nobility subject to taxation.
    c. made people the basis for the taxation system in Russia, not land.
    d. was vigorously resented by peasant and noble alike, and led to serious civil unrest throughout Russia.

62. Perhaps the most important consequence of Peter I's reforms was the
    a. creation of a middle class.
    b. widening gap between the elite and commoners.
    c. use of French as the language of state.
    d. imposition of royal justice in the provinces.

63. The most serious problem for Russian autocracy during the Time of Troubles was the
    a. invasion by Swedes and Poles.
    b. peasant rebellion.
    c. political intrigues of the royal family.
    d. reforms of Patriarch Nikon.

64. The baroque palaces of central and eastern European princes were modeled on
    a. Notre Dame de Paris.
    b. the Louvre.
    c. Versailles.
    d. the Kremlin.

65. Perhaps the most important consequence of Stenka Razin's uprising was the
    a. creation of the myth of rebellion that would inspire future generations.
    b. abolition of serfdom.
    c. establishment of the Cossack tradition.
    d. overthrow of the Mongol Yoke.

66. All of the following were characteristic of the new royal cities *except*
    a. broad avenues.
    b. imposing government buildings.
    c. speeding carriages.
    d. wide sidewalks.

67. The population of St. Petersburg was
    a. compelled by Peter to reside there.
    b. drawn to the new capital by its beauty.
    c. composed almost exclusively of government officials.
    d. composed of mostly foreigners who had built the city.

68. According to Olearius''s description of Russian society, presented in "Listening to the Past," the Russians were
    a. generally cowards.
    b. independent, industrious people.
    c. barbarians.
    d. a great threat to civilized Europe.

History and Geography

69. The Ottoman Empire was considered a major threat to Europe. Based on Map 17.1, describe the expansion of the Ottoman state into Europe.

70. What were the three territorial parts of the Habsburg state? How did they come to be united?

71. After studying Map 17.3, describe the growth of Muscovy. How did Peter the Great add to the Muscovite base? Do his territorial acquisitions support the notion of Peter the Great as a "westernizer"? Why or why not?

CHAPTER 18

TOWARD A NEW WORLD-VIEW

Key Terms

1. Nicolaus Copernicus
2. Johannes Kepler
3. scientific method
4. *Principia*
5. Gresham College
6. Duc d'Orléans
7. Partition of Poland
8. Bernard de Fontenelle
9. Joseph II
10. *Essay on Human Understanding*
11. *philosophes*
12. Montesquieu
13. Denis Diderot
14. Madame du Châtelet
15. David Hume
16. J.- J. Rousseau
17. Mme. Geoffrin
18. War of the Austrian Succession
19. Emelian Pugachev
20. "Enlightened Absolutism"

Essay Questions

21. The Scientific Revolution transformed the way Europeans perceived the world around them. Discuss this change in detail. How did this new way of thinking spread?

    This essay asks the student to examine the Scientific Revolution rather closely. There should be a narrative tracing the developments from the pre-Copernican roots through the publication of Newton's synthesis. Focus should be placed on the heliocentric view of the universe, the belief in general theories of physics, attack on authority and use of reason, and the evolution of the scientific method; the fundamental shift from a preoccupation with the metaphysical universe to the physical universe must be fully covered. The discussion of the spread of this intellectual revolution should include both the exchange of ideas and inventions exemplified by Galileo's acquisition of a Dutch telescope, and the role of the Enlightenment (especially the early figures such as Fontenelle) in disseminating the new world-view.

22. Some monarchs of the eighteenth century have been called *enlightened despots*. Who were these rulers? What did their contemporaries mean when they called them *enlightened*? How have historians treated these rulers and their policies? Were they really enlightened? Explain your answer.

The essay should begin with a traditional definition of an enlightened monarch; following the definition, the careers of the various rulers (Frederick II, Catherine II, Maria Theresa, Joseph II) presented in this chapter should be considered, along with the basis for the perception of the rulers' enlightened nature or lack thereof. In this section, the reform efforts should be emphasized as should the impact of one's reputation for espousing Enlightenment ideals. Next, the historical interpretations of the concept should be considered, beginning with those of the nationalistic German historians of the nineteenth century to the current interpretation; stress must be placed on the role of the international system. Finally, the student is asked to assess the monarchs' enlightened nature; in this respect emphasis should be placed on the lack of attention given to reform of the social structure and the reasons for this inaction.

23. The Enlightenment had a profound effect on politics in France and in the rest of Europe. Compare the impact of the Enlightenment on French absolutism with its impact on the eastern absolute monarchies. How can we account for the differences?

One should begin with a brief description of the eastern monarchs' use of Enlightenment concepts while shielding their societies from the more dangerous aspects, such as questioning authority, of the Enlightenment; this should be compared to the emergence of a political culture in France that incorporated a much broader spectrum of the population and had as a central element the resistance to absolutism. This political culture discussion should include "public opinion," the "reading revolution," and the *salons*; the role of the Parlement of Paris in its active resistance to royal reform efforts is a critical aspect as well. Thus, in eastern Europe the monarchs were strengthened while in France the opposite occurred. In the assessment of why this occurred, the personalities of the monarchs should be considered as well as the differences in social and economic development between France and eastern Europe.

24. Historians disagree as to the nature of the Scientific Revolution, whether it was an *internal* or *external* phenomenon. What are the premises of each interpretation? Which one seems most valid and why?

First, the essay should describe each interpretation: internal refers to the Scientific Revolution as a product of the evolution from Copernicus to Newton, based upon the scientific interchange between scientists; external focuses on the social, economic, cultural, and political situations in Europe in the sixteenth and seventeenth centuries. Next, the essay should identify those conditions as they relate to the emergence and evolution of the Scientific Revolution. Finally, the student must choose an interpretation and support that choice by referring to the nature of the Revolution presented in the text.

25. The text maintains that international competition was the primary motivation behind the reforms of monarchs such as Frederick II and Catherine II. Is this an accurate assessment? How do the careers of the Austrian rulers Maria Theresa and Joseph II support or refute this assertion?

In this essay, the nature of international competition must first be described, being sure to include the wars at mid-century as well as the territorial aggrandizement that continued up to the end of the century. The reforms of Frederick II and Catherine II should be included. Next, include a thorough description of the various reforms initiated by Maria Theresa and her son, being sure to indicate the timing and motivation of these efforts. Although it is obvious that Maria Theresa's reforms are certainly motivated by the desire to improve the state in order to exact revenge on Frederick II, Joseph II's reforming efforts are rather harder to characterize in the same manner. Moreover, the reforms of both addressed the major issue, serfdom; this aspect should be assessed.

26. The scientists of the seventeenth century constructed a new world-view; the *philosophes* of the eighteenth century popularized it. How? Why did the *philosophes* pursue this effort?

This answer must focus on the spread of the new world-view. Include a thorough discussion of the efforts of Bayle, Fontenelle, Montesquieu, Voltaire, and Diderot, to popularize the Scientific Revolution through their writings. In addition, the impact of learned societies, literary clubs, and especially salons must be discussed; the concept of "public opinion" should be included as should the "reading revolution." In this discussion, indicate the types of people involved: representatives from virtually all layers of the educated classes.

27. Trace the evolution of the Enlightenment from its late-seventeenth-century roots through the later Enlightenment. Based on this discussion, can an argument be made that the mechanistic philosophy espoused by Baron d'Holbach was the logical outcome of the core beliefs of the Enlightenment? Why or why not?

The essay should begin with a description of the works of Fontenelle, Bayle, and Locke; Montesquieu, Voltaire, and the Encyclopedists should be covered next; finally, the later writers such as Hume, d'Holbach, Condorcet, and Rousseau should be discussed. In this section, the essay should indicate the three central concepts of the Enlightenment: the use of Reason, ability to discover the laws of human behavior, and Progress. The essay should then consider d'Holbach's *System of Nature*, indicating the mechanistic, atheistic base of this philosophy; finally, the student should offer an interpretation of whether or not d'Holbach's philosophy was the logical outcome of the Enlightenment, or something new.

28. Enlightenment political thought was clustered into two distinct schools, epitomized by the beliefs of Montesquieu and Voltaire. What were those beliefs? What impact did their thinking have on the governments of western and eastern Europe?

Initially, describe the political thought of Montesquieu and Voltaire, emphasizing the constitutional restraint urged by one and the reliance on benevolent reform supported by the other. There should certainly be mention of the role of the nobility in Montesquieu''s political system. The influence of Montesquieu and his school of thought in France should then be discussed; its rejection in the east must also be discussed and explained. Next, the influence of Voltaire''s ideas in the east should be discussed. A discussion of the role of social and economic development on the relative influence of each school of thought should conclude the essay.

MULTIPLE-CHOICE QUESTIONS

29. The illegal book trade in France featured all of the following types of literature *except*
    a. works by famous *philosophes*.
    b. scandalmongering denunciations of important political figures.
    c. technical journals on agriculture and industry.
    d. pornography.

30. Catherine II's greatest territorial triumph was the
    a. conquest of the Caucasus.
    b. partition of Poland.
    c. annexation of Siberia.
    d. seizure of Silesia.

31. Galileo's greatest achievement was his
    a. synthesis of the new scientific discoveries.
    b. refinement of the scientific method.
    c. invention of the telescope.
    d. postulation of a heliocentric universe.

32. All of the following played a role in the erosion of French absolutism *except* the
    a. political resurgence of the nobility.
    b. inattentiveness of Louis XV.
    c. rise of the middle class.
    d. growth of judicial power in the parlements.

33. The accomplishments of Frederick II included all of the following *except*
    a. territorial expansion.
    b. judicial and bureaucratic reform.
    c. economic improvements.
    d. restructuring the Prussian social system.

34. Before the Scientific Revolution, Europeans' view of the universe was based on the ideas of
    a. Plato.
    b. medieval scholastics.
    c. Aristotle.
    d. Isaac Newton.

35. The causes of the Scientific Revolution include all of the following *except* the
    a. development of philosophy as an academic discipline in medieval universities.
    b. navigational problems of ship captains.
    c. Renaissance recovery of ancient Greek mathematical texts.
    d. extensive support and funding provided by European governments.

36. All of the following were political consequences of the Enlightenment *except*
    a. a weakening of absolutism in France.
    b. the idea that government was a science.
    c. attempts to reform from above.
    d. a growing respect among monarchs for individual rights.

37. The most important and original idea of the Enlightenment was
    a. that reform had to come from the monarch.
    b. that the scientific method should be used to examine all aspects of life.
    c. the belief that progress was possible.
    d. that the laws of human society could be discovered.

38. All of the following astronomers contributed to the destruction of the Aristotelian view of the universe *except*
    a. Nicolaus Copernicus.
    b. Galileo Galilei.
    c. Johannes Kepler.
    d. Bernard de Fontenelle.

39. Copernicus's theory of the universe
    a. destroyed the distinction between earthly and heavenly worlds.
    b. was endorsed by John Calvin.
    c. postulated an earth-centered view of the universe.
    d. strengthened the Ptolemaic theory of the universe.

40. The synthesis of the Scientific Revolution was
    a. John Locke's *Essay Concerning Human Understanding*.
    b. Bernard de Fontenelle's *Conversation of the Plurality of Worlds*.
    c. Isaac Newton's *Principia*.
    d. Nicolaus Copernicus's *On the Revolution of the Heavenly Bodies*.

41. The key feature of Newton's system was the law of
    a. planetary motion.
    b. universal gravitation.
    c. reciprocity.
    d. constant acceleration.

42. One of the few attempts to link theoretical science with applied science took place at
    a. the French Academy.
    b. the Sorbonne.
    c. Gresham College.
    d. the University of Berlin.

43. Empiricism emphasized
    a. the use of deductive reasoning.
    b. reliance on the authority of other scientists.
    c. the actual examination of phenomena.
    d. greater reliance on mathematical equations.

44. The two men generally given credit for creating the modern scientific method were Francis Bacon and
    a. Johannes Kepler.
    b. Nicolaus Copernicus.
    c. John Locke.
    d. René Descartes.

45. The primary purpose of Fontenelle''s *Conversations on the Plurality of Worlds* (1686) was to
    a. popularize the findings of the Scientific Revolution.
    b. attack French absolutism.
    c. adapt scientific thought to Christian doctrine.
    d. counteract the influence of the Enlightenment.

46. The Enlightenment reached its highest development in France for all the following reasons *except*
    a. French was the international language of the educated classes.
    b. French scientists and universities were the most preeminent in the Scientific Revolution.
    c. the level of censorship and repression was somewhat less than that in most of Europe.
    d. French *philosophes* asked fundamental questions and sought actively to influence the educated public.

47. Pierre Bayle is famous for his
    a. skeptical view of absolute certainty.
    b. theories on political organizations.
    c. reconciliation of religious belief and science.
    d. synthesis of Enlightenment thought.

48. In his *Essay Concerning Human Understanding,* John Locke claimed that
    a. sovereign authority rests in the hands of the people.
    b. all people are born with certain ideas and ways of thinking.
    c. human development is determined by education and society.
    d. people are born corrupt and society must re-educate them.

49. The concept of a "reading revolution" asserts all of the following *except*
    a. reading became an individual process.
    b. that the reading public was very selective in its choice of reading material.
    c. that educated classes were reading insatiably and carelessly.
    d. the process of reading became desacralized, less accepting of authority.

50. All of the following are later Enlightenment *philosophes except*
    a. Baron Paul d'Holbach.
    b. Madame du Châtelet.
    c. David Hume.
    d. Marquis de Condorcet.

51. In his *Spirit of Laws*, Montesquieu argued for
    a. direct democracy.
    b. enlightened absolutism.
    c. popular sovereignty.
    d. the separation of governmental powers.

52. Politically, Voltaire believed that
    a. reform could come only from enlightened rulers.
    b. revolution was the best source for societal reform.
    c. social and political equality were necessary.
    d. Christian morality should be the basis for reforms.

53. D'Holbach's *System of Nature* presented a
    a. democratic basis for political organization.
    b. mechanistic, atheistic philosophy.
    c. popular account of the Scientific Revolution.
    d. pornographic attack on the French nobility.

54. According to its editor, the fundamental goal of the *Encyclopedia* was to
    a. popularize the Scientific Revolution.
    b. improve the material life of Europeans.
    c. change the general way of thinking.
    d. undermine French absolutism.

55. Madame du Châtelet
    a. believed women's limited contribution to science was the result of unequal education.
    b. was the first woman admitted into the Royal Academy of Sciences.
    c. was the powerful mistress of Louis XV.
    d. inspired Jean-Jacques Rousseau's ideas on education and emotion.

56. Rousseau's concept of the "general will" asserts that
    a. enlightened monarchs protect the interests of the entire society and should be relied upon for reform.
    b. only by direct democracy can the people's political wishes be conveyed.
    c. authentic, long-term needs of the people can be correctly interpreted by a farseeing minority.
    d. sovereignty resides in the people.

57. Moses Mendelsson's "On the Immortality of the Soul" developed the idea that
    a. philosophers should attack organized religion.
    b. the French Enlightenment had nothing to offer Jews.
    c. reason could complement and strengthen religion.
    d. Jews should assimilate into Christian society.

58. A striking feature of the salons was that
    a. women participated as equals.
    b. *philosophes*, nobles, and members of the upper middle class intermingled.
    c. they were often sponsored by the government.
    d. members of the working classes often attended.

59. The intellectual uncertainties of the late seventeenth century included all of the following *except*
    a. skepticism about the existence of religious truth.
    b. a great increase in information about non-European cultures, producing a tendency to adopt a relativistic approach to truth and morality.
    c. the scientific assertion that men and women were equals.
    d. the destruction of the Aristotelian universe.

60. Absolute monarchs like Catherine II and Frederick II pursued reform primarily
    a. because they believed in the Enlightenment.
    b. to compete in the fierce international system of the European states.
    c. to improve the lives of their subjects.
    d. to lessen the power of their nobles.

61. After the Seven Years' War, Frederick II set out to
    a. punish the states that had attacked him.
    b. partition Poland with the Russians.
    c. restructure the Prussian social system.
    d. rebuild the Prussian economy and improve the lives of his subjects.

62. Enlightenment thinkers relied on the reforming efforts of monarchs for all of the following reasons *except*
    a. so that individual *philosophes* could claim credit for such efforts.
    b. that absolute monarchy was a fact of political existence.
    c. the monarchs seemed to be listening to the *philosophes*.
    d. the belief that the common people were like children in need of firm guidance.

63. The least realized of Catherine II's chief goals was
    a. domestic reform.
    b. the spread of Western culture in Russia.
    c. suppression of the Russian nobility.
    d. territorial expansion.

64. As a result of Pugachev's rebellion, Catherine II
    a. initiated modest reform of the feudal system.
    b. abolished serfdom.
    c. gave the nobles more power over their serfs.
    d. created special army units to deal with unruly serfs.

65. After the death of Louis XIV, the French parlements
    a. typically supported the reform efforts of the monarchy.
    b. were undermined by the appointment of conservative nobles.
    c. effectively challenged royal absolutism.
    d. attempted to quash the Enlightenment.

66. Louis XV's abolition of the Parlement of Paris
    a. was generally approved by public opinion.
    b. provoked widespread criticism.
    c. solved the financial problems of the French government.
    d. reasserted the prestige of the monarchy.

67. The conflict between Louis XV and the Parlement of Paris centered on the issue of
    a. taxation.
    b. serfdom.
    c. political sovereignty.
    d. judicial independence.

68. To improve the rural economy and lives of the peasants, Empress Maria Theresa
    a. regulated the church more closely.
    b. ordered the adoption of scientific farming techniques.
    c. abolished serfdom.
    d. reduced nobles' power over their serfs.

69. Joseph II's conversion of labor obligations to cash payments
    a. had the support of the nobles.
    b. transformed a barter economy into a monetized one.
    c. was opposed by both nobles and peasants.
    d. was the basis for the future evolution of Austrian society.

70. The passage from Voltaire's *Philosophical Dictionary*, presented in "Listening to the Past," indicates that Voltaire
    a. detested the hypocrisy and violence associated with organized religion.
    b. was an atheist.
    c. was sympathetic to Roman Catholicism.
    d. believed that the lower classes should be controlled by the use of religion.

History and Geography

71. Where is Silesia and why did Frederick II want to seize it from Maria Theresa of Austria?

72. On the blank outline map of Europe, mark the three partitions of Poland. What does the experience of Poland reveal about the nature of the international system at the time?

73. Describe the imperial expansion of Russia under Catherine II. Where were the greatest gains made?

CHAPTER 19

THE EXPANSION OF EUROPE IN THE EIGHTEENTH CENTURY

Key Terms

1. "famine foods"
2. fallow
3. *The Gleaners*
4. nitrogen-storing crops
5. commons
6. invisible hand
7. Cornelius Vermuyden
8. Charles Townsend
9. wander rat
10. putting-out system
11. Marquis de Montcalm
12. plantation agriculture
13. "The Clothier's Delight"
14. "holy Monday"
15. Navigation Acts
16. *asiento*
17. Seven Years' War
18. Atlantic economy
19. *creoleos*
20. debt peonage

Essay Questions

21. During the eighteenth century, the population of Europe underwent a sharp increase. What factors influenced that growth? What were the social consequences of population expansion?

    This essay should begin with a brief mention of population growth before the eighteenth century. For the growth during the eighteenth century, some statistical evidence should be included. Second, the factors which caused this change must be considered, including natural factors as well as political, economic, and military changes. Finally, the impact of population growth must be discussed, as it related to agriculture, cottage industry, and the Atlantic economy.

22. French historian Marc Bloch described the agricultural revolution as "one of the noblest stories that can be told." What were the most important elements of this revolution? What factors explain the Dutch leadership in this revolution? Why and how did it spread to England?

This essay should begin with a consideration of why agricultural change was necessary. Second, the advent of scientific farming (including mention of such aspects as new crops, crop rotations, and animal husbandry) should be discussed; enclosure must be discussed fully. Third, the push/pull factors of the Dutch economy, emphasizing urbanization, must be discussed. Finally, English emulation should be described and analyzed: the obvious similarities to Dutch society and economy must be mentioned; the role of English commercial competition with the Dutch Republic is another aspect which should be discussed.

23. The period between 1650 and 1763 was characterized by nearly continual imperial competition, a competition which England ultimately won. Why?

This essay should begin by discussing the role of European politics, including not only the imperial competition that involved England, the Dutch Republic, and France, but also the role of mercantilism. The impact of European wars on the colonial competition should be stressed. The trading patterns of the Atlantic economy should then be described. Following this description, British mercantilistic policies, especially the Navigation Acts, must be discussed. In addition, the capitalistic spirit, amply demonstrated by Adam Smith, should also be discussed. Finally, the student should refer to the excerpt from Defoe; this certainly provides a fine description of the importance of trade, but is perhaps less worthwhile in presenting the complete picture of English economic dominance, a failing which should be mentioned.

24. While England was building the preeminent world empire and greatest economic power base in Europe, its society was undergoing profound changes. Describe these changes, being sure to identify the causes and consequences of these changes.

The description should include the impact of the agricultural revolution on the rural population, including peasants, tenant farmers, and land owners. The creation of a landless rural proletariat is a key component. Scientific farming and destruction of the commons are major causes of these changes. The population explosion of the eighteenth century must also be discussed, with the impact on rural population and the inability to employ the new population. Rise of the putting-out system, growing out of the changes caused by the agricultural changes, should be discussed, with the role of family-based employment being a key component; introduction to production techniques, wage labor, etc., are all worthy of mention. The negative aspects of the system (labor relations, drunkenness and other familial problems, quality control, and production bottlenecks) should be included. The longer-term impact on the industrial revolution would provide a solid conclusion.

25. Despite the success of English mercantilist policies, many chafed under this regulatory system. What were the criticisms of mercantilism? What was Adam Smith's answer to mercantilism? Would the application of Smith's theories result in English domination of the Atlantic economy? Why or why not?

This essay should begin with a brief description of mercantilism, followed by the criticisms of the system, especially the artificial restrictions imposed by governmental regulation. Next, Smith's economic theories must be discussed thoroughly. Finally, to analyze the effectiveness of Smith's theories for enabling English domination of the Atlantic economy, one must consider those policies, such as the Navigation Acts, which helped assure English ascendancy, and the capitalist spirit so evident in English commercial activities. The role of continental mercantilistic policies might also be mentioned.

26. The enclosure movement has been the subject of much debate among historians. Trace this movement from its origins through the end of the eighteenth century. What impact did enclosure have on the society and economy of England?

The essay should begin with a narrative of the enclosure movement, from its sixteenth-century wool industry origins to the end of the eighteenth century. Second, one must describe the distinctive pattern of landownership and production in England. Third, the rise of market-oriented agriculture and the emergence of a landless rural proletariat must be fully described; rising agricultural productivity, rising population, export markets, cottage industry, and urbanization should all be addressed in the context of the transformation of English society.

MULTIPLE-CHOICE QUESTIONS

27. Before 1700, the total European population
    a. followed an irregular cycle of slow growth.
    b. always grew too fast.
    c. grew steadily and moderately.
    d. followed a cyclical pattern of steady decline.

28. The agricultural revolution was first manifested in
    a. England.
    b. the Low Countries.
    c. Sweden.
    d. North America.

29. The expansion of Europe in the eighteenth century featured all of the following *except*
    a. growing population.
    b. increased world trade.
    c. expansion of agriculture.
    d. relatively peaceful international relations.

30. The most prevalent system of land usage in Europe in the early modern era was known as the
    a. estate system.
    b. tenant system.
    c. fallow-rotational system.
    d. open-field system.

31. The English Navigation Acts not only mandated that all English imports and exports had to be transported on English ship, they also
    a. restricted English banks from making foreign loans.
    b. initiated English involvement in the transatlantic slave trade.
    c. restricted manufacturing in the colonies.
    d. created an alliance with the Dutch against the French.

32. Traditional agricultural practices included all of the following *except*
    a. division of land into strips which were then parceled out to individual families.
    b. crop rotations to allow the soil to rest.
    c. common lands set aside for pasturage and complement to peasant household economy.
    d. fenced fields and long-term tenureship of plots of land by peasants.

33. The most persistent problem with the open-field system of agriculture was
    a. the scarcity of labor.
    b. bad weather.
    c. soil depletion.
    d. inequitable land distribution among the peasants.

34. The subject of Millet's masterpiece *The Gleaners* was the
    a. tranquility of rural life.
    b. precarious nature of agrarian life.
    c. resentment of feudal obligations.
    d. bounty of Dutch agriculture.

35. According to Adam Smith, the duties of government included all of the following *except*
    a. defense against foreign invasion.
    b. maintenance of civil order.
    c. sponsorship of certain indispensable public works.
    d. pursuit of policies favorable to large-scale manufacturing and commerce.

36. The key to the agricultural revolution was the
    a. elimination of fallow lands.
    b. discovery of animal husbandry.
    c. expropriation of noble and church lands.
    d. introduction of the longer crop rotations.

37. Dutch leadership in farming can be attributed primarily to
    a. the exceptional fertility of their lands.
    b. a large urbanized population.
    c. the leadership of the Dutch scientific community.
    d. their strong nobility.

38. Lord Charles Townsend is famous for
    a. the introduction of the Navigation Acts.
    b. the development of the putting-out system.
    c. his advocacy of scientific farming.
    d. his attack on mercantilism.

39. Cornelius Vermuyden
    a. invented the seed drill.
    b. developed new methods of breeding livestock.
    c. reintroduced the tulip to Holland.
    d. was a Dutch land reclamation expert.

40. Jethro Tull's contributions to English agriculture were the product of
    a. good luck.
    b. empirical research.
    c. deductive reasoning.
    d. speculative reasoning.

41. The social group upon which the success of the English agricultural revolution depended was the
    a. land-owning aristocracy.
    b. landless peasants.
    c. tenant farmers.
    d. independent peasant farmers.

42. The enclosure acts of 1760 and later
    a. were responsible for the enclosure of almost 90 percent of English farmland.
    b. only completed a process begun much earlier.
    c. resulted in a newly created army of landless cottagers.
    d. forced people to move to the cities.

43. The eighteenth-century enclosure movement in England was responsible for the rise of market-oriented estate agriculture and the
    a. emergence of a landless rural proletariat.
    b. destruction of cottage industry.
    c. declining power of the English aristocracy.
    d. collapse of tenant farming.

44. Probably the most important competitive advantage of the putting-out system was its
    a. cheap labor costs.
    b. unregulated production techniques.
    c. support of the guilds.
    d. responsiveness to demand.

45. The tremendous population growth of the eighteenth century resulted from all of the following *except*
    a. earlier marriages.
    b. advances in medical science.
    c. improvements in transport and storage of grain.
    d. the disappearance of the bubonic plague.

46. All of the following were shortcomings of the putting-out system *except*
    a. bottlenecks in the production process.
    b. rigid production techniques.
    c. quality control.
    d. labor relations.

47. The term *spinster* referred to
    a. a widowed or unmarried woman who spun cloth for a living.
    b. the putting-out merchant.
    c. the wife of a weaver.
    d. a female member of a textile guild.

48. Plantations in the Virginia lowlands, by 1730, were worked entirely by
    a. indentured servants.
    b. American Indians.
    c. African slaves.
    d. free whites.

49. Typically the putting-out industry employed
    a. only women.
    b. rural families.
    c. urban workers.
    d. men and older boys.

50. Virginia plantation owners and New England merchants were
    a. not an integral part of the mercantile system.
    b. both damaged by the mercantile system.
    c. protected and restricted by the mercantile system.
    d. the greatest beneficiaries of the mercantile system.

51. For cottage workers, "holy Monday" was
    a. payday.
    b. the delivery day for raw materials.
    c. a day spent in church.
    d. a day of relaxation.

52. The Navigation Acts were a form of economic warfare that initially targeted the
    a. Dutch.
    b. French.
    c. Spanish.
    d. colonists.

53. Montcalm's mistake at the battle of Quebec was his decision to
    a. continue his defense of the fortress.
    b. attack the British lines in a frontal assault.
    c. refuse to use Canadian militiamen.
    d. continue the guerrilla tactics utilized by the Canadians and Indians.

54. The theaters of operations for the century-long competition between England and France included all of the following *except*
    a. North America.
    b. India.
    c. Europe.
    d. South America.

55. The *asiento* was
    a. a tax on imports into the Spanish colonies.
    b. the upper class in Brazil.
    c. the West African slave trade.
    d. the system of debt peonage in South and Central America.

56. The decisive round in the colonial conflict between England and France was the
    a. Seven Years' War.
    b. Thirty Years' War.
    c. War of the Austrian Succession.
    d. War of the Spanish Succession.

57. The British won the American component of the Seven Years' War because
    a. the French military leadership was ineffective.
    b. their Prussian ally won the European component.
    c. the French did not have an adequate navy.
    d. they diverted men and money from Europe to the American theater.

58. The factor that most limited the growth of industry in the British colonies was
    a. the Navigation Acts.
    b. a lack of raw materials.
    c. a lack of investment capital.
    d. a labor shortage.

59. Most British colonists were motivated to settle in the colonies by
    a. the availability of cheap land.
    b. political freedom.
    c. religious freedom.
    d. a sense of adventure.

60. On the eve of the American Revolution, the average standard of living in the British colonies was
    a. much lower than that of Britain.
    b. about the same as Britain's.
    c. the highest in the world.
    d. falling as a result of the Navigation Acts.

61. By the 1770s, the bulk of British foreign trade was with
    a. France.
    b. its colonial empire.
    c. Africa and the Middle East.
    d. the European continent.

62. According to Adam Smith, harmony and progress would result from
    a. laws to regulate economic behavior.
    b. the decline of warfare and improved health care.
    c. the government's maintenance of civil order and public works.
    d. the pursuit of self-interest in a competitive market.

63. Spanish-American society included all of the following groups *except*
    a. creoles.
    b. mestizos.
    c. Indians.
    d. conquistadors.

166 / *The Expansion of Europe in the Eighteenth Century*

64. From 1600 on, the typical system of labor control in Spanish America was
    a. raced-based slavery.
    b. debt peonage.
    c. forced labor.
    d. indentured servitude.

65. Defoe's description of the social status of the English commercial classes, presented in "Listening to the Past," indicates that
    a. the nobility still enjoyed a monopoly on power.
    b. tradesmen were unlikely to be able to raise their social standing.
    c. commercial activity was no barrier to elevated social status.
    d. English traders enjoyed the same prestige as did those of France.

History and Geography

66. Describe the physical layout of a typical, traditional farming community, based upon the description in the text of the open-field system. How would an enclosure act change the description?

67. According to the text and Map 19.3, describe the impact of the Seven Years' War on the British empire.

68. Chart the Atlantic economy. What products composed the various legs of this so-called triangular trade?

CHAPTER 20

THE CHANGING LIFE OF THE PEOPLE

Key Terms

1. St. Vincent de Paul
2. illegitimacy explosion
3. wetnursing
4. "overlaying"
5. Daniel Defoe
6. nuclear family
7. "just price"
8. scurvy
9. midwife
10. blood-letting
11. white bread
12. Carnival
13. lunatic
14. Hôtel Dieu
15. "charity schools"
16. Edward Jenner
17. territorial churches
18. popular culture
19. pietism
20. John Wesley

Essay Questions

21. In recent years, scholars have successfully challenged many of the old generalizations made about the past. What were those generalizations and how have recent studies modified our views of the family in pre-industrial Europe? How and why did the European family begin to change in this period?

    The essay should identify the generalizations, such as large families, early marriage, and extended family structure. Next, the manner by which recent historical studies have come to challenge these generalizations, including the sources utilized (parish records), should be discussed; this section should include a full discussion of our understanding of the European family in the early modern period: nuclear family, number of children, late marriage for both men and women. Finally, the

168 / The Changing Life of the People

impact of economic and societal change on such things as family size, age of marriage, and choice of spouse should conclude the essay.

22. "Pre-industrial Europe was clearly a hierarchical society." Assess the validity of this statement, being sure to support your assertions with germane examples from the text in this chapter.

    For this essay, there are several good examples: the diets of Europeans, emphasizing the differences between that of upper class and common people; the differences between upper-class and lower-class families, in terms of size, affectional relations, marriage choices, age of marriage, child abandonment, wet nursing, and education; the dichotomy between popular culture and high culture represents a third area of differentiation between upper class and common people.

23. One of the most neglected groups in historical study has been children. Correct this oversight by writing a brief history of children during the eighteenth century. What was their life like? Be sure to consider educational opportunities, health, medical care, and diet. What was the attitude of their parents toward them? How would Jean-Jacques Rousseau's ideas on child rearing and education have affected them? What would they have done for entertainment and courtship as they approached adulthood? Finally, what changes had they experienced in these areas?

    This essay should provide a thorough description of childhood in early modern Europe, following the outline in the question; sensitivity to class differences will greatly enhance the effectiveness of the essay. Rousseau's ideas, on more affectionate child rearing, breast feeding, experiential education, and separate spheres, should also be discussed. One can discuss the transition from childhood to adulthood by considering the courtship practices at the time. The essay should conclude by placing emphasis on the changes, such as greater educational opportunities, experienced.

24. While the Enlightenment was spreading among the educated elites, religion remained a strong force in the lives of the common people. What were the patterns of popular religion for both Catholics and Protestants in the late eighteenth century? How did the church leaders, Protestant and Catholic, respond to popular religion?

    Begin by stressing the fact that religion not only offered answers but was deeply embedded in local traditions, experiences, and culture. Next, the pattern should be described; this section must include a discussion of the institutional church, focusing on the role of the parish church. In Catholic regions, the local cults of the saints and other such practices must be discussed. The discussion of the Protestant revival should include the central concerns and beliefs of the revivalists, such as Wesley. The Catholic leadership's attempts to purify Catholicism of the many dubious, pagan practices should then be discussed as should the "smug complacency" of the Protestant establishment; indicate the class basis of this dichotomy between the official theology and popular practices and how this is evidence of the distance between the elite and the common people of Europe.

25. The eighteenth century was an era of improving health and increased life expectancy. Why? What impact did the improving health and longevity have on European society?

    A thorough discussion of diet and nutrition must be included in this essay. The role of medical science, limited though it was, should also be included; mention of the improving abilities of surgeons, and midwives (using Martha Ballard as an example) would be helpful. A brief discussion of the role of Mary Montague and Edward Jenner in the control of smallpox should also be included. In discussing the impact, population growth is an obvious factor; more complicated is the impact on land tenure and inheritance, age of marriage and choice of partner, illegitimacy, relationship to one's children.

26. By the eighteenth century, a "popular culture" had evolved. What is "popular culture"? What were its typical manifestations? Why would the elites be critical of popular culture?

    Describe fully popular culture; consider the interplay between popular religion and the other aspects of the popular culture of Europe. Include the role of the parish church, the calendar, blood sports, superstitious ritual, and Carnival; include group basis of behavior. This group behavior, especially at Carnival time, can be used to underscore the tension between elites and common people. This tension is certainly one aspect of elite criticism of popular culture, but one should also include the superstitious, frivolous, and sometimes brutal aspects of popular culture to which the educated elites of Europe would react negatively.

MULTIPLE-CHOICE QUESTIONS

27. The first European state to mandate compulsory elementary education was
    a. Prussia.
    b. the Netherlands.
    c. England.
    d. France.

28. The reading material of the popular classes included all of the following *except*
    a. practical material, such as almanacs.
    b. entertaining, humorous, escapist stories.
    c. works on Christian theology.
    d. chapbooks with religious contents.

29. The *Edict on Idle Institutions* outlawed
    a. the Jesuits.
    b. contemplative monastic orders.
    c. foundling homes.
    d. territorial churches.

30. In seventeenth- and early-eighteenth-century Europe, most couples
    a. married in their teens.
    b. lived together before marriage.
    c. included an older husband and young wife.
    d. married in their late twenties.

31. Most girls who sought work outside their families found jobs as
    a. workers in textile factories.
    b. teachers.
    c. domestic servants.
    d. shop clerks.

32. The pattern of late marriage in early modern Europe resulted primarily from the
    a. necessary precondition of economic independence.
    b. prevalence of the extended family structure.
    c. fear of overpopulation.
    d. availability of premarital sex.

33. Prior to 1750, premarital sex
    a. was nonexistent.
    b. occurred only among upper classes.
    c. was commonplace.
    d. resulted in a high percentage of illegitimate children.

34. Violations of social norms of traditional lower-class communities were punished by
    a. banishment.
    b. public humiliation.
    c. public corporal punishment.
    d. fines and imprisonment.

35. In the second half of the eighteenth century, couples married younger, primarily in response to
    a. the emergence of the cottage industry.
    b. the Enlightenment.
    c. state policies encouraging larger families.
    d. the depopulation caused by the wars of the eighteenth century.

36. Popular leisure and entertainment included all of the following *except*
    a. blood sports.
    b. Carnival.
    c. social gatherings in groups, for drinking and story-telling.
    d. dinner parties.

37. The illegitimacy explosion in the second half of the eighteenth century was the result of
    a. later marriage among the rural and urban poor.
    b. urban migration.
    c. stringent laws against birth control.
    d. the establishment of foundling homes all over Europe.

38. In his work on education and children, Jean-Jacques Rousseau urged all of the following *except*
    a. equality of education for boys and girls.
    b. maternal breast-feeding.
    c. experiential education for children.
    d. greater tenderness for children.

39. The neglectful attitudes toward children in pre-industrial Europe were conditioned by
    a. high infant mortality rates.
    b. church doctrine.
    c. Enlightenment philosophy.
    d. their economic value.

40. The practice of wet-nursing benefited
    a. the infants placed in the care of wet-nurses.
    b. the working-class mothers who had to go to work.
    c. the infants of the wet-nurses.
    d. nobody but selfish upper-class mothers.

41. The term "overlaying" refers to
    a. the rape of domestic servants.
    b. parents' suffocating young children in bed.
    c. wet-nurses who took on too many infants.
    d. the practice of abandoning children on the steps of churches.

42. St. Vincent de Paul is most famous for his
    a. efforts to outlaw the Society of Jesus.
    b. perfection of the smallpox vaccination.
    c. establishment of foundling homes.
    d. establishment of churches in new, working-class neighborhoods in cities.

43. The English author Daniel Defoe is used to illustrate
    a. harsh, often brutal discipline inflicted on children.
    b. financial opportunities available in the eighteenth century.
    c. standards of health care available to the rich in eighteenth-century London.
    d. emotional power of the Protestant revival.

44. The most important factor influencing increased life expectancy for pre-industrial Europeans was
    a. better wet-nursing techniques.
    b. more and better food.
    c. improved medical care.
    d. fewer wars.

45. All of the following are accurate about midwives in the eighteenth century *except* that they
    a. faced growing criticism and discrimination from the medical profession.
    b. received practical training.
    c. were of modest social origins, and were typically mothers themselves.
    d. could earn professional credentials.

46. A rich person's dinner party was characterized by copious consumption of meat and
    a. vegetables.
    b. bread.
    c. fruit.
    d. wine.

47. The diet of the poorer classes consisted of bread and
    a. meat and eggs.
    b. dairy products.
    c. vegetables.
    d. wild game.

48. A severe deficiency in vitamin C results in the disease known as
    a. anemia.
    b. gout.
    c. dysentery.
    d. scurvy.

49. The American crop that became an important dietary supplement by the end of the century was
    a. winter wheat.
    b. the tomato.
    c. rice.
    d. the potato.

50. Medical practitioners who were most likely to rely on drugs were called
    a. faith healers.
    b. apothecaries.
    c. surgeons.
    d. physicians.

51. In the eighteenth century, faith healers
    a. had disappeared.
    b. usually prescribed herbal remedies.
    c. believed disease was caused by imbalance in the humors.
    d. used exorcism to treat illness.

52. Changes in the food consumption habits of Europeans in the eighteenth century included all of the following *except*
    a. declining consumption of alcoholic beverages.
    b. the replacement of coarse whole-wheat bread with white bread.
    c. greater variety and availability of vegetables.
    d. increased consumption of sugar.

53. Many surgeons gained anatomical knowledge and practical experience
    a. on the many battlefields of Europe.
    b. by apprenticing themselves to physicians.
    c. as a result of the legalization of dissection.
    d. from the rediscovery of Greek and Roman medical writings.

54. For a sick person in the eighteenth century, the best advice would have been to
    a. check into a hospital.
    b. visit an apothecary.
    c. visit a physician.
    d. hope the condition improves on its own.

55. The term *lunatic* refers to
    a. someone who drank too much.
    b. traditional village punishments for those who violated local customs.
    c. popular belief that mental illness was caused by moonlight.
    d. German Protestants who joined the Pietist movement.

56. The greatest achievement of eighteenth-century medical science was the
    a. control of venereal disease.
    b. elimination of the bubonic plague.
    c. rise of the animistic school of medicine.
    d. conquest of smallpox.

57. Lady Mary Wortley Montague is most famous for
    a. spreading the practice of smallpox inoculation in England.
    b. the establishment and support of foundling homes all over England.
    c. her efforts at establishing universal elementary education.
    d. her amazing career as a midwife.

58. Smallpox vaccination was developed by
    a. John Wesley.
    b. St. Vincent de Paul.
    c. Edward Jenner.
    d. Jean-Jacques Rousseau.

59. The term *territorial churches* refers to
    a. Catholic churches still controlled by the pope.
    b. large parish churches of any denomination.
    c. churches outside the control of the state.
    d. churches controlled by the state.

60. The dissolution of the Jesuit order in 1773 is a striking indication of the
    a. decline of religious feeling in the eighteenth century.
    b. resurgent power of the papacy.
    c. power of the state over the church.
    d. vitality of the Protestant revival.

61. The popular strength of religion in Catholic countries reflected
    a. the desires of secular authorities.
    b. its importance in community life.
    c. the decline of papal and clerical abuses.
    d. the role of the parish clergy in the state bureaucracy.

62. Martha Ballard's credentials as a midwife included all of the following *except*
    a. practical training received from other, experienced midwives.
    b. her own experience, giving birth to nine children.
    c. her maturity, self-confidence, and physical and moral strength.
    d. a certificate of professional competence.

63. All of the following were aspects of the celebration of Carnival *except*
    a. drinking and dancing.
    b. mocking the established order.
    c. begging forgiveness for one's sins.
    d. masquerading.

64. All of the following were aspects of the Protestant revival in Germany *except*
    a. rationalism.
    b. religious enthusiasm.
    c. stress on the priesthood of all believers.
    d. the practical power of Christian rebirth in everyday affairs.

65. John Wesley's religious revival
    a. emphasized Calvin's belief in predestination.
    b. preached free will and universal salvation.
    c. took place within the organized Anglican church.
    d. incorporated aspects of Enlightenment deism.

66. In the excerpt from *Emile*, reproduced in "Listening to the Past," Rousseau argued that
    a. education for boys and girls should be the same.
    b. the strict discipline of children was necessary.
    c. reliance on emotion crippled the intellect.
    d. experience and emotion are the best teachers.

History and Geography

67. How did land-owning patterns and inheritance practices affect marriage and population growth in the eighteenth century? How did the urban migration and new employment opportunities in the countryside affect marriage practices and relations between men and women generally?

68. What were the most important food crops introduced into Europe from the Americas?

CHAPTER 21

THE REVOLUTION IN POLITICS, 1775-1815

Key Terms

1. Declaration of Independence
2. Coercive Acts
3. liberalism
4. anti-Federalists
5. Marquis de Lafayette
6. *A Vindication of the Rights of Woman*
7. Bastille
8. Maximilien Robespierre
9. Marie Antoinette
10. Abbé Sieyès
11. Jacobins
12. "second revolution"
13. sans-culottes
14. Committee of Public Safety
15. Thermidorian reaction
16. Civil Code (1804)
17. Grand Empire
18. Waterloo
19. German Confederation of the Rhine
20. Law of the Maximum
21. "war of liberation"
22. women's march on Versailles

Essay Questions

23. Liberalism inspired the political revolutionaries in both North America and France. How can we define this political philosophy? How was it manifested in the American and French Revolutions?

    First, there should be a definition of liberalism, stressing individual political rights and private property. Then the student should indicate the liberalism of each revolution, manifested in the beliefs of the leadership of each revolution and certain fundamental documents such as the American Declaration of Independence, Constitution and Bill of Rights, and the French Declaration of the Rights of Man, Constitution of 1791, and the Civil Code of Napoleon.

24. Compare the origins of the American and French Revolutions. In what ways do the factors behind each revolution reflect the situation in each country? How did these factors influence the course of each revolution?

In this comparative essay, the student should describe the origins of each revolution; one should be certain to include factors (especially the Enlightenment) common to both revolutions as well as the unique aspects of each. For the American Revolution, the role of political control must be addressed; the lack of any serious economic and social problems must be considered. For the French Revolution, one should certainly discuss the political conflict between the various rival elites, but one must also discuss the economic problems, the archaic social structure, and the resultant social conflict. The role of economic and social relations is critical to the explanation of why the French Revolution was so much more violent than the American.

25. The era of the French Revolution also saw the birth of the modern feminist movement. Who were the leaders in this movement? What were their beliefs? What was the role of average women? How did the men of the Revolution react to these women?

The essay should begin with a description of Mary Wollstonecraft's positions, outlined in her *Vindication of the Rights of Woman*; one should be sure to stress the logical implications of natural-law philosophy. Then the essay should refer to Olympe de Gouge's "Declaration of the Rights of Woman and the Female Citizen"; this more detailed presentation should be discussed fully as it relates to women's position in society. Here again one should be sure to consider its connection to natural-law philosophy. The role of women in important revolutionary events should be noted, as should women's participation in political clubs. Next one should present the record of both revolutionary governments and Napoleon in terms of women's rights; one must provide specific examples of the expected role of women as the various constitutions and governments defined it, ranging from the greater protection of property rights granted by the National Assembly through the institutionalization of women's secondary status in the Civil Code. Finally, the arguments of both Wollstonecraft and de Gouge should be assessed as logical extentions of the natural-law philosophy of all men enjoying inalienable rights.

26. "The primary impetus for action during the Revolution came from the common people of France, both rural and urban." Assess the role of sans-culottes and peasants in the French Revolution. What impact did popular participation have on the success (or failure) of the Revolution?

To begin, this essay must discuss fully the storming of the Bastille as the event that turned a competition among elites for political power into revolution. Second, the Great Fear and its impact must be described, and analyzed for its impact on the role of the peasantry during the subsequent course of the Revolution. Next, such events as the Women's March on Versailles should be covered. The storming of the Tuileries on 10 August 1792 is another such moment that should be included. The September Massacres should be stressed. With the onset of the Reign of Terror, the role of the Parisian population (and elsewhere) in influencing the revolutionary tribunals must be stressed. The ongoing influence of the Parisian population on the successive legislative bodies until 1795 should also be described. The quiesence of the Parisians following the overthrow of Robespierre is yet another moment that bears discussion. The support of peasants for counterrevolutionary insurgencies in various regions should also be discussed. In terms of motivation, one should certainly emphasize the role of economic collapse on the events of 1789 and the continuing role of the economy in subsequent years; one should also discuss the creation of political parties and how these parties' competition helped to politicize and radicalize the

Parisians, to such an extent that the Parisians became aware of their political power. Finally, one must provide an opinion as to the impact of the people on the Revolution; one's discussion of the role of the people on the course of the Revolution should reveal their crucial role.

27. "Napoleon was a child of the Enlightenment." Assess the validity of this statement through a careful consideration of his domestic policies and military campaigns. In light of your analysis, how accurate is this statement?

One should begin with a definition of what would constitute a child of the Enlightenment; astute students would also indicate the difference between early and late Enlightenment. In the next section of the essay, one should analyze Napoleon's career; the Civil Code must be stressed as an obvious example of Enlightenment thinking while his imperialist and rapacious foreign adventures coupled with his dictatorial government run counter to Enlightenment principles. One's analysis should attempt to go beyond these obvious aspects and consider his efforts at conciliation in France and his reorganization of Germany. The student should defend a position.

28. In the Constitution of 1791, the leaders of the National Assembly rejected wars of conquest, yet one could argue that, by as early as 1795, the Revolution was engaged in just such adventures. Why did the various French governments from 1792 to 1815 pursue such imperialistic activities? What were the consequences of French military activities?

To explain the continual resort to war, and to a system of military conquest and oppression, by revolutionary governments and Napoleon, one should refer to foreign hostility (from aristocrats, monarchs, and nationalists); another factor was the pressure of counter-revolutionary activity and subsequent political competition in Paris; France's ongoing financial problems is yet another factor; Napoleon's militaristic attitude and megalomania should also be included; to a certain extent, at least in the early years, there was also a genuine belief in the propagation of the revolution through waging war against the monarchies of Europe. Consequences include: the political reorganization of much of the map of Europe; the emulation of the large French military techniques; abolition of serfdom and extension of administrative and legal reforms in many parts of Europe; and the emergence of nationalistic sentiments throughout the Continent.

29. It has been argued that the financial problems of the royal government were a major cause of the French Revolution. What were these problems? How did Louis XVI's government attempt to deal with the financial crisis? How did these problems precipitate the Revolution?

This question demands a rather thorough examination of the financial problems of the French government during the eighteenth century; although the question specifies the governmental problems, a good essay will relate governmental financial problems to the general economic problems of France. In the enumeration of these problems, one should emphasis the long-term nature of this issue; emphasis should be placed on the burgeoning royal debt (the various sources of this debt should be noted) and the shrinking tax base, the difficulty of acquiring new sources of credit, and the limited options available to Louis XVI. The king's efforts to reform the tax system (mention could be made of the efforts of Louis XV in this regard) and resistance of the Parlement of Paris must next be considered. Ultimately, one should conclude the essay with the calling of the Assembly of Notables, and the resultant attempt by the nobles to destroy the remnants of absolutist monarchy in France; the economic distress of the people of Paris and many in the countryside would push the French into revolution.

30. The French Revolution and the Napoleonic era produced profound change in Europe. What were the gains and losses of the various social groupings—nobility, bourgeoisie, workers, peasants, women—in this era? Who gained the most? The least?

This essay should describe and analyze the impact of the revolutionary and Napoleonic eras on the social groupings enumerated in the question. One should be sensitive to changes in political power, economic well-being, educational opportunity, and social status; the essay should indicate whether or not groups experienced consistent improvement or decline, that is, one must discuss the ebb and flow of events as they affected each social grouping. Finally, the winners and losers must be identified; for example, the gains of the peasantry resulting from abolition of feudalism and the protection of these gains by the Civil Code identify this group as a winner but, on the other hand, recruitment into the army and civil war were both negative factors for the peasants.

31. Debate over the French Revolution continues today. In many ways this debate revolves around the causes of the Revolution. What are the two major positions in the debate? What were the causes of the Revolution? How did these causes affect the course of the Revolution? Based upon your consideration of the causes and their impact, which of the interpretations seems most valid?

The essay should begin with a brief definition of the Marxist notion of the bourgeois revolution and the revisionist critique of the interpretation. Next, the essay must carefully and fully describe the long-term causes of the Revolution: financial crisis, economic problems, social structure, Enlightenment political culture, weakness of the monarchy. Then the immediate causes should be related to the long-term causes: economic disasters of the last years of the decade, price of bread, bankruptcies and unemployment, Louis XVI's political incompetence, middle-class uneasiness, resistance of the Parlement of Paris and the Assembly of Notables. The violent and erratic course of the Revolution should be related to the long-term causes, especially economic collapse, social tensions, and Enlightenment political culture. Finally, the essay should then determine which interpretative paradigm seems most accurate.

Multiple-Choice Questions

32. The group that met in 1787 to discuss tax reform was the
    a. Estates General.
    b. Assembly of Notables.
    c. National Assembly.
    d. National Convention.

33. During the Reign of Terror, the dominant person on the Committee of Public Safety was
    a. Abbé Sieyès.
    b. Napoleon Bonaparte.
    c. Georges Danton.
    d. Maximilien Robespierre.

34. During the Hundred Days,
    a. the sans-culottes committed the September Massacres.
    b. Napoleon was driven from Russia.
    c. Napoleon returned from exile to rule France briefly.
    d. the Reign of Terror executed 30,000 people.

35. The republic proclaimed by the National Convention in 1792 sought to
    a. create a new culture and make a complete break with the past.
    b. establish economic and social equality.
    c. reconcile the component parts of French society to the Revolution.
    d. consolidate the revolutionary accomplishments of the National Assembly.

36. The Declaration of Pillnitz
    a. was issued by Austria and Prussia to intimidate French revolutionaries.
    b. abolished the Holy Roman Empire.
    c. affirmed the rights of French men and women.
    d. insured the continuation of slavery in French colonies.

37. All of the following were aspects of the influence of the American Revolution on the French Revolution *except*
    a. providing young men with a taste of revolutionary action and ideals.
    b. providing a revolutionary role model.
    c. increasing the class conflict between nobility and bourgeoisie.
    d. increasing the financial burdens of the state.

38. The furor over the Stamp Act of 1765 resulted from the
    a. fact that American colonists were overtaxed.
    b. high-handed attitude of King George III.
    c. fear that Americans' liberties were threatened.
    d. use of troops to collect the tax.

39. Mary Wollstonecraft argued that
    a. women were naturally inferior to men.
    b. thorough-going reform in France would lead to anarchy.
    c. women's place in society was in the private sphere.
    d. men and women would benefit from sexual equality.

40. The battle that prevented Napoleon's planned invasion of England was
    a. Waterloo.
    b. Trafalgar.
    c. Borodino.
    d. Jemappes.

41. Napoleon's Civil Code of 1804
    a. granted women the right to vote.
    b. insured a continuation of revolutionary equality between men and women.
    c. insured political but not economic equality.
    d. institutionalized women's secondary status.

42. The social groups that benefitted most from the Revolution and Napoleon were the middle class and the
    a. peasants.
    b. aristocracy.
    c. workers.
    d. women.

43. The Directory was popular with the
    a. peasants.
    b. sans-culottes.
    c. clergy.
    d. virtually no one.

44. Women were ultimately excluded from the political process during the Revolution for all of the following reasons *except*
    a. the belief that a woman's place was in the home.
    b. the belief that immoral aristocratic women had used sexual charms to manipulate the kings.
    c. the desire to have women raise the high-minded citizens needed to govern the nation.
    d. that women themselves rejected participation in the political sphere.

45. The Charter issued by Louis XVIII in 1814 established a(n)
    a. democratic republic.
    b. limited constitutional monarchy.
    c. military dictatorship.
    d. absolutist monarchy.

46. In *Reflections on the Revolution in France*, Edmund Burke defended
    a. radicalization, exemplified by the Reign of Terror.
    b. the direct actions of the peasants and sans-culottes.
    c. traditional, monarchical government and inherited privileges.
    d. the liberal ideology that led to the Revolution.

47. Eighteenth-century liberalism called for all of the following *except*
    a. individual human rights.
    b. economic equality.
    c. the people's sovereignty.
    d. equality of opportunity.

48. Abbé Sieyès's answer to the question of what is the third estate was
    a. a bunch of rabble-rousers.
    b. the most useful component of French society.
    c. those who adhered to liberalism.
    d. the business and professional elite.

49. Jakob Walter's memoirs of the 1812 campaign is dominated by his tales of
    a. the struggle to find food.
    b. probably fictionalized, heroic actions.
    c. his increasing intellectual discontent with the policies of Napoleon.
    d. his hatred for both the Russians and the French.

50. Liberalism appealed strongly to the ambitious bourgeoisie and
    a. the peasants.
    b. the clergy.
    c. the sans-culottes.
    d. much of the aristocracy.

51. The situation in Paris on the eve of the Revolution included all of the following *except*
    a. faith in the king, if not his government.
    b. high unemployment.
    c. high food prices.
    d. fear of a royal and aristocratic attack on the city.

52. The distinctiveness of the North American society included all of the following *except*
    a. its greater political equality.
    b. a high degree of social and economic equality.
    c. economic, religious, and ethnic homogeneity.
    d. a tradition of self-government.

53. The Declaration of Independence
    a. included a denunciation of slavery.
    b. proclaimed the natural rights of all humankind.
    c. was primarily a list of American grievances against the British.
    d. proclaimed the formation of a democratic republic.

54. Opponents of the U.S. Constitution were called
    a. Loyalists.
    b. Federalists.
    c. Anti-Federalists.
    d. Liberals.

55. In the 1780s, over 50 percent of France's annual budget was expended on
    a. the military.
    b. the royal court.
    c. administrative functions.
    d. interest payments on the debt.

56. The legal definition of the composition of the prerevolutionary third estate included
    a. everyone who was not a noble or member of the clergy.
    b. the clergy.
    c. the peasantry.
    d. the nobility.

57. Revisionist historians of the French Revolution stress all of the following *except* the
    a. fluidity and relative openness of the nobility.
    b. adoption of liberalism by many nobles.
    c. common economic goals of the nobility and the middle class.
    d. conflict between the nobility and the bourgeoisie.

58. The men elected to represent the third estate at the Estates General were primarily
    a. provincial nobles.
    b. businessmen.
    c. lawyers and government officials.
    d. sans-culottes.

59. The grievance petitions from all three estates called for all of the following *except*
    a. an American-style republic.
    b. a constitutional monarchy.
    c. the guarantee by law of individual liberties.
    d. economic reforms.

60. The events in France became a revolution with the
    a. swearing of the Oath of the Tennis Court.
    b. storming of the Bastille.
    c. declaration of war against Austria and Prussia in 1792.
    d. execution of the king.

61. The term "Great Fear" refers to the
    a. Reign of Terror.
    b. murder of thousands of detainees in Paris prisons.
    c. paranoia in the countryside that fanned the flames of rebellion.
    d. horrific retreat of the Great Army from Russia in 1812.

62. The Declaration of the Rights of Man and Citizen guaranteed all of the following *except*
    a. equality before the law.
    b. economic equality.
    c. representative government.
    d. individual freedom.

63. The accomplishments of the National Assembly included all of the following *except* the
    a. administrative reorganization of the provinces.
    b. introduction of the metric system.
    c. introduction of universal compulsory education.
    d. abolition of monopolies, guilds, and internal tariffs.

64. Perhaps the most serious error of the National Assembly was the
    a. reorganization of the Catholic church.
    b. adoption of the revolutionary calendar.
    c. retention of Louis XVI as a constitutional monarch.
    d. declaration of war against Austria and Prussia.

65. During the September Massacres,
    a. Robespierre crushed the Conspiracy of Equals.
    b. the Directory suppressed popular revolts.
    c. the king fled France.
    d. Parisian crowds slaughtered prison inmates.

66. The life-and-death political struggle between the Girondins and the Mountain resulted mainly from the
    a. profound differences on questions of policy.
    b. Girondins' rejection of war.
    c. Girondins' radical economic and social policies.
    d. personal hatred and jealousy.

67. The elemental force that drove the Revolution forward was
    a. liberal ideology.
    b. the radical politicians of the Mountain.
    c. the laboring men and women of Paris.
    d. the class conflict between nobility and bourgeoisie.

68. The Committee of Public Safety was able to defeat the armies of the First Coalition by harnessing all of the following *except*
    a. modern nationalism.
    b. religious zealotry.
    c. revolutionary terror.
    d. a planned economy.

69. The Reign of Terror was directed primarily at
    a. the aristocracy.
    b. monarchists and Girondins.
    c. members of the middle class.
    d. any and all enemies of the Revolution.

70. French policies in areas conquered by French armies resulted in
    a. a deep affection felt by those liberated by the French.
    b. strong, nationalistic resentment against the oppressive French.
    c. the establishment of thriving, capitalistic economies.
    d. the establishment of strong, viable republics throughout Europe.

71. The common people were wary of liberalism because it
    a. did not address their economic needs.
    b. was irreligious.
    c. attacked the monarchy.
    d. supported religious toleration.

72. The legacy of Napoleon's Grand Empire included all of the following *except*
    a. the abolition of serfdom.
    b. legal and administrative reform.
    c. the popular belief in Napoleon as the enlightened liberator.
    d. resentment against foreign domination.

73. According to Olympe de Gouges,
    a. women should enjoy special rights and privileges.
    b. men and women should be equal in the eyes of the law.
    c. monarchy was the most oppressive form of government.
    d. it was natural to exclude women from the political process.

History and Geography

74. What were the three basic components of the Napoleonic empire? How did this imperial organization affect the future course of European history?

75. What were the geographic and climatological factors that helped transform Napoleon's 1812 campaign into a complete disaster?

76. On the blank outline map of Europe, mark the boundaries of France in 1789 and 1814. What does this reveal about both the power unleashed by the Revolution and the conciliatory gestures of the victorious Quadruple Alliance?

CHAPTER 22

THE REVOLUTION IN ENERGY AND INDUSTRY

Key Terms

1. hand-loom weavers
2. Richard Arkwright
3. Thomas Savery
4. James Watt
5. James Stephenson
6. Crystal Palace
7. Thomas Malthus
8. William Cockerill
9. Fritz Harcort
10. Friedrich List
11. Crédit Mobilier
12. Factory Act
13. *Condition of the Working Class in England*
14. Andrew Ure
15. pauper apprentices
16. Robert Owen
17. Mines Act
18. class consciousness
19. "new model unions"
20. sexual division of labor

Essay Questions

21. Technological innovation played a critical role in the industrial development of Britain. Assess the impact of technology on the British economy by examining the innovations in textile production.

    Begin by identifying the need for technological innovation: the production bottlenecks in the cottage system and the inability to keep up with rising demand, for example. Following this, there should be a narrative of the technological innovations, with references to the specific inventions and their practical applications: Hargreaves, Arkwright, Crompton should all be included as should Watt. Next, one should assess the impact of this technology on the productivity of the British textile industry and what this meant for subsequent growth (in textiles and other industries) and competition with other economies. Then the impact on the workforce must be fully assessed; this assessment should be sure to address the proletarianization of artisanal workers and the urbanization of rural workers. There should also be a discussion of the increased role of factory discipline. Finally, one should attempt to generalize about the British economy, based upon the assessment of the textiles industry.

22. Britain was the first industrial nation. Why?

The essay should begin with a thorough description of these factors, including the physical environment (the importance of water transport should be stressed), the impact of the Agricultural Revolution (which should be stressed), Atlantic economy, cottage industry, government stability and positive attitude toward commercial and industrial expansion, unified national market, capitalistic spirit, human capital in terms of labor and technological innovators, and credit facilities and instruments (such as the Bank of England, limited liability) . Following this descriptive section, the student should identify those unique to Britain. Finally, one must decide which factor was most important, and justify this decision.

23. The Industrial Revolution profoundly affected the British working classes. Describe the impact of the Industrial Revolution on working-class men, women, and children. What is meant by the concept of class consciousness and how did this reflect the reality of the situation in Britain during this period? Overall, was the Industrial Revolution beneficial or harmful for the working class?

This essay should describe the lives of the working class, in terms of such things as employment opportunities, working and living conditions, sexual division of labor, education, political rights; one should be sure to discuss the psychological transvaluations resulting from changes in the work process and the new urban environment. Reference to the testimony to the Ashley Mines Commission would reinforce one's arguments. The changing patterns of employment in the factory system, from pauper apprentices to family units to the male-dominated workforce, and the role of kinship networks in the labor market should be addressed. Next, there should be a discussion of class consciousness, including a definition of the term and scholarly understanding of how it developed. In this section, one should compare the concept of class consciousness to the very stratified society created by the Industrial Revolution. Finally, the student is asked for an informed opinion on the optimist/pessimist debate on the benefits of the Industrial Revolution for the working people of Britain.

24. Historians have argued fiercely over the social costs of the British Industrial Revolution. What are the issues in this debate? What were the viewpoints of contemporaries? How have historians attempted to resolve this debate?

One way to approach this question is to outline the parameters of the optimist/pessimist debate, in terms of contemporary adherents, points of contention, modern scholars' viewpoints, and evidence used in recent studies to assess the social cost. Thus one should discuss Ure, Chadwick, and Engels; then one should consider the standard of living, including living and working conditions, decline of village life, labor discipline, and evolution of working-class life in the cities. For one's discussion of attempts to resolve the debate, consider statistical reports on real wages, unemployment, consumption, and boom/bust economic curves.

25. What was the impact of industrialization on the women of Britain? How does the evidence of the Ashley Mines Commission (in "Listening to the Past") broaden our understanding of this process? How have historians interpreted these changes? Were these changes positive or negative? Why?

In this essay one should describe the employment opportunities and working conditions for working-class women at the outset of the Industrial Revolution. Reference should be made to the early use of women in textile factories and the tendency to hire family units. Next, one should describe the changes, resulting from both parliamentary legislation and labor leaders' efforts, in the employment opportunities available to women; one should also acknowledge the changes in family and marriages which affected women. Ashley Commission evidence should be referenced to support the generalizations made in the essay. Following this, the student should describe the various historical interpretations, from patriarchal-dominated labor movements to the requirements of running an urban household. To conclude, one must take and defend a position as to the positive or negative nature of these changes.

26. Britain was the "workshop of the world" but soon after the fall of Napoleon in 1815, industrialization began to spread to the Continent. Trace the course of industrial development on the Continent. What were the key features of this development? What were the positive and negative aspects of being a "follower" nation?

After the narrative description of industrial development on the Continent, being sure to emphasize the key features (emigration of British experts, importance of government policy, use of foreign specialists, spread of industrial technology, expense of newest technology, etc.), one should discuss the unique aspects of Continental industrialization and why changes took place. In this section, the role of the state must be stressed, in light of the greater expense associated with railroad construction on the Continent and the generally greater expense of later industrialization and the more powerfully entrenched nobility; that is, one should stress the generally greater role of the state in the industrial development of the Continent than that of Britain. Finally, one should conclude with the beneficial and detrimental aspects of being a "follower" economy; include strong, stable governments, artisanal laboring tradition, wealth, natural resources, blueprint to follow for avoiding the problems of early British industrialization, and access to the latest technology; negative aspects include such things as greater costs, resistance of entrenched nobility and fear of the social problems evident in Britain.

27. "Steam is an Englishman." Assess the validity of this quotation, especially in reference to the resolution of the British energy crisis, the spread of the factory system, and railroads.

In general, this essay should discuss thoroughly the energy crisis and its resolution, beginning with the reliance on charcoal, early steam engines, deforestation, and Watt's perfection of the steam engine using a separate condenser. One should be sure to indicate that the early steam engines were employed primarily in the coal mines; the much greater efficiency of the Watt's engine allowed it to be installed in the new textile factories. The role of the steam engine in enabling the British textiles industry to respond to burgeoning demand must be stressed; one should be able to discuss the production innovations that could only come about by harnessing the efficiency, speed, and power of the steam engine. Next, one should make a similar discussion for application of steam power to the steel industry and, of course, the evolution of the railroads.

28. The Industrial Revolution not only transformed British industry and society, it also called forth a multifaceted reform effort to cope with the societal problems created by industrialization. What

were the goals and motivations of both the parliamentary reform movement and the labor movement in nineteenth-century Britain? What were the successes and failures?

This essay should begin with a brief description of the problems: working conditions, living conditions, class conflict, exploitation. Next, one should discuss the parliamentary reform effort, including leadership, goals, and motivations, information-gathering, and relevant legislation; one should be sure to discuss the role of upper-middle-class women as well as the role of party politics in the efforts of the reformers. Then one should turn to the labor movement; in this section one must discuss the efforts of such reformers as Owen as well as the efforts of the working class itself, to organize politically, to improve working and living conditions, insure higher wages, job security and the like. The rise of class consciousness, the Combination Acts, and the emergence of the "new model unions" should be discussed. One should be sure to include the political balance between Whigs and Tories that often enabled the working classes to make gains. Successes would include such things as the Factory Act and Mines Act, repeal of the Corn Laws, and formation of the labor movement in general; failures would include, of course, Owen's grandiose schemes of societal reform, and the primary aim of the Chartist movement, the right to vote. An astute essay would conclude by assessing the impact of these early efforts on subsequent developments in labor relations.

29. The railroad has been called the crowning glory of the Industrial Revolution. Describe the impact of the railroad on the development of industry in Britain and on the Continent.

This essay calls for a discussion of the railroads as a leading sector of a developing economy. One should begin with a definition of what a leading sector does for an economy, in terms of creating demand across a broad spectrum of the economy. Next, one should look at the impact specifically of the railroads in Europe at the time. There should certainly be mention of the ravenous appetite of the railroad industry for steel, wood products, coal, machined parts, capital, and labor. Next, one must emphasize the role of the railroad in nation-building; in this respect one should focus on such aspects as the railroads' creation of nationally unified markets and the decline of regional particularism, the increased pace of rural to urban migration; on the Continent the central position of the national capital in the rail network should be indicated, leading to a discussion of the role of the railroad in extending the power of the central government. Finally, the conquest of distance and the practical and psychological impact should be discussed.

MULTIPLE-CHOICE QUESTIONS

30. Elizabeth Strutt's role in the family business included all of the following *except*
    a. seeking investment.
    b. representing the company in its patent case in local court.
    c. soliciting orders for the company's products.
    d. recruiting sales agents for the company.

31. British economist Thomas Malthus argued that
    a. population pressure would always force wages down to subsistence levels.
    b. using young children in factories was immoral.
    c. population always grew faster than the food supply.
    d. the standard of living was a reflection of industrial capacity.

32. A comparison of European per capita levels of industrialization reveals all of the following *except* that
    a. the British model of industrialization was the only one to follow.
    b. in 1750 all countries were fairly close together.
    c. Britain had opened a lead by 1800 that continued to widen until 1860.
    d. the timing and extent of industrialization on the Continent varied.

33. For industrialization, the Continental countries had all of the following advantages *except*
    a. a well-developed cottage industry and urban artisan tradition.
    b. the chance to "borrow" British technology.
    c. unified national markets.
    d. strong, independent governments.

34. The Amalgamated Society of Engineers was an example of the
    a. grandiose national unions envisioned by Robert Owen.
    b. monopolitistic organizations of factory owners.
    c. factory-based unions.
    d. craft-based, new model unions.

35. The tendency to hire family units in the early factories was
    a. originally a government-sponsored response to urbanization.
    b. usually a response to the wishes of the families.
    c. replaced by the system of pauper apprenticeship.
    d. outlawed by the Combination Acts.

36. The tremendous growth of the textile industry resulted from all of the following *except*
    a. government subsidies to textiles manufacturers.
    b. increased demand.
    c. technological innovation.
    d. emergence of cotton.

37. The first modern factories arose in the
    a. furniture-making industry.
    b. steel industry.
    c. textile industry.
    d. railroad industry.

38. All of the following were consequences of revolutionary changes in the textile industry *except*
    a. cheaper cotton goods.
    b. a dramatic increase in weavers' wages.
    c. the movement of large numbers of agricultural workers into the industry.
    d. a reduction in child labor.

39. The most serious obstacle impeding industrial development in Britain was
    a. lack of investment capital.
    b. the wars of the French Revolution and Napoleon.
    c. a shortage of energy.
    d. a lack of human capital.

40. The earliest steam engines were
    a. used to pump water out of coal mines.
    b. developed by James Watt.
    c. those used to propel locomotives.
    d. used as central power sources for the new factories.

41. The difficulties faced by the Continental economies in their efforts to compete with the British included all of the following *except* the
    a. low prices of British mass-produced goods.
    b. complexity and expense of the new technology.
    c. resistance of landowning elites.
    d. scarcity of human capital.

42. The labor force of the early rural textile factories was recruited primarily from
    a. cottage industry workers.
    b. orphaned children.
    c. African slaves.
    d. Irish immigrants.

43. In order to make his steam engine a practical success, James Watt needed all of the following factors of production *except*
    a. investment capital.
    b. skilled workers.
    c. experienced sales and marketing agents.
    d. precision parts.

44. James Watt solved the inefficiency problems of early steam engines by
    a. increasing the size of the engines.
    b. adding a separate condenser.
    c. using a better grade of coal for fuel.
    d. using accurate, precision parts.

45. The world's first important railroad, the *Rocket*, was built by
    a. James Watt.
    b. William Cockerill and Fritz Harcort.
    c. the British government.
    d. George Stephenson.

46. By reducing the cost of overland freight, the railroad
    a. created national markets.
    b. reduced the volume of world trade.
    c. strengthened regional economies.
    d. strengthened rural cottage industry.

47. The men who built the European railroads were typically
    a. slaves imported from Africa.
    b. army soldiers.
    c. rural laborers and peasants.
    d. urban factory workers.

48. The Crystal Palace exhibition of 1851 commemorated the
    a. industrial dominance of Britain.
    b. half-century of labor reforms in Britain.
    c. creation of the German Zollverein.
    d. Battle of Peterloo.

49. Prior to 1815, the spread of industrialization to the Continent was impeded most by
    a. a lack of investment capital.
    b. the instability of the revolutionary and Napoleonic eras.
    c. governmental interference and aristocratic resistance.
    d. a lack of natural resources.

50. The careers of William Cockerill and his sons indicate
    a. the difficulties facing Continental industrialists.
    b. how technology was transferred from Britain to Europe.
    c. the declining social mobility after 1830.
    d. how family-owned businesses prospered and declined.

51. The difficulties faced by Fritz Harcort in his attempt to build steam engines in Germany included all of the following *except* the
    a. lack of highly skilled laborers needed in this industry.
    b. lack of specific materials required in the production process.
    c. reluctance of German manufacturers to buy the home-grown product.
    d. terrible conditions of German roads.

52. Friedrich List was an early proponent of
    a. economic liberalism.
    b. working-class unions.
    c. factory regulation and reform.
    d. economic nationalism.

53. The key development that allowed Continental banks to shed their earlier conservative nature was the
    a. industrialization of the Continent.
    b. establishment of limited liability investment.
    c. replacement of the old managers with young, aggressive investment bankers.
    d. recruitment of bank deposits from the landed aristocracy.

54. As industrial development continued in the nineteenth century, opportunities for success
    a. became more dependent on formal education.
    b. equaled those of earlier days.
    c. increased.
    d. became more dependent on securing government financing.

55. In *The Condition of the Working Class in England*, Friedrich Engels stated that
    a. the social problems in Britain were not a product of the Industrial Revolution.
    b. the British middle classes were guilty of "mass murder" and "wholesale robbery."
    c. in general, the living conditions of the working class were slowly improving.
    d. the class consciousness of the working class would lead to social revolution.

56. The greatest change workers faced with the shift from cottage industry to factory was
    a. lower wages.
    b. harder work.
    c. the destruction of family-unit labor.
    d. a new tempo and discipline.

57. Scholarly statistical studies of the condition of the British working class indicate that
    a. their standard of living improved steadily from the beginning of industrialization.
    b. improvement did not come until the period after 1820.
    c. the standard of living for British workers deteriorated throughout the nineteenth century.
    d. only skilled workers enjoyed improvements in their standard of living.

58. Labor legislation in the first half of the nineteenth century
    a. was nonexistent.
    b. attempted to control the labor union movement.
    c. curtailed child and female labor.
    d. supported family-unit employment.

59. The Scottish industrialist Robert Owen is remembered for all of the following *except*
    a. his establishment of a model, utopian community at New Harmony, Indiana.
    b. his opposition to the employment of young children.
    c. founding the Grand National Consolidated Trades Union.
    d. supporting Engels's denunciation of the British middle class.

60. The system of subcontracting indicates that
    a. labor discipline was becoming more humane.
    b. the exploitation of workers was becoming worse.
    c. middle-class owners increasingly lacked the will and energy to manage their own affairs.
    d. employment opportunities depended on blood and kinship ties.

61. A newer interpretation of the sexual division of labor argues that it occurred for all of the following reasons *except*
    a. an effort by older people to help control the sexuality of working-class youth.
    b. the conflict between child care and factory discipline.
    c. the conscious efforts of women to escape the horrors of the factory system.
    d. the difficulty of managing an urban household.

62. The law which outlawed labor unions and working-class political activities was the
    a. Factory Act of 1833.
    b. Mines Act of 1842.
    c. Coercive Acts of 1766.
    d. Combination Acts of 1799.

63. The key demand of the Chartist movement was
    a. that all men have the right to vote.
    b. an eight-hour workday and a minimum wage.
    c. a ban on women and children working in the factories.
    d. repeal of the Combination Acts.

64. During the era of industrial transition, skilled workers in the artisanal trades
    a. were eliminated by technological innovations.
    b. developed very little class consciousness.
    c. identified with the problems of their small-scale employers.
    d. had their traditional work practices transformed by organizational changes.

65. Railroad construction on the Continent
    a. was much cheaper than it had been in Britain.
    b. featured varying degrees of government involvement.
    c. was generally the work of private entrepreneurs.
    d. generally followed the British pattern.

66. The British railroads
    a. improved the economic independence of cottage workers.
    b. were regulated by Parliament.
    c. were a major factor in the urbanization of labor.
    d. dispersed workers across the countryside.

67. The testimony of the young, female mine workers, presented in "Listening to the Past," illustrates
    a. the long hours, hard labor, and harsh working conditions.
    b. the improving moral and religious instruction available to the working class.
    c. that these women preferred working in the mines to agricultural labor.
    d. the ongoing technological innovation in British industry and its impact on employment opportunities.

History and Geography

68. Compare the population and industrial distribution of Britain in 1750 and in 1850, presented in Maps 22.1 and 22.2. How can we explain the changes in this distribution?

69. What factors affected the location of the first railroads on the Continent?

70. How does geography help explain Britain's early industrial development?

CHAPTER 23

IDEOLOGIES AND UPHEAVALS, 1815-1850

Key Terms

1. balance of power
2. congress system
3. Saint-Simon
4. Klemens von Metternich
5. *laissez-faire*
6. Jules Michelet
7. Louis Blanc
8. Karl Marx
9. *Lyrical Ballads*
10. George Sand
11. Walter Scott
12. Victor Hugo
13. Germaine de Staël
14. Ludwig von Beethoven
15. Chartist movement
16. Reform Bill of 1832
17. national workshops
18. June Days
19. "sentinel on the Rhine"
20. Frankfurt Parliament

Essay Questions

21. "The Congress of Vienna represented the highest achievements of European balance-of-power politics: faced with the task of creating a lasting peace following the generation of warfare, the statesmen at Vienna succeeded admirably." Assess the validity of this quotation. Who were the leaders at the Congress? What principles guided their actions? What were the primary elements of the peace settlement? How successful was the Congress at creating a stable Europe?

    Begin the essay by identifying the chief players: Metternich, Castlereagh, Talleyrand, Alexander I. Next, there should be a brief narrative of the problems: control of France, Russian ambitions, redrawing the map of central Europe, preventing further wars. Next, discuss fully the underlying principles; simply mentioning balance of power is not enough; include a discussion of legitimacy, equilibrium, compensation, and conservatism. Following this theoretical discussion, describe how these theories were followed or ignored in practice by considering how the balance was restored to Europe and future security insured; this section should include a consideration of the treatment of France, security measures instituted, and compensation made to restore the balance of power. Finally, an assessment of the effectiveness of the Congress should be made, based upon the goals of the diplomats, their effectiveness in achieving the goals, and, generally, whether or not Europe enjoyed an era of peace; the astute essay will not only mention the decades without a general European war, but will also discuss the role of intervention in internal affairs to forestall or put down revolution as evidence of an era lacking stability.

22. The years 1815 to 1848 saw the rise and evolution of the ideology of socialism. Describe this evolution, being sure to emphasize the principal components. How did socialism reflect the attitudes and aspirations of working people of the time? How did the Revolution of 1848 reflect the impact of socialist ideals?

Describe the various beliefs of the leading utopians (Saint-Simon, Fourier, Owen, Cabet), Louis Blanc, and Marx, being sure to indicate the connections between and modifications made by these thinkers. A consideration of what prompted the emergence of this ideology and why it took hold in France should be included. Next, there should be a discussion of how adequately the movement related to working-class existence in terms of accurately describing working-class life, addressing the needs of the working class, and the level of support among the working class. Finally, discuss its role in the Revolutions of 1848, based upon the role of the workers, the socialists, and the middle classes.

23. Although the Revolutions of 1848 took place at roughly the same time and in reasonable proximity to one another, in certain ways they were very different from one another. Compare the 1848 uprisings in France and Austria, in terms of causation, participants, goals, and outcomes of each revolution. What were the key differences? In what ways were they similar?

Initially, identify the causes of revolution in each state, being sure to stress the role of nationalism, socialism, liberalism, economics, and level of repression in each. Next, identify the components of the revolutionary coalition, and their respective goals, in both states. A brief narrative, indicating successes and failures in each state, should follow, including the reasons for the overall failure. In the assessment of similarities and differences, there should be a discussion of coalition composition, the reactionary responses, and the impact of historically conditioned economic and social structures.

24. Many would argue that Nationalism was and remains the most powerful of the nineteenth-century ideologies. What are the roots of this ideology? What are the basic tenets? Who were the principal spokesmen and adherents? How does Mazzini's *The Duties of Man*, presented in "Listening to the Past," enhance our understanding of nationalism? How can we account for the power of this ideology?

In this essay, the narrative should describe the roots (during the French Revolution and Napoleonic era) and evolution (List's economic nationalism, underground efforts, role in 1848). Next should be a discussion of the component parts: the cultural, linguistic, and historical roots of the nation must be stressed, along with the desire to transform cultural unity into political unity. Spokesmen, such as Michelet and Mazzini, should follow; reference to Mazzini's *The Duties of*

Man is crucial to providing a thorough discussion of nationalism; there should be an acknowledgment of the difference within nationalism, between liberals and democrats. Then identify the social groupings - middle class, lower middle class, artisans - that supported nationalism. Finally, the essay should attempt to explain nationalism's power; a discussion of the we/they mentality is a starting point.

25. Austrian chancellor Metternich and other conservatives fought a tenacious battle to resurrect and maintain the pre-revolutionary Old Regime. What were the motivations, methods, successes, and failures of Metternich and the conservatives?

Begin with a description of the components of the ideology, stressing the rejection of modern political and social movements and the embrace of the past. In the second section, identify the motivations, especially the disruptive impact that such movements as nationalism could have on multinational states (such as Metternich's Austria,) threats to the balance of power, social upheaval and revolution. Next, describe the efforts made in international and domestic politics to preserve the old order; the Holy Alliance, armed intervention in Italy and Spain, Carlsbad Decrees, repressive police measures are all good examples. Finally, a substantiated assessment of the success of the conservative effort must be made, emphasizing the generally unsuccessful efforts of conservatives to hold back the dual revolution.

26. The uprisings of 1848 enjoyed early success only to see their gains destroyed by counterrevolution. How do we account for the early success and later collapse of the revolutionary movements of 1848?

The essay should begin with a narrative of the course of the Revolutions of 1848 from origins to eventual collapse. Next, in the explanation of the early success, emphasis should be placed on the problems of the existing governments and the vitality of the revolutionary coalitions. In the assessment of the collapse, emphasis should be placed on the problems of building new governments, rival goals of coalition members, and resurgence of the forces of order.

27. The first half of the nineteenth century is often called the Age of Ideology. Describe briefly the primary ideological movements. How can we explain this phenomenon?

Begin with a description of the various movements (including its origins, beliefs, adherents): conservatism, liberalism, nationalism, socialism, Romanticism; a good essay would note the connections between various ideologies, such as liberalism and nationalism. Next, the essay should provide an analysis of why these ideologies appeared; the impact of the upheaval of the revolutionary era, the economic and social transformations being wrought by the Industrial Revolution, and the continuing impact of Enlightenment thought is one way to approach this.

MULTIPLE-CHOICE QUESTIONS

28. The tendency for economic and political changes to reinforce and strengthen each other is referred to as the
    a. dual revolution.
    b. Marxist dialectic.
    c. French Revolution.
    d. *Sturm und Drang*.

29. At the Congress of Vienna, the victorious allies
    a. were guided by the principle of the balance of power.
    b. resurrected the Holy Roman Empire.
    c. treated France very harshly.
    d. established constitutional monarchies in the areas conquered by Napoleon.

30. The peace settlement arranged at Vienna in 1815 included all of the following *except*
    a. Prussia was given extensive territories in the Rhineland.
    b. acceptance of an enlarged France.
    c. national self-determination.
    d. numerous territorial exchanges to maintain the equilibrium.

31. The compensation issue that endangered the peace settlement was the
    a. Rhineland.
    b. distribution of French overseas colonies.
    c. Polish-Saxon exchange.
    d. northern Italian provinces.

32. Austria and France intervened in Italy and Spain, respectively, in order to
    a. prevent foreign conquest of these two.
    b. suppress liberal and nationalistic revolutions in both areas.
    c. enforce the compensation agreements agreed to at Vienna.
    d. divert attention from economic problems in Vienna and Paris.

33. The Carlsbad Decrees
    a. sparked the Revolutions of 1848.
    b. instituted repressive measures in the German Confederation.
    c. were the artistic manifesto of the Romantic movement.
    d. established a constitutional monarchy in France.

34. Metternich's hatred of liberalism was based on all of the following *except*
    a. his belief in a hierarchically organized society.
    b. his belief that liberals had stirred the lower classes to rebellion.
    c. its link to nationalism.
    d. its connection to English economic power.

35. The demands of liberalism included all of the following *except*
    a. social welfare reform.
    b. representative government.
    c. individual freedoms, such as freedom of speech, press, assembly.
    d. no government interference in the economy.

36. The success of the Revolution of 1830 was due primarily to the
    a. shrewd political genius of Louis Philippe.
    b. Lafayette's unwavering leadership.
    c. revolutionary actions and leadership of the upper-middle-class liberals and nationalists..
    d. revolutionary actions of the artisans, shopkeepers, and workers of Paris.

37. All of the following men contributed to economic liberalism *except*
    a. Adam Smith.
    b. Thomas Malthus.
    c. Jules Michelet.
    d. David Ricardo.

38. All of the following groups played a role in the popular uprising in Paris in February 1848 *except*
    a. shopkeepers.
    b. artisans.
    c. peasants.
    d. unskilled workers.

39. The writings of the Czech historian Francis Palacky exemplified the
    a. harmony of all peoples in the symphony of nations.
    b. transforming power of the dual revolution.
    c. continued vitality of conservatism.
    d. "we/they" outlook inherent in nationalism.

40. For both liberals and nationalists, the basic unity of a people was based on
    a. a common history.
    b. a shared language.
    c. a common religion.
    d. geographic contiguity.

41. All of the following statements about nationalism are true *except* that
    a. it evolved from cultural unity.
    b. it was weak in central Europe.
    c. its roots lay in the French Revolution and Napoleonic wars.
    d. nationalists tried to create a political entity based on culture.

42. Early French socialists believed in all of the following *except*
    a. economic planning.
    b. helping and protecting the poor.
    c. state ownership of property.
    d. violent class warfare.

43. Typically, the specific programs of the French utopian socialists
    a. all called for violent clashes with the ruling elites.
    b. lacked realistic measures to bring about a socialistic society.
    c. rejected industrialization.
    d. were based on solid economic theory.

44. The intellectual roots of Karl Marx's philosophy were in all of the following *except*
    a. Enlightenment political liberalism.
    b. English classical economics.
    c. German philosophy.
    d. French utopian socialism.

45. Karl Marx argued that socialism would be established
    a. through electoral victories and control of legislatures.
    b. by violent revolution.
    c. by the cooperation of all classes to alleviate poverty and exploitation.
    d. through the efforts of enlightened rulers.

46. Romanticism was characterized by
    a. restraint.
    b. conservatism.
    c. imagination.
    d. convention.

47. The message of the French utopian socialists
    a. found very little audience in France.
    b. had a profound influence on the English reform movement.
    c. found its greatest spokesperson in Karl Marx.
    d. interacted with the aspirations of French urban workers to create a socialist movement in Paris.

48. Germaine de Staël's *On Germany*
    a. urged French artists and writers to embrace German romanticism.
    b. warned of the danger of the "sentinel on the Rhine."
    c. called for the unification of Germany.
    d. denounced the conservative repression led by Metternich.

49. Romanticism generally portrayed nature
    a. as merely a backdrop for human dramas.
    b. as awesome and tempestuous.
    c. as beautiful and chaste.
    d. only in paintings.

50. George Sand's novel *Lélia* explored
    a. the world of urban working women.
    b. her life as a prostitute in Paris.
    c. the role of a provincial wife and mother.
    d. her own quest for sexual and personal freedom.

51. Eugène Delacroix's greatest masterpiece celebrated the
    a. nobility of popular revolution.
    b. sensuality of women.
    c. transforming power of industrialization.
    d. exoticism of the Romantic movement.

52. All of the following are aspects of Karl Marx's philosophy *except* that
    a. all history is the history of class struggle.
    b. the bourgeoisie had played a revolutionary role.
    c. change results from a dialectic driven by the conflict of ideas.
    d. the proletariat would overthrow the bourgeoisie in violent revolution.

53. The revisions to the Corn Law in 1815 were intended to
    a. ease the economic problems of the working classes.
    b. promote free trade.
    c. make England agriculturally self-sufficient.
    d. protect the economic interests of the aristocracy.

54. The beliefs and aspirations of the Romantics included all of the following *except*
    a. a rejection of materialism.
    b. a rejection of nature.
    c. that personal fulfillment was the supreme purpose in life.
    d. a spontaneity in life and art.

55. As a result of the English Reform Bill of 1832,
    a. the Commons became the most important legislative body.
    b. all males gained the right to vote.
    c. the Tories emerged as the dominant political party.
    d. the role of the monarch was reduced.

56. The Battle of Peterloo refers to
    a. Napoleon I's last-gasp attempt to retain his empire.
    b. the working-class demonstration which was broken up by cavalry charges.
    c. the bloody repression of the Parisian workers during the Revolution of 1848.
    d. the victory of the Anti-Corn Law League.

57. The repeal of the Corn Laws ushered in an era of
    a. agricultural depression.
    b. famine and economic depression.
    c. free trade.
    d. remarkable expansion of British agriculture.

58. The most important factor influencing the peaceful mid-century reforms in Great Britain was
    a. the fear of working-class revolution.
    b. political competition between the aristocracy and the middle class.
    c. the outbreak of revolution on the Continent.
    d. the moderating influence of the monarch.

59. The bloody June Days in Paris in 1848
    a. resulted from middle-class fears of socialist revolution.
    b. destroyed the monarchy of Louis Philippe.
    c. resulted in the establishment of national workshops.
    d. was a short-lived victory for the working class.

60. The "winners" of the Revolution of 1830 in France were the
    a. peasants.
    b. urban laboring poor.
    c. shopkeepers.
    d. notables.

61. All of the following were causative factors of the Revolution of 1848 in Paris *except*
    a. rising grain prices.
    b. high unemployment.
    c. government refusal to consider electoral reform.
    d. the closing of the national workshops.

62. The Revolution of 1848 in Paris was distinct from the uprisings in the rest of Europe because
    a. the revolutionaries were all socialists.
    b. nationalism was not a key aspect of the uprising.
    c. of the brutality of the June Days.
    d. the revolutionary coalition collapsed.

63. The person most responsible for suppressing the revolution in the Habsburg lands faced was
    a. Archduchess Sophie.
    b. Emperor Franz Joseph.
    c. Germaine de Staël.
    d. Metternich.

64. The Prussian workers' demands included all of the following *except*
    a. universal male suffrage.
    b. a ministry of labor.
    c. abolition of private property.
    d. a minimum wage.

65. The primary goal of the Frankfurt assembly was the
    a. liberation of Schleswig and Holstein.
    b. exclusion of Austria from German affairs.
    c. establishment of a democratic republic in Prussia.
    d. creation of a unified German state.

66. In Mazzini's *The Duties of Man*, presented in "Listening to the Past," he argued that social justice could only be achieved
    a. by the establishment of a utopian socialist society.
    b. by the establishment of a democratic, national state.
    c. under an enlightened absolute monarch.
    d. by the establishment of a Marxist dictatorship of the proletariat.

History and Geography

67. Describe the geopolitical factors which affected the German Confederation. What were the two leading powers?

68. What impact would nationalism have on the political boundaries in Italy, central Europe, and the Balkans?

69. Describe briefly the territorial changes resulting from the Congress of Vienna. What were the most significant changes and why?

CHAPTER 24

LIFE IN THE CHANGING URBAN SOCIETY

Key Terms

1. sanitary idea
2. middle-class feminism
3. Louis Pasteur
4. Michael Faraday
5. Georges Haussmann
6. labor aristocracy
7. sweated industries
8. kinship ties
9. "servant-keeping classes"
10. Gustave Droz
11. psychoanalysis
12. law of conservation of energy
13. white-collar workers
14. positivism
15. Charles Darwin
16. *The Human Comedy*
17. *My Secret Life*
18. George Eliot
19. Social Darwinism
20. zoning expropriation laws

Essay Questions

21. What were the major problems facing nineteenth-century European cities? How and with what degree of success were these problems addressed?

    Begin the essay with a thorough description of the urban problems: overcrowding and housing shortages, transportation, pollution, disease, and crime. Next, identify the specific remedies applied to each major problem area: sewage systems, urban renewal and housing projects, zoning laws, public health and scientific research, improved lighting, urban mass transit. Haussmann's Paris should be used as the prime example of rebuilt cities. Finally, the assessment should indicate the advances of science and role of government in the improvements.

22. Discuss the role European governments played in improving the urban environment. What were the most important aspects of their involvement?

Begin with a discussion of the motivation behind government involvement in improving the urban environment; a brief consideration of the problems besetting the cities should be included. Next, the various ways in which governments played a role should be thoroughly discussed; this should include a consideration of such things as government finance, new regulations, and building programs. The efforts of Baron Haussmann in Paris provides an excellent case study to support generalizations.

23. Marx had predicted in 1848 that European society would be increasingly polarized into two classes: bourgeoisie and proletariat. What was the reality of the European social structure in the second half of the nineteenth century?

Initially, describe Marx's prediction; that is, how this polarization would come about, and the composition and characteristics of the two classes should be described. Next, carefully describe the actual stratification of the European social structure, based on employment, education, standard of living, and attitudes of the various strata. Finally, assess the role of industrialization on the creation of this class structure; a consideration of the creation and destruction of employment opportunities would help explain this process.

24. The place for women in the latter half of the nineteenth century seemed to be the home. Why? What other options did European women have? How did economic considerations affect women's career decisions?

To begin, assess the general accuracy of the statement, being sensitive to how applicable it is to women in different levels of society and at different stages of life. Next, discuss thoroughly the concept of "separate spheres" as it was applied at the time. In the next section describe the employment opportunities available to European women, being aware of differences resulting from social status. Finally, assess the impact of economic necessities on women's career and life choices.

25. European attitudes toward children seemed to change from the eighteenth to the nineteenth century. What were these changes? Why did attitudes and practices change?

Begin with a description of the eighteenth-century attitude; then describe the nineteenth-century attitude, placing emphasis on the changes; be sure to include such things as levels of affection, education, parental roles, and discipline. Next assess why these changes occurred, indicating the manner in which the generalized changes affecting European society were manifested in this area. Finally, there should be a discussion of attitudes toward children within the various strata of European society; this discussion could flow from the preceding consideration of the causation of change.

26. Family life in the second half of the nineteenth century was profoundly different from that of pre-industrial Europe. Describe the changes—including attitudes toward sexuality, illegitimacy, kinship ties, parenting, and standards of living—along class lines. In what ways does Stephan Zweig's *The World of Yesterday*, excerpted in "Listening to the Past," illuminate attitudes towards sexual morality and gender? How does the history of the family in the nineteenth century exemplify the gap between elites and common people?

Following the directions in the question, describe the various aspects of family life among the classes in European society, being sure to note how life had changed for each class; this should especially include marriage and reproduction patterns, relationships with relatives and neighbors, standards of living. Indicate instances in which a social grouping did not experience change in a particular area. Zweig should be used to provide substantiation. This essay should be concluded by addressing the gap between elites and common people, and comparing the family life of each and how it changed.

27. Much of the change in urban life in the 1800s was the result of scientific advances. What were the contributions of science to the improved urban environment and the economic and social structure of Europe?

In this essay, one should describe the role of science in the transformation of the urban environment and the ongoing economic transformation of Europe. The narrative should include the impact of scientific discoveries (for example, those of Pasteur, Lister, and Faraday) and the application of new technologies to the urban environment, including such things as sewer systems, street lighting, public health, and urban rail networks. Next, discuss the growth of industrial sectors, such as the chemical and electrical industry, resulting from scientific discoveries. Finally, assess the impact of these two - applications of scientific discoveries to the improvement of the urban environment and the emergence of new industries - on the social structure of Europe.

28. The second half of the nineteenth century has been called the Golden Age of Science. How was this reflected in the literature and philosophy of the time?

This essay should begin with a description of the scientific discoveries, in many fields, that revolutionized not only European lifestyles and economies but also European thought in general. The rise of science to near religious status must then be assessed; mention of the Enlightenment concept of Progress can be used as a beginning point. In the discussion of the predominant position enjoyed by science, describe such aspects as positivist philosophy, evolutionary theory, and realism in literature. The careers of such individuals as Comte, Zola, Darwin, and Freud should then be used to substantiate the generalizations made in the previous section of the essay.

Multiple-Choice Questions

29. Perhaps the most crucial cause of the urban problems in the first half of the nineteenth century was
    a. population pressure.
    b. lack of public sanitation.
    c. unresponsive government.
    d. substandard housing.

30. In the nineteenth century, the labor aristocracy
    a. aligned with the middle classes.
    b. rejected the working-class movement.
    c. saw themselves as the leaders of the laboring classes.
    d. virtually disappeared under the onslaught of industrialization.

31. Georges Haussmann is remembered for
    a. developing the antiseptic method.
    b. rebuilding Paris.
    c. his realistic novels of lower-class life.
    d. enunciation of the positivist philosophy.

32. Nineteenth-century women
    a. had a slightly lower legal status than men.
    b. were typically second-class citizens.
    c. were the legal equals of men.
    d. were adequately protected by the judicial system.

33. Honoré de Balzac's *The Human Comedy*
    a. was a best-selling marriage manual.
    b. described the role of religion in everyday life.
    c. was a Romantic history of the Napoleonic era.
    d. was a hundred-volume masterpiece of realism

34. The conquest of the urban environment featured all of the following *except*
    a. improved sanitation.
    b. urban planning and zoning laws.
    c. exclusion of taverns and houses of prostitution.
    d. mass public transportation.

35. Joseph Lister is responsible for the
    a. development of the germ theory.
    b. popularization of the miasmatic theory.
    c. practice of antiseptic sterilization.
    d. the theory of genetics.

36. Job opportunities for women outside the home typically included all of the following *except*
    a. professional careers.
    b. sweated industries.
    c. domestic service.
    d. prostitution.

37. The common aspects that united the middle classes included all of the following *except*
    a. keeping servants.
    b. commitment to frugal living.
    c. belief in education.
    d. a strict code of behavior.

38. The decline in working-class church attendance has been attributed to all of the following *except*
    a. the influence of Auguste Comte's writings.
    b. a lack of clergymen.
    c. responsibilities at home and the factory.
    d. the identification of organized religion with the ruling elites.

39. Edwin Chadwick believed that
    a. poverty was the result of lower-class immorality.
    b. individuals were responsible for their economic success.
    c. death and disease caused poverty.
    d. Christian morals should be the basis of urban reform.

40. The feminist movement of the second half of the nineteenth century resulted from the discrimination women suffered in all of the following areas *except*
    a. military and government service.
    b. education.
    c. employment.
    d. legal rights.

41. The breakthrough development of germ theory was the work of
    a. Georges Haussmann.
    b. Louis Pasteur.
    c. Joseph Lister.
    d. Robert Koch.

42. Napoleon III believed that rebuilding Paris would lead to all of the following *except*
    a. increased employment.
    b. a more equitable division of wealth.
    c. glorification of his empire.
    d. improved living conditions.

43. As the nineteenth century progressed, the upper middle class
    a. tended to merge with the old aristocracy.
    b. formed tighter bonds with the rest of the middle class.
    c. expressed a high degree of social conscience.
    d. retained its frugal attitudes.

44. The comfortable, "middle" middle class added all of the following professions *except*
    a. engineers.
    b. white-collar employees.
    c. schoolteachers.
    d. managers.

45. The white-collar employees identified with the
    a. working class.
    b. labor aristocracy.
    c. middle class.
    d. union movement.

46. In the second half of the nineteenth century, the labor aristocracy was
    a. constantly changing its composition.
    b. stable.
    c. destroyed by industrialization.
    d. merging with the middle class.

47. Middle-class families spent their money on all of the following *except*
    a. education for the children.
    b. public charities.
    c. home and home furnishings.
    d. servants, food, and drink.

48. The "world of drink and hard liquor" was civilized by
    a. the religious revival among the working classes.
    b. the greater participation of women.
    c. state regulation.
    d. the efforts of middle-class reformers.

49. The decline in illegitimacy rates after 1850 was probably the result of
    a. higher incidence of marriage for expectant mothers.
    b. decreased premarital sexual activity.
    c. urban renewal.
    d. increased availability of contraception and abortion.

50. *My Secret Life* describes the
    a. harsh world of sweated industries.
    b. search for scientific discoveries.
    c. seamy, underground sex live of a Victorian rake.
    d. psychological stress created by the new, stifling family structure.

51. After 1850, husbands and wives, in the cities, were able to work together only in
    a. factories.
    b. sweated industries.
    c. white-collar jobs.
    d. small-scale retail trade.

52. The middle-class feminists of England in the late nineteenth century
    a. worked for property rights and then voting rights for women.
    b. were influenced by utopian socialism.
    c. focused on the problems of working-class women.
    d. were most concerned with moral standards.

53. One positive aspect of the rigid separation of men and women was
    a. that women were no longer exploited in sweated industries.
    b. a decline in the rape and abuse of young women.
    c. a larger role for women in managing the household.
    d. the relative decline of prostitution.

54. Gustave Droz is cited for his
    a. discoveries in the fields of biology.
    b. *Mr., Mrs., and Baby*, a family manual.
    c. leadership of the Realist movement.
    d. rebuilding of Paris.

55. The revolutionary reduction in the size of European families was in large part caused by
    a. the family's desire to improve its economic and social position.
    b. the effectiveness and availability of birth control.
    c. women wanting to pursue careers outside the home.
    d. oppressive Victorian morality.

56. One of the more disturbing changes in the attitudes toward children was the tendency to
    a. spoil them.
    b. suppress their sexuality.
    c. use corporal punishment.
    d. use psychological punishment.

57. Generally, Freud postulated that
    a. people were motivated by reason.
    b. sexual desires are a minor component in the behavior of people.
    c. human behavior is motivated by unconscious emotional needs.
    d. heredity was the key factor in explaining incidences of mental illness.

58. Theoretical science found practical applications almost immediately in all of the following areas *except*
    a. biology.
    b. chemistry.
    c. genetics.
    d. thermodynamics.

59. All of the following were consequences of the triumph of science and technology *except*
    a. the popular realization of the importance of science.
    b. seemingly endless and automatic progress.
    c. the belief that science was the only reliable route to truth.
    d. the growth of the idea of cultural relativity.

60. Comte believed that application of the positivist method would result in
    a. discovery of the eternal laws of human behavior.
    b. social revolution.
    c. economic growth.
    d. the establishment of socialism.

61. The trait shared by Charles Lyell, Jean-Baptiste Lamarck, and Auguste Comte was
    a. the evolutionary aspect of their theories.
    b. that they were all French social reformers.
    c. their rejection of positivist science.
    d. their role in the biological revolution.

62. The originality of Charles Darwin's theory lay in the concept of
    a. the struggle for survival.
    b. common ancestral heritage.
    c. natural selection.
    d. genetic mutation.

63. Franziska Tiburtius, despite the social pressures to the contrary, became a licensed
    a. train engineer.
    b. teacher.
    c. medical doctor.
    d. governess.

64. According to the realists,
    a. human individualism was a powerful force.
    b. heredity and environment determined behavior.
    c. all humans had the free will to choose good or evil.
    d. the universe was limited only by one's imagination.

65. America also produced realist writers, including the author of *Sister Carrie*,
    a. George Eliot.
    b. Leo Tolstoy.
    c. Gustave Droz.
    d. Theodore Dreiser.

66. In *War and Peace*, Tolstoy presents a philosophy of history which was, in essence,
    a. individualistic.
    b. Marxist.
    c. fatalistic.
    d. optimistic.

67. In the excerpt from *The World of Yesterday*, presented in "Listening to the Past," Stephan Zweig maintained that
    a. prostitution was very prevalent.
    b. social morality was the same for men and women.
    c. middle-class ideas on marriage and morality had been adopted by the laboring classes.
    d. only very rich men were able to satisfy their sexual desires before marriage.

History and Geography

68. What was the most significant geographic/demographic development of this period? What proof can you offer for your answer? What regions of Europe were most affected?

CHAPTER 25

THE AGE OF NATIONALISM, 1850-1914

Key Terms

1. Napoleon III
2. Camillo de Cavour
3. "blood and iron"
4. Hermann Baumgarten
5. king cotton
6. Abraham Lincoln
7. The Great Reforms
8. Third Reform Bill
9. Sergei Witte
10. Bloody Sunday
11. Social Democratic Party
12. social security laws
13. *Kulturkampf*
14. nation-state
15. Austro-Prussian War
16. Ulsterites
17. Dreyfus Affair
18. People's Budget
19. Magyars
20. *Evolutionary Socialism*

Essay Questions

21. The two dominant ideologies of the second half of the nineteenth century were nationalism and socialism. What were the key tenets of each ideology, and its leading thinkers or leaders? How did each of these ideologies change over the course of the second half of the nineteenth century? Which of these movements seems to have been stronger?

    The essay should begin with a description of the basic tenets: for nationalism, this should include the establishment of a nation-state reflecting historical, cultural, and linguistic affinities; there should also be a clear indication of the we/they dichotomy in nationalism. For socialism, the concepts of bourgeois domination, proletarianization/pauperization, role of class struggle, state ownership of property, and necessity for political revolution should be discussed. Leaders of nationalism include: Mazzini, Gioberti, Garibaldi; Napoleon III, Cavour, even Bismarck can be included as representatives of later development of authoritarian nationalism. For socialism: Marx and Engels, Lenin, Bernstein, and Jaurès can be included as revisionist leaders. The essay should next trace the evolution of each ideology, from early nineteenth-century roots through the 1890s. Emphasize the changes: for nationalism the emergence of authoritarian nationalism exemplified by Napoleon III and the shading into social Darwinism, with Lueger being a prime example; for socialism, revisionism exemplified by both the labor union movement and Bernstein. Finally, the essay should indicate which movement was stronger; the successes of authoritarian nationalism (unification of Germany, Italy, Second Empire) should be stressed; the best essay will also indicate the problems: militarism, xenophobia (Dreyfus Affair), and radicalism (Lueger). For socialism, the essay should indicate the emergence of socialist parties throughout Europe and their size, the creation of the first and second Internationals, the Paris Commune, rise of labor unionism and revisionism should be mentioned as examples of weaknesses in socialism.

22. The decade of the 1860s saw the success of the nation-building efforts of Bismarck and Cavour in Germany and Italy, respectively. Choose either case and describe the process by which unification was achieved, assess the reasons for success, and indicate the consequences.

For Germany, the essay should discuss: the constitutional struggle between Bismarck and the parliament over taxation and sovereignty; the previous efforts of German liberals at unification should then provide a transition to Bismarck's efforts: Danish War, Austro-Prussian War, and Franco-Prussian War. Success stemmed from the earlier efforts at unity (i.e., Zollverein) which laid a foundation for Prussian leadership, Bismarck's diplomacy, and Prussian military reforms and expertise. Consequences include: German Empire as the most powerful state in Europe, upsetting the balance of power; intoxication of nationalistic pride in Germany; the destruction of German liberalism as a political opposition force in the new German Empire; Prussian domination of Germany. For Italy, one should discuss the failures of 1848 and emergence of Sardinia-Piedmont, Cavour's diplomacy, warfare, urban uprisings, and Garibaldi. Consequences include: Italian unification; impact on German desires; weakening of France; "colonial" subjugation of southern Italy by the north.

23. Napoleon III provided the model for the authoritarian nationalist state. Describe the state created by Napoleon III. How do we explain his rise to power and the success of the Second Empire?

The description should include the political structure of the Second Empire, including the role of the central government in controlling elections, the aggressive state intervention in the French economy, and the use of nationalism to create a consensus. Haussmannization should be used to indicate the interventionist aspect of Napoleon III's regime. Next assess the rise to power (including such things as his name, his reputation as a tough policeman, and his promise to restore order and protect property) and the continued success of his regime (based on economic policies, nationalistic support, and political opportunities.)

24. For both the United States and Russia, the evolution toward a modern nation-state was conditioned by the response to the systems of unfree labor found in both states. How did each state come to grips with this issue? How successful was each?

This essay should begin with a brief description of slavery and serfdom in the two states. Next, there should be a description of the manner in which these two forms of unfree labor were transformed, through civil war on the one hand and government-imposed reform on the other; for the Russian example, the Crimean War and the concept of modernization should also be discussed. Next, the shortcomings of both Reconstruction in the U.S. South and the Great Reforms must be discussed.

25. The nation-state was believed to be the crowning glory of the political evolution of Europe. Why? What were the common features of the modern nation-state? How do the experiences of the German Empire, Great Britain, and France exemplify the modern nation-state?

The essay should connect the belief in the nation-state as the evolutionary epitome of a political entity to the dominant scientific theories of the period. Next, one should provide a general definition of the nation-state. Then the essay should describe the German, British, and French experiences in the attempt to build nation-states, focusing on reformist efforts (Third Reform Bill, Home Rule, People's Budget; Bismarck's constitution, *Kulturkampf*, social welfare legislation; the emergence of a democratic Third Republic, through the efforts of politicians such as Jules Ferry and Léon Gambetta in France) as well as those forces which resisted nation-building (civil war in Ireland, socialist movements, Dreyfus Affair, Lueger). General characteristics should also be discussed: emergence of political parties, education as a unifying force, use of international affairs to distract populations, and especially militarism.

26. Discuss the changing face of socialism in Europe. What factors influenced these changes? What was the role of Karl Marx, labor unions, Edward Bernstein, the First International, the Paris Commune, and the Second International in the evolution of socialism? What was the impact of economic expansion and the aggressive nation-state? How does the experience of Adelheid Popp, presented in "Listening to the Past," illuminate the personal reasons for becoming a socialist?

The essay should begin by tracing the evolution of socialism from its utopian roots through the split between evolutionary and revolutionary socialists in the last decades of the century. One must accurately identify those factors which influenced change; one way to identify these is to discuss the roles of the individuals and events listed in the question, paying special attention to the impact on the development of socialism. One must also consider the interplay between socialism, economic transformation, and the nation-state as a transforming agent. Finally, in order to put a human face on your essay, explain why a person might choose to become a socialist, using the evidence provided in the text and in Popp's testimony.

MULTIPLE-CHOICE QUESTIONS

27. The first state to enact social welfare legislation was
    a. England.
    b. Germany.
    c. France.
    d. the United States.

28. The negative aspect of the emergence of the responsive national state was its
    a. responsiveness to parliamentary government.
    b. inculcation of loyalty to the state.
    c. expansion of the electoral franchise.
    d. channeling of national sentiment in a militaristic direction.

29. The first and most important of the Great Reforms in Russia was the
    a. abolition of serfdom.
    b. creation of the *zemstvos*, the local, elected governmental councils.
    c. granting of a constitution.
    d. nationalization of church property.

30. The Russian Revolution of 1905 resulted from all of the following causes *except*
    a. business and professional classes' desire for political modernization.
    b. the assassination of Alexander III.
    c. a radicalized and unhappy working class.
    d. growing nationalism among subject peoples of the empire.

31. Edward Bernstein argued
    a. for a return to revolutionary tactics.
    b. that economic reform in Russia should be financed by the West.
    c. that the working class should use the electoral process.
    d. that the Jews were a threat to the Austrian Empire.

32. The Russian *zemstvo* was the
    a. peasant commune which owned the land distributed by the Great Reforms.
    b. new Russian parliament established after the Revolution of 1905.
    c. institution for local government established by the Great Reforms.
    d. name of the currency issued when Russia adopted the gold standard.

33. Bismarck's phrase "blood and iron" referred to the
    a. future general war in Europe.
    b. racial conflict between Germans and Jews.
    c. establishment of worldwide empire.
    d. unification of Germany.

34. Karl Lueger, the popular mayor of Vienna, espoused
    a. anti-Semitism.
    b. evolutionary socialism.
    c. revolutionary Marxism.
    d. parliamentary democracy.

35. A typical example of the conversion of German liberals to Bismarck's brand of nationalism was
    a. Sergei Witte.
    b. Edward Bernstein.
    c. Karl Lueger.
    d. Hermann Baumgarten.

36. Bismarck's *Kulturkampf* was directed primarily against German
    a. socialists.
    b. Catholics.
    c. liberals.
    d. intellectuals.

37. Guiseppe Garibaldi, the liberator of southern Italy, supported all of the following *except*
    a. emancipation of women.
    b. unification of Italy under the leadership of the pope.
    c. social reforms.
    d. universal suffrage.

38. Louis Napoleon's election as president of the Second Republic and then hereditary emperor was a product of all of the following *except* his
    a. famous name.
    b. protection of property.
    c. anti-Catholic beliefs.
    d. positive program.

39. The stability of Napoleon III's regime was undermined by all of the following *except*
    a. Italian unification.
    b. growing criticism from the liberals.
    c. emergence of Prussia as a dominant power.
    d. working-class rebellion.

40. The success of Napoleon III's system was based on all of the following *except*
    a. a successful foreign policy.
    b. economic intervention.
    c. close attention to electoral politics.
    d. sensitivity to public opinion.

41. Pope Pius IX's *Syllabus of Errors* was a scathing denunciation of
    a. Bismarck's *Kulturkampf*.
    b. everything modern.
    c. the efforts of Cavour and Garibaldi to unify Italy.
    d. both American slavery and Russian serfdom.

42. Sardinia-Piedmont became the leader of the Italian unification as a result of all of the following factors *except*
    a. the failure of Mazzini's style of democratic nationalism in 1848.
    b. Pope Pius IX's rejection of Italian unification.
    c. the endorsement of Napoleon III.
    d. Victor Emmanuel's granting of a liberal constitution.

43. In order to force Austria to give up its territory in Italy, Cavour secured an alliance with
    a. the pope.
    b. Prussia.
    c. the Hungarians.
    d. France.

44. The leader of the "Red Shirts" was
    a. Giuseppe Garibaldi.
    b. Camillo de Cavour.
    c. Father Gioberti.
    d. Victor Emmanuel.

45. The long-established customs union among the German states was known as the
    a. Zemstvo.
    b. Zollverein.
    c. Reichstag.
    d. North German Confederation.

46. The cash crop that revitalized the slave economy of the southern United States in the nineteenth century was
    a. tobacco.
    b. sugar cane.
    c. cotton.
    d. rice.

47. Bismarck's constitution for the North German Confederation featured all of the following *except*
    a. a lower house elected by universal, male suffrage.
    b. local control of local affairs.
    c. Prussian control of the federal government, army, and foreign affairs.
    d. an elected president.

48. The life of Garibaldi, presented in "Individuals in Society," represents the
    a. power of ideas and ideals.
    b. supremacy of pragmatism in politics.
    c. failure of revolutionary movements.
    d. allure of wealth and power.

49. In response to the Austro-Prussian War of 1866, German
    a. workers rebelled.
    b. middle-class liberals called for the impeachment of Bismarck.
    c. middle-class liberals adopted Bismarck's brand of nationalism.
    d. Catholics formed a political party to protect their interests.

50. All of the following are consequences of the Franco-Prussian War *except*
    a. the completion of German unification.
    b. the collapse of the French Second Empire.
    c. an upsurge of German nationalistic pride.
    d. a wave of social reform in Germany.

51. The Great Reforms in Russia included all of the following *except*
    a. a national parliament.
    b. abolition of serfdom.
    c. establishment of a new institution of local government.
    d. reform of the legal system.

52. The greatest impediment to nation-building in the United States was
    a. its weak "colonial" economy.
    b. regional differences exacerbated by slavery.
    c. the lack of common ancestry among its citizens.
    d. the intellectual legacy of the American Revolution.

53. Factors that contributed to the North's victory in the American Civil War included all of the following *except*
    a. the ineffective leadership of Southern generals.
    b. Northern industrial superiority.
    c. the larger population of the North.
    d. the sense of national purpose in the North.

54. The consequences of the U.S. Civil War included all of the following *except*
    a. the emergence of powerful business corporations.
    b. reinforcement of the concept of free labor.
    c. equality for its black citizens.
    d. the confirmation of the concept of "manifest destiny."

55. Narrowly defined, modernization refers to the
    a. industrialization of a state.
    b. movement toward the creation of a nation-state.
    c. changes which have occurred in the past 500 years.
    d. changes that enable a country to compete with leading countries at a given time.

56. Witte's greatest innovation was
    a. using the West to catch up with the West.
    b. putting Russia on the gold standard.
    c. protecting Russian industry with tariffs.
    d. constructing the trans-Siberian railroad.

57. The French Third Republic urged young teachers to marry for all of the following reasons *except*
    a. to provide a contrast to the celibate nuns and priests who had dominated primary education.
    b. the belief that married couples could cope with potential isolation in provincial France.
    c. to appease Catholic criticism of the secular schools and teachers.
    d. the hope that these women would set a good example.

58. Bismarck's social reforms were motivated primarily by
    a. the Long Depression.
    b. his fear and distrust of socialism.
    c. humanitarian concern for the suffering of the urban poor.
    d. the failure of his *Kulturkampf* against German Catholics.

59. All of the following were important factors in the stability of the Third Republic in France *except*
    a. the abolition of trade unions.
    b. sweeping educational reform.
    c. colonial expansion.
    d. the skill and moderation of political leaders in the early years of the Republic.

60. The Dreyfus Affair
    a. revived the prestige of the French army.
    b. drove a wedge between Catholics and anti-Semites.
    c. revived republican distrust of Catholicism.
    d. fanned the flames of French imperialism.

61. Between 1906 and 1914, the Liberal party in Britain was able to accomplish all of the following *except*
    a. eliminate the House of Lords as a real power in British politics.
    b. substantially increase taxes on the rich.
    c. pass extensive social welfare measures.
    d. resolve the violent problems of Ireland.

62. The British failed to resolve the problem of Ireland because of
    a. the rivalry between Irish Catholics and Protestants.
    b. the Long Depression.
    c. World War I.
    d. the poverty in Ireland.

63. The establishment of the Dual Monarchy in the Habsburg empire resulted in all of the following *except*
    a. an autonomous Hungarian state.
    b. a relaxation of extremist nationalism in the provinces.
    c. Magyar repression of the ethnic minorities in Hungary.
    d. an intensification of nationalist agitation among the subject nationalities.

64. The Second International
    a. was dominated by labor unionism from its beginnings.
    b. was a well-organized, centrally controlled revolutionary movement.
    c. had a powerful psychological impact on the workers and socialists of Europe.
    d. had little impact on Europeans of the late nineteenth century.

65. The decline of worker radicalism resulted from all of the following *except*
    a. improved standard of living.
    b. states outlawing socialist parties.
    c. patriotic education and indoctrination.
    d. increased political participation.

66. According to Adelheid Popp, presented in "Listening to the Past," her political views
    a. had at first been very nationalistic.
    b. were formed by her father's socialist past.
    c. remained very sympathetic to the royal families.
    d. were the result of her expulsion from the Catholic church.

History and Geography

67. On the blank outline map mark the boundaries of the new Germany of 1871. How did this affect the European balance of power?

68. Cavour originally was only interested in uniting northern Italy. Why?

69. In what ways was Paris transformed by Baron Haussmann?

CHAPTER 26

THE WEST AND THE WORLD

Key Terms

1. Panama Canal
2. Treaty of Nanking
3. machine gun
4. "African fever"
5. Mohammed Ali
6. Colonel Ahmed Arabi
7. "swallows"
8. chain migration
9. Cecil Rhodes
10. Pierre de Brazza
11. effective occupation
12. Omdurman
13. quinine
14. Heinrich von Treitschke
15. Rudyard Kipling
16. Joseph Conrad
17. Indian National Congress
18. Meiji Restoration
19. Open Door policy
20. 100 Days of Reform

Essay Questions

21. Historians have called the extension of European hegemony after 1882 the *new imperialism*. What were the key components of the new imperialism? How does the case of Egypt exemplify the transition from the old to the new form of imperialism?

    This essay must begin with a definition of the new imperialism, indicating that which differentiates it from the older version; one can argue that the newer version is not fundamentally different, but one must indicate the variations nonetheless. Be sure to stress the role of political and military power, and the nature of the societies brought under European control at the end of the nineteenth century. Egypt should be used as a case study to underscore the key components of the new imperialism, such as formal political control, military force, and self-justifying ideology.

22. Both Egypt and Japan, to different degrees and at different times, attempted to modernize their states. Describe these attempts. How can we account for the failure of one and the success of the other?

The essay should begin with a brief narrative of the modernizing efforts in both states: in Egypt one should discuss the efforts of Mohammed Ali and the failures of Ismail Ali; for Japan, the Meiji Restoration should be the focus. Second, explain the different outcomes; attention should be given to the role of native elites and the actions of the European (including the United States) powers. A consideration of geography, economics (especially Japanese industrializing efforts), and social structure of the two states helps explain the different outcomes.

23. How did Asians and Africans respond to the establishment of European imperialism? Using specific examples, describe these responses. What factors seem to have influenced the choice of a particular response?

The essay should begin with a brief description of the various responses along the spectrum from armed resistance to complete collaboration. Next, specific examples must be provided: the Sudanese efforts under the Mahdi are an excellent example of armed resistance, as is the opium war, the Great Mutiny, Arabi's uprising; Indian service in the army and as civil servants is a good example of cooperation; Japan represents the most successful "westernization" response. Finally, the essay should assess the factors - such as proximity to Europe, level of European penetration, native leadership, and economic and social development - which affected the choice of a response.

24. The Great Migration of the second half of the nineteenth century was one of the most dramatic events in human history. How extensive was this movement of people? Where did they come from and where did they go? What were the social origins of the various groups of migrants? What were the motivations of the migrants? Finally, what impact did this movement of people have on imperialist expansion?

The essay should begin with an overall description, which should include the extent of the Great Migration, in general terms. Next, the destinations should be identified: North and South America, Australia, parts of Africa. The next section should describe these migrants fully, considering their social status (being sure to focus on the industrious nature of most groups of immigrants) and geographic origins. In the consideration of motivation, the essay should indicate the various reasons for migration, ranging from economic dislocation to political/racial oppression, and how different motivations affected the permanence of migration, a point which can be illustrated by indicating those emigrants that rarely returned to their original homes and why (availability of land, political and racial oppression). Finally, the essay should assess the role of migration on imperial expansion and the economic development of the destination countries.

25. How can we explain the historical phenomenon of the *new imperialism*? What were the causes? Which seems to have been the most significant?

This essay should outline the various causes thoroughly: economic competition among the European powers and especially British adherence to the policy of free trade, the search for new markets, raw materials, and outlets for excess capital; European governments using imperial triumphs to divert attention from domestic problems, the primacy of international politics and need to retain one's relative position, a cause to which strategic needs are connected; weakness of non-European states; cultural and religious zeal. After this description, the essay should assess the relative strength of each factor, being sure to stress the interconnections between various causes, and then indicate the most significant factor.

26. European imperialism was not only resisted by the colonial peoples but criticized by some Europeans. What were the arguments of these critics? How would Arminius Vambery, whose viewpoint is presented in "Listening to the Past," respond to these critics? How did these criticisms influence native resistance to European domination?

    The essay should present the criticisms of imperialism offered by such individuals as Joseph Conrad, J. A. Hobson, and V. I. Lenin; these criticisms include: the expense, the barbarity, the racism, and the hypocrisy undermining European civilization itself. Next, the essay should present Vambery's justification of imperialism. Finally, indicate the manner in which European ideologies of liberation, such as nationalism and socialism, helped influence native resistance and independence movements.

27. The "Scramble for Africa" is the most striking example of the European rush for empire. Trace the history of imperialism in Africa, being sure to identify the key developments and events. How did it epitomize the new imperialism?

    The narrative of the events should include the occupation of Egypt, establishment of Leopold II's claims on the Congo, the Berlin Conference, the Boer War, and the Fashoda crisis. The essay should then explain how the Scramble epitomized the new imperialism; a brief listing of the characteristics of the new imperialism should be included, with the various aspects of the "Scramble for Africa" used as examples of those characteristics.

28. "One of the most disquieting aspects of the era of the new imperialism was the general belief among Europeans of their superiority." How accurate is this quotation? What were the causes and consequences of this belief?

    In this essay, the student should present a thorough discussion of the European-wide feeling of superiority to Africans and Asians; germane examples should be provided: British discrimination in India; "civilizing mission," white man's burden, etc. The role of technological and economic superiority giving rise to feelings of cultural and racial superiority should be explored. The essay should conclude with an attempt to estimate the consequence of this attitude: deep and abiding resentment of colonialized peoples for their European rulers as well as an intangible but nonetheless real loss for the Europeans as well, exemplified by Conrad's *Heart of Darkness* and denounced in Hobson's *Imperialism*.

MULTIPLE-CHOICE QUESTIONS

29. Ahmed Arabi represents the
    a. collaborationist response to Western imperialism.
    b. armed resistance response to Western imperialism.
    c. cooperative, but uncommitted, response to Western imperialism.
    d. Westernizer response to Western imperialism.

30. The most striking difference between the new imperialism and the old was the new imperialism's
    a. violence.
    b. economic domination.
    c. formal political control.
    d. efforts to civilize native peoples.

31. All of the following technological innovations were crucial to European imperialistic expansion *except*
    a. the machine gun
    b. the telegraph.
    c. quinine.
    d. the airplane.

32. The model for the new imperialism was the takeover of
    a. Egypt.
    b. Japan.
    c. South Africa.
    d. China.

33. The typical European immigrant was often a(n)
    a. middle-class professional.
    b. urban factory worker.
    c. small farmer or rural craftsman.
    d. landless peasant.

34. The largest share of European foreign investment went to
    a. sub-Saharan Africa.
    b. Asia.
    c. European states and North America.
    d. the Third World.

35. The Sino-Japanese War led to
    a. the collapse of Japanese imperial designs.
    b. a fresh round of imperialistic activity in China.
    c. a brief naval war between Japan and England.
    d. a successful program of modernization in China.

36. Britain and France almost went to war over the incident at
    a. Lake Chad.
    b. Omdurman.
    c. Canton.
    d. Fashoda.

37. Jews made up the immigrant group least likely to return to their native land, primarily because of the
    a. violent anti-Semitism in eastern Europe.
    b. success they enjoyed in their new homes.
    c. laws against such repatriation.
    d. high cost of travel back to Europe.

38. The United States's imperial acquisitions included all of the following *except*
    a. Guam.
    b. China.
    c. Samoa.
    d. the Philippines.

39. Rudyard Kipling's works were indicative of the
    a. economic desirability of empire.
    b. Marxist critique of imperialism.
    c. civilizing mission of imperialism.
    d. popular opposition to imperialism.

40. All of the following were decided on at the Berlin Conference *except*
    a. effective occupation as the basis of territorial claims.
    b. internationalization of the Suez and Panama canals.
    c. pledges to stop the slave trade.
    d. recognition of Leopold II's personal rule over the Congo.

41. In the Open Door policy, the United States argued that
    a. effective occupation should be the basis for territorial claims.
    b. all countries should willingly accept all immigrants, regardless of race.
    c. South America would not be subjected to European imperialism.
    d. Chinese territory should not be annexed by the European powers.

42. While Europeans migrated for a variety of reasons, most did so for
    a. economic reasons.
    b. political reasons.
    c. religious reasons.
    d. personal reasons.

43. The Sino-British war which ended with the Treaty of Nanking in 1842 was caused by
    a. British attempts to break the Chinese monopoly on the tea trade.
    b. the brutal massacre of Christian missionaries by the Chinese army units.
    c. British attempts to intimidate the Manchu emperor.
    d. Chinese attempts to stop the British-controlled opium trade.

44. The influx of Asian immigrants into Australia and North America was blocked at the turn of the century by
    a. the restrictions on emigration enacted by Asian governments.
    b. discriminatory immigration laws.
    c. cultural disincentives in Asian societies.
    d. the crushing poverty of Asia.

45. Lake Chad, the object of France's three-pronged imperialistic advance into Africa, was a major source of
    a. malaria-infested swamp water.
    b. gold and silver.
    c. diamonds.
    d. oil.

46. Gaps in average wealth and well-being among countries and regions is the result of
    a. imperialism.
    b. urbanization.
    c. population growth.
    d. industrialization.

47. By 1900, the only areas of Africa not controlled by European states were
    a. Algeria and Angola.
    b. South Africa and the Sudan.
    c. Liberia and Ethiopia.
    d. Zanzibar and Morocco.

48. The writings of Heinrich von Treitschke reflected the
    a. anti-imperialist critique.
    b. nationalist drive for colonies.
    c. economic interpretation of imperialism.
    d. missionary aspect of imperialism.

49. The principle by which the European powers established their claim to an African territory was known as
    a. extraterritoriality.
    b. annexation.
    c. effective occupation.
    d. military subjugation.

50. The primary factor that influenced whether or not European immigrants returned to their native land was
    a. their degree of success in the New World.
    b. family connections in Europe.
    c. the strength of their nationalism.
    d. the possibility of buying land in the home country.

51. All of the following facilitated the growth of world trade after 1840 *except*
    a. steamship and telegraphy development.
    b. the Suez and Panama canals.
    c. Britain's commitment to free trade.
    d. economic nationalism in Europe.

52. In his book *Imperialism*, J. A. Hobson maintained all of the following *except* that imperialism
    a. was justified by Darwin's theory of natural selection.
    b. diverted attention from much-needed domestic reform.
    c. resulted from capitalists' search for profitable investments.
    d. benefited only a small number of private interests.

53. Japan opened its shores to Western trade
    a. because it wanted to enter the world economy.
    b. in response to U.S. military pressure.
    c. as a result of the Meiji Restoration.
    d. under the influence of Dutch missionaries there.

54. Cecil Rhodes, the founder of the DeBeers Diamond Company and the state of Rhodesia, believed progress resulted from
    a. technological innovation.
    b. political liberalism.
    c. racial competition and territorial expansion.
    d. social welfare reforms and religious training.

55. Anti-imperialist leaders in Africa and Asia
    a. typically rejected all aspects of Western culture.
    b. used Western ideologies to shape their movements.
    c. were usually of lower-class origins.
    d. rejected violence as a tool for independence.

56. All of the following were products of British rule in India *except*
    a. economic development.
    b. an improved educational system.
    c. a powerful unified state.
    d. social equality.

57. The Meiji Restoration featured all of the following *except*
    a. a military modeled along European lines.
    b. borrowing of Western science and technology.
    c. a democratic political system.
    d. a free, competitive, government-stimulated economy.

58. Japan's arrival as world-class power was signaled by its
    a. conquest of Korea.
    b. victory in the Sino-Japanese War.
    c. victory in the Russo-Japanese War.
    d. role in suppressing the Boxer Rebellion.

59. The overthrow of the Manchu Dynasty in 1912 was the result of all of the following factors *except*
    a. U.S. invasion and annexation of Chinese territory.
    b. increased intensity and radicalism of Chinese traditionalists.
    c. the Sino-Japanese War.
    d. enhanced imperialistic activities by the European powers.

60. Winston Churchill's description of the battle of Omdurman
    a. revealed his horror of the carnage.
    b. praised the bravery of the Sudanese warriors.
    c. contained a strong criticism of imperialism.
    d. exemplified the European attitude of superiority.

61. All of the following were characteristics of the new imperialism *except*
    a. military force.
    b. racial equality.
    c. political domination.
    d. self-justifying ideology.

62. By 1913, world trade had
    a. increased by 25 percent over the 1800 level.
    b. almost tripled that of 1800.
    c. more than doubled that of 1800.
    d. grown twenty-five times that of 1800.

63. The German migration pattern illustrates that
    a. migration was linked to the level of industrial development.
    b. very few migrants returned to Europe.
    c. migration was most strongly affected by political events in Europe.
    d. the European share of the world population declined at the end of the nineteenth century.

64. In the battle of Omdurman, the British lost twenty-eight troops, while Sudanese forces lost
    a. one thousand.
    b. six hundred.
    c. one hundred.
    d. eleven thousand.

65. The Christian missionary effort was characterized by all of the following *except*
    a. a high degree of success in China.
    b. a Eurocentric, racist attitude.
    c. some success in sub-Saharan Africa.
    d. general failure in India, China, and the Islamic world.

66. According to Arminius Vambery, whose views are presented in "Listening to the Past," European imperialism was
    a. dangerous to European civilization.
    b. justified by European military superiority.
    c. justified by its spread of culture and liberty.
    d. a barbaric and destructive abuse of power.

History and Geography

67. On the blank outline map of Africa, indicate those areas which were brought under British control. How does this support the military-strategic interpretation of imperialism?

68. Trace the general migration patterns of most European emigrants. What are the implications of these patterns?

69. On the blank outline map of Africa, indicate the locations of Lake Chad and Fashoda. Why were the French so interested in reaching these two locations and what does this reveal about the new imperialism?

CHAPTER 27

THE GREAT BREAK: WAR AND REVOLUTION

Key Terms

1. First Balkan War
2. Congress of Berlin
3. Three Emperor's League
4. Algeciras Conference
5. Archduke Franz Ferdinand
6. "blank check"
7. trench warfare
8. submarine
9. Erich Ludendorff
10. Schlieffen Plan
11. "total war"
12. Walter Rathenau
13. Georges Clemenceau
14. David Lloyd George
15. Petrograd Soviet
16. home front
17. Leon Trotsky
18. Cheka
19. League of Nations
20. reparations

Essay Questions

21. Some historians have argued that the First World War was the logical, perhaps inevitable, outcome of the revolutionary changes of the nineteenth century. Discuss this assertion by examining both the origins of and the destructive ferocity of the war. In light of this discussion, how accurate is the statement?

    The essay should begin with an examination of the long-term causes of the war: as economic transformation and competition; ideological movements, especially nationalism with its social Darwinist variant; population growth; arms race; expansion and centralization of state power; unresolved domestic tensions; and the international tension emanating from imperial squabbles and the bloc system of alliances. Second, the essay should indicate how these factors contributed both to the outbreak of the war (especially nationalism) and its evolution into total war. The ability of powerful state governments to mobilize society to fight, through the skillful manipulation of nationalist sentiment and the marshaling of economic resources, a total war must be discussed. The use of up-to-date technology enabled people to kill each other at an unprecedented rate, while young men were led to the slaughter.

22. The end of World War I was accompanied by revolutions and revolutionary activity throughout Europe. Describe this activity and identify the causes. How can we explain the failure of more radical revolutionary actions, such as occurred in Russia?

The essay should describe the socialist revolution in Germany, the nationalist revolutions in Poland, Austro-Hungarian Empire, Ottoman Empire; an astute essay will also mention the mutinies in French army units and the uneasiness in Italy. Causation is, of course, the war; in all cases, war-weariness is prime factor; for Germany, Austria-Hungary, and the Ottoman state, defeat added to the social unrest. To explain why a Bolshevik-style revolution did not occur, the essay should identify the revisionist nature of the German Social Democratic Party and its alliance with right-wing elements against Communist uprising; it should also indicate the greater degree of economic development in Germany. For the nationalist uprisings, the generally more limited desires of nationalist movements should be indicated.

23. According to Article 231 of the Versailles settlement, Germany was principally responsible for the war. Was this judgment valid? If not, who else shared responsibility for the war? Support your conclusions, being sure to refer to the memorandum of Bethmann-Hollweg presented in "Listening to the Past".

To answer this question, the essay should examine the long-term causes of the war (economic competition, international rivalries, arms race, nationalism), which should indicate that every European state shared in this aspect. Next, the essay should consider the immediate causes of the war; in this section the complicity of the Serbs in the assassination of Archduke Franz Ferdinand, Austrians blithely choosing war to settle their nationalities problems, the Germans' "blank check" to the Austrians and the German invasion of Belgium, Russian support of Serbia, British reluctance to indicate its position on the possibility of war should all be discussed. The Bethmann-Hollweg memorandum offers valuable insight into German thinking on the eve of the war. Finally, the essay must decide the question of guilt.

24. Discuss the phenomenon of "total war" and its impact on the social, political, and economic structure of Europe during and after the war.

First, the essay should define what is meant by the term "total war": full mobilization of society, including the industrial and agricultural sectors of the economy, finances, and especially the population, both soldiers and civilians to make supreme sacrifices to win the war, an effort to which all else was subordinated. The carnage of the Western Front, with its insatiable demand for men and supplies, should also be mentioned. Next, using the British and German experiences, the essay should describe how society was mobilized in terms of psychology, economy, labor, and politics; the efforts of Walter Rathenau in Germany and David Lloyd George should be emphasized. Finally, the essay should assess the impact of total war mobilization on labor unions and labor leaders, class distinctions, women, and large- and small-scale businesses. Finally, indicate the lessons that the total war experience provided for subsequent European governments.

25. The textbook asserts that World War I represented the triumph of nationalism. In what ways did nationalism contribute to the origins of the war, its outbreak and the course of the war? How did nationalism affect the Versailles settlement?

First, a brief definition of nationalism as it existed on the eve of the war is necessary. Second, the essay should describe and assess the impact of nationalism on both the long-term tensions in Europe and the fateful events of the summer of 1914. Third, the essay should describe how nationalism was used by governments to prosecute the war and its role on individuals' beliefs and actions. Finally, the impact of nationalism at the Versailles Conference as it related to French security concerns and the creation of successor states, both through nationalist revolution and Versailles diplomacy, in central and eastern Europe must be considered.

26. In January 1917, Russia was an autocratic empire; by the end of 1920, it was a socialist state. Trace the course of the Russian Revolution from March 1917 through 1920. How can we explain the ultimate victory of Lenin's Bolsheviks?

In tracing the events of the Russian Revolution, the essay should first identify the main causes and events: causation includes exigencies of war effort, incompetent leadership, social and economic conditions; events include popular uprising in Petrograd and elsewhere in February (March) 1917, establishment of Provisional Government and Petrograd Soviet, arrival of Lenin, Bolshevik's June Days, Kornilov's attempted coup, Bolshevik seizure of power in October (November), Treaty of Brest Litovsk, civil war. In assessing the success of the Bolsheviks, the essay should indicate the mistakes of the Provisional Government, especially continuing the war effort and failing to crush opposition parties, the anarchic situation in Russia, the inspired leadership of Lenin and Trotsky; Trotsky's Red Army and Lenin's War Communism and revolutionary terror should be emphasized; weakness of white armies and feeble, half-hearted interventions of Western allies should also be mentioned.

27. The First World War was a pivotal event in the course of European history. What were the social, political, economic, and psychological consequences of the war on Europe?

For this question, the answer should address the impact of the war: the relative leveling of society; the demographic loss of 10 million dead and the economic cost of some $33 billion; increased acceptance of labor leaders in government circles; emancipation of women and the right to vote; new states in central and eastern Europe and the increased power and role of the state in western Europe; the insignificance of human life resultant from the carnage; generation of 1914 disgust with and inability to reenter civilian life; rejection of liberalism.

28. The statesmen who gathered at Versailles hoped to establish a lasting peace. Why did they fail?

The essay should first outline the goals and principles of the Big Four, indicating the areas where conflict would arise: Italian territorial demands, French security concerns, British economic interests, Wilsonian idealism. The dilemma of controlling Germany without leaving her subject to a Bolshevik revolution should be included. The essay should then discuss the key provisions, referring to the excerpt presented in "Listening to the Past," and how each of these failed to build a secure peace: war guilt clause; reparations; taking German colonial possessions and territories in Alsace-Lorraine and Poland; military restriction; all were designed to restrain German aggression, but were too weak to accomplish that goal, and only increased German resentment at the "diktat" of Versailles. U.S. failure to sign the peace should conclude the essay.

COPYRIGHT © HOUGHTON MIFFLIN COMPANY. ALL RIGHTS RESERVED.

Multiple-Choice Questions

29. Civil war against the Bolshevik regime was sparked by
    a. Lenin's ratification of land confiscation by the peasants.
    b. the signing of the Treaty of Brest Litovsk with Germany.
    c. the disbanding of the Constituent Assembly by the Bolsheviks.
    d. the Bolshevik overthrow of the Provisional Government.

30. Grigorii Rasputin was assassinated by
    a. Bolshevik revolutionaries.
    b. agents of the tsarist police force.
    c. German mercenaries.
    d. nationalistic aristocrats.

31. The Bethmann-Hollweg memorandum, presented in "Listening to the Past," indicated that the
    a. Germans had not wanted to go to war.
    b. Germans intended to establish their economic domination.
    c. Austrians were most responsible for the war.
    d. Germans were not interested in a war for material and territorial gain.

32. The German revolution did not radicalize, like Russia's, for all of the following reasons *except*
    a. the moderate nature of the leadership of the German socialists.
    b. acceptance of defeat by the German provisional government.
    c. less popular support for extreme radicals in Germany.
    d. the lack of any attempts to overthrow the German Social Democrats.

33. The spark that ignited the Balkan "powder keg" was the assassination of
    a. Archduke Francis Ferdinand.
    b. Emperor Francis Joseph.
    c. Chancellor Bethmann-Hollweg.
    d. Tsar Nicholas II.

34. Germany's initial offensive was stopped on the outskirts of Paris at the Battle of
    a. Verdun.
    b. the Somme.
    c. the Marne.
    d. Ypres.

35. The Schlieffen plan indicated that the Germans
    a. did not expect to go to war with Russia.
    b. were relying heavily on Italy and the Ottoman Empire.
    c. expected a long, bloody war.
    d. anticipated war on two fronts.

36. President Wilson believed that future wars could best be averted by
    a. the creation of a League of Nations.
    b. rebuilding Germany.
    c. continuation of the wartime alliance.
    d. a restored balance of power.

37. In addition to U.S. President Woodrow Wilson, the Big Four at Versailles included all of the following *except*
    a. Leon Trotsky of Russia.
    b. David Lloyd George of Great Britain.
    c. Vittorio Orlando of Italy.
    d. Georges Clemenceau of France.

38. The Petrograd Soviet's Army Order No. 1
    a. launched the disastrous July offensive.
    b. led to a total collapse of discipline in the Russian army.
    c. resulted in a counter-revolutionary attack on Petrograd.
    d. reinvigorated morale in the Russian army.

39. For the generation of 1914, the survivors of slaughter in the trenches on the Western Front, all of the following are accurate *except* that they
    a. emerged committed to the pre-war world of order and progress.
    b. resented those who had not experienced the trenches.
    c. lost faith in the pre-1914 consensus of progress.
    d. viewed the sacrifice and comradeship of the trenches as life's crucial experience.

40. Walter Rathenau is remembered for his
    a. May Day rally in opposition to the German war effort.
    b. assassination of Archduke Franz Ferdinand.
    c. role in Germany's total war mobilization.
    d. anti-war novels which he wrote after the war.

41. The United States entered the war as a result of the
    a. German invasion of Belgium.
    b. Russian Revolution.
    c. mutinies in the French army.
    d. resumption of unrestricted submarine warfare.

42. Trotsky's role in the early years of the Bolshevik regime included all of the following *except*
    a. the creation of the Red Army.
    b. chief economic policy adviser to Lenin.
    c. negotiating the Brest-Litovsk Treaty with Germany.
    d. controlling the Petrograd Soviet prior to the seizure of power.

43. Lenin's contribution to Marxist theory included all of the following *except* the
    a. importance of violent revolution.
    b. possibility of social revolution in a backward country.
    c. necessity of a disciplined workers' party.
    d. historically determined nature of revolution.

44. The Triple Entente, on the eve of war, included all of the following states *except*
    a. Italy.
    b. Great Britain.
    c. France.
    d. Russia.

45. Bismarck's alliance system was designed to isolate France and
    a. expand German territory eastward.
    b. challenge Britain's dominant world position.
    c. create rival diplomatic blocs in Europe.
    d. maintain peace between Russia and Austria-Hungary.

46. By early 1917, the excessive strains of the war were manifest in all of the following *except*
    a. mutinies in the French army.
    b. nationalist agitation in Austria-Hungary.
    c. agitation among the colonial peoples of the British Empire.
    d. strikes and parliamentary resistance in Germany.

47. The legacy of Rosa Luxembourg, presented in "Individuals in Society," is that she
    a. personified resurgent radicalism in the Marxist movement after 1905.
    b. personified the moderate leadership of German socialism during the war.
    c. exemplified the suffering of average, working women in Germany during the war.
    d. exemplified the courage of nurses on the fields of battle during the war.

48. A recent interpretation, by anti-conservative German historians, on the origins of the war stresses
    a. the role of Bismarck's alliance system.
    b. the role of domestic problems and social tensions on German diplomacy.
    c. the declining status of Germany as a world power.
    d. the anti-German efforts of the Triple Entente.

49. The efforts of wartime governments to wage total war resulted in all of the following *except*
    a. a shortening of the war.
    b. an effective and destructive war effort on both sides.
    c. a blurring of the distinction between soldiers and civilians.
    d. the emergence of socialism as a realistic economic blueprint.

50. Austria-Hungary deliberately chose war in July 1914
    a. to annex Serbia.
    b. against the desires of their German allies.
    c. because they believed Russia would not intervene.
    d. to stem the tide of hostile nationalism within their borders.

51. The social impact of total war included all of the following *except*
    a. greater power and prestige for labor unions.
    b. greater acceptance of ethnic minorities.
    c. dramatic changes in the role of women.
    d. greater social equality.

52. The Bolsheviks won the civil war for all of the following reasons *except*
    a. German support of the Bolsheviks against Allied intervention.
    b. Trotsky's creation of an effective army.
    c. weakness and disunity of their White opponents.
    d. the use of terror to crush opponents.

53. Generally, the offensives on the Western Front
    a. made significant territorial gains.
    b. relied heavily on flanking movements of cavalry units.
    c. were depressingly similar slaughters of massed infantry units.
    d. were won by the army on the offensive.

54. All of the following were Western Front battles, resulting in hundreds of thousands of casualties, *except* the Battle of
    a. the Somme.
    b. Verdun.
    c. Passchendaele.
    d. the Masurian Lakes.

55. Italy entered the war on the Allied side
    a. to fulfill treaty commitments before the outbreak of war.
    b. following her betrayal by the Germans.
    c. to protect its vital colonial interests in southwest Africa.
    d. in order to gain territory from the Austrians.

56. Pre-war tensions were generated by all of the following *except*
    a. conflict among the leaders of the European banking community.
    b. the bloc system of international relations.
    c. imperial rivalries in Africa and Asia.
    d. nationalism.

57. For Clemenceau, the key issue at the Versailles Conference was
    a. extracting revenge on Germany.
    b. firmly establishing future French security.
    c. stopping the spread of communism.
    d. insuring national self-determination.

58. All of the following were consequences of the Great War *except*
    a. an administrative revolution, born of the total war effort.
    b. the realization of the dream of national unity for almost all Europeans.
    c. the return of Britain to its status as the leading industrial state.
    d. the radical Bolshevik revolution in Russia.

59. The German total war effort included all of the following *except*
    a. total mobilization of human resources.
    b. rationing of food.
    c. production of substitute raw materials.
    d. strict control of war profits.

60. Hindenburg and Ludendorff were the
    a. German diplomats who signed the Versailles Treaty.
    b. two generals who essentially ruled Germany from the end of 1916 until the end of the war.
    c. leaders of the failed communist uprising in Germany.
    d. primary conspirators in the plot to assassinate Archduke Franz Ferdinand.

61. The Great War
    a. reduced the power of labor unions.
    b. brought women into the work force.
    c. strengthened class distinctions.
    d. destroyed the labor aristocracy.

62. During the war, social distinctions were blurred by all of the following *except*
    a. death at the front.
    b. rationing of scarce goods.
    c. shared hardships.
    d. government decrees.

63. The Progressive Bloc in Russia
    a. called for responsible parliamentary government.
    b. was dominated by Bolsheviks.
    c. opposed the war.
    d. formed an alliance with the tsar to mobilize society.

64. In Austria-Hungary the revolutions of 1918 and 1919 were primarily
    a. Bolshevik movements.
    b. conservative and aristocratic movements.
    c. revisionist socialist revolutions.
    d. nationalist revolutions.

65. The greatest mistake of the Russian provisional government was
    a. continuing the war effort.
    b. confiscating and redistributing noble lands.
    c. instituting legal and political equality.
    d. suppressing the Petrograd Soviet.

66. The Bolsheviks were able to seize power in November 1917 for all of the following reasons *except*
    a. anarchy in Russia.
    b. the leadership of Lenin and Trotsky.
    c. their appeal to soldiers and urban workers.
    d. the threat of counter-revolution.

67. The key issue in the U.S. rejection of the Treaty of Versailles was
    a. American indignation at the amount of German reparations.
    b. fear of the Bolshevik Revolution.
    c. the Senate's fear of losing control of the right to declare war.
    d. Wilson's conflict with Clemenceau over Germany's borders.

68. The Versailles settlement included all of the following except
    a. the imposition of huge reparations on Germany.
    b. generalized arms control in Europe.
    c. the creation of the League of Nations.
    d. a clause placing blame for the war on Germany.

History and Geography

69. In World War I, the Western Front became an immovable mass of heavily armed, defensive trenches, while in the east the front remained very fluid. What geographical factors helped foster these developments?

70. The Wilsonian concept of national self-determination was applied, to a considerable extent, in the Versailles settlement regarding eastern Europe. Identify the states created on the basis of national self-determination and explain the limitations of the concept in establishing stable, democratic states in eastern Europe.

71. Many influential Germans believed that Germany was surrounded by hostile states that were preventing the Germans from achieving their destiny as a world power. Indicate the geographical and diplomatic basis of this belief. How was the Schlieffen Plan to resolve the apparent "encirclement"?

CHAPTER 28

THE AGE OF ANXIETY

Key Terms

1. Friedrich Nietzsche
2. existentialsim
3. Ludwig Wittgenstein
4. Søren Kierkegaard
5. Albert Einstein
6. "stream of consciousness"
7. *1984*
8. Bauhaus
9. *Triumph of the Will*
10. Vincent van Gogh
11. expressionism
12. Labour Party
13. Charlie Chaplin
14. John Maynard Keynes
15. radio
16. Dawes Plan
17. "spirit of Locarno"
18. "on margin"
19. Agricultural Adjustment Act
20. Popular Front

Essay Questions

21. How did the Age of Anxiety manifest itself in the artistic style called *modernism*? What were the new schools of artistic interpretation and who were the leading artists? What were their artistic principles? How did they express these principles in their respective media? What factors influenced the emergence and development of modernism?

    First, the essay should define modernism, with its rejection of past artistic rules and conventions. Next the essay should describe the various schools of artistic expression (including painting, music, literature, and architecture): functionalism, expressionism, cubism, dadaism, surrealism, "stream of consciousness" literature. The essay should include reference to artists such as van

Gogh, Gauguin, Cézanne, Matisse, Picasso, and Kandinsky; writers such as Proust, Woolf, Faulkner, and Joyce; architects such as Le Corbusier, Frank Lloyd Wright, Gropius, Mies van der Rohe; musicians such as Stravinsky, Berg, and Schönberg. The essay should then turn to an analysis, based upon the rejection of nineteenth-century bourgeois society, to explain the emergence of these new styles in art.

22. The Age of Anxiety was, in many ways, ushered in by developments in the fields of physics, philosophy, and psychology. How did these developments contribute to the Age of Anxiety?

First, the essay should describe the various discoveries and developments in these three fields. In physics, the work of Curie, Planck, and Einstein in subatomic and astronomic physics effectively destroyed the certainties of the Newtonian synthesis; the work of Rutherford and Heisenberg completed the destruction. In philosophy, the rise of both logical empiricism in the Anglo-Saxon world, led by Wittgenstein, and that of existentialism on the Continent shook people's belief in the hope of finding answers to the fundamental questions of human existence. In psychology, Freud's theories on the basic irrationality of human kind destroyed the belief, dating from the Enlightenment, that humans are reasoning creatures. Taken together, developments in these three fields destroyed the Age of Reason's certainties concerning the physical, mental, and metaphysical universe. The good essay will indicate how World War I underscored these developments, making uncertainty a reality.

23. Although anxiety seems to have affected everyone in the 1920s, upper and lower classes retained a sharp division between high and popular culture. Which aspects of the developments in arts, literature, entertainment, and philosophy had an impact on the common person?

The essay should describe and assess the developments that affected popular culture and its lower-class audience; radio and motion pictures should be especially stressed. The essay should also discuss the religious revival of the era as well.

24. In the late twenties and early thirties, the world suffered through the Great Depression. What were the causes of the economic collapse? How did the United States and the European states respond to this crisis? How effective were their responses? What were the consequences of the Great Depression?

The essay should discuss the causes, both long-term and immediate, of the Great Depression; this discussion should include reference to circular flow of money created by the Dawes Plan, the basic fragility of the post-war economic boom, and the speculative fever which gripped investors in the American stock market and ultimately caused the crash. The spread of the depression, resulting from nationalistic economic policy, should also be described. Next the essay should discuss fully Roosevelt's New Deal, including the NRA, WPA, and the Agricultural Adjustment Act; British focus on the home market should also be considered, as should the Scandinavian "middle way." Finally, the impact of the Great Depression should be assessed, including the psychological trauma, the ruined bank accounts of many middle-class families, endemic unemployment, and the rise of radical movements with new solutions to the problem.

25. During the middle years of 1920s Europe underwent a remarkable transformation in domestic politics and in international relations. Describe these changes. Why did this new found stability fail to prevent the rise of radical movements at the end of the decade?

The essay should discuss the emergence of the Labour government in Britain and its social welfare policies, Stresemann's middle-of-the road government in Germany. The role of democratic reforms in the establish of MacDonald's party in power should be mentioned; for Germany, the economic recovery occasioned by the Dawes Plan reforms should be mentioned. The "spirit of Locarno" represents the stability in international relations, resulting from the general weariness of Europeans with continued tension and the concerted efforts of leaders such as Stresemann and Chateaubriand to bring such tensions to an end. To assess the failure, one should indicate the fragility of the German political scene, where the Weimar Republic never enjoyed enthusiastic support, the dangers of the circular money flow of the Dawes Plan, and, of utmost importance, the Great Depression, which raised the old issues of economic nationalism and class conflict.

26. The word used to define architecture in the 1920's was *functional*. What is functionalism? How was it manifested in the Bauhaus and the Chicago school? In what ways did this trend mirror developments in art in general?

First, the essay should define functionalism, with its rejection of useless ornamentation; Le Corbusier's quotation "a house is a machine for living in" exemplifies the movement. Using specific examples, such as the Fagus Shoe Factory and industrial-style chairs, the essay should then describe the implementation of the concept of functionalism in both the Bauhaus movement and the Chicago school of architecture; this should include the use of modern materials and the dictum that form follows function. Then relate the functionalist movement to the broader themes manifested in the rise of modernism, the rejection of the certainties of nineteenth-century bourgeois Europe.

27. In many ways this chapter is about World War I. Discuss this statement critically, being sure to address both the impact of the Great War on European society, politics, economy, and culture and the prewar origins of postwar developments in science, art, and philosophy. Do you agree with the assertion? Why or why not?

For this question, the essay should indicate the consequences of the carnage of the war and of the flawed Versailles settlement on Europe in the 1920s and early 1930s. The essay should address the role of massive death and total war mobilization on social structures, the political instability and weakness of newly created representative governments, the continued tension among the European states, the economic problems associated with wartime destruction and postwar reparations. The irrationality of the Great War which seemed to provide validity to the developments in physics, philosophy, and psychology should be included. Finally, the rejection of the bourgeois certainties concerning politics, economics, and science, and the representation of these consequences in the artistic movements of the era should be fully discussed. Finally, the essay should take a position on the validity of the statement.

Multiple-Choice Questions

28. Picasso's masterpiece *Guernica* portrays the
    a. ups and downs of everyday life.
    b. artist's romantic nature.
    c. brutality and darkness of the twentieth century.
    d. suffering brought on by the Great Depression.

29. To resolve the economic problems of Germany and international tensions in Europe, the U.S. developed the
    a. Agricultural Adjustment Act.
    b. Dawes Plan.
    c. League of Nations.
    d. New Deal.

30. The parliamentary governments of Germany in the mid- to late 1920s were dominated by
    a. Social Democrats.
    b. right-wing nationalists.
    c. moderate businessmen.
    d. conservative aristocrats.

31. The biography of Eleanor Roosevelt, in "Individuals in Society," reveals all of the following *except*
    a. the level of personal sadness in her life.
    b. her commitment of social reform.
    c. her efforts as the "eyes and ears" of President Franklin D. Roosevelt.
    d. her search for sexual fulfillment, ignited by her loveless marriage.

32. The "middle way" refers to the
    a. Scandinavian response to the Great Depression.
    b. design philosophy of the Bauhaus.
    c. reform of German reparations payments.
    d. new literary efforts of writers such as Joyce and Faulkner.

33. The world of music was transformed by the works of all of the following composers *except*
    a. Alban Berg.
    b. Igor Stravinsky.
    c. Ludwig Wittgenstein.
    d. Arnold Schönberg.

34. At its height during the Great Depression, unemployment in the United States reached
    a. 10 percent.
    b. 25 percent.
    c. 33 percent.
    d. 50 percent.

35. Anglo-French unity after the war was damaged by all of the following *except*
    a. disagreement over the implementation of the Versailles treaty.
    b. French refusal to repay British war loans.
    c. British suspicions of French foreign policy.
    d. conflicts over their League of Nations mandates in the Middle East.

36. All of the following artistic styles emerged in the Age of Uncertainty *except*
    a. surrealism.
    b. cubism.
    c. dadaism.
    d. impressionism.

37. The British political party that emerged during the 1920s as the champion of the working class and the main opposition to the Conservative party was the
    a. Liberal party.
    b. Labour party.
    c. Social Democratic party.
    d. Communist party.

38. All of the following aspects of the Bauhaus movement are accurate *except* that it
    a. combined fine and applied arts.
    b. stressed functional design.
    c. combined expressionism and cubism to form surrealism.
    d. was led by Walter Gropius.

39. Authors such as Marcel Proust, James Joyce, and William Faulkner wrote about
    a. societal problems.
    b. utopian escapist themes.
    c. romantic themes of love and personal fulfillment.
    d. the complexity and irrationality of the human mind.

40. The development that revived the national film industries of Europe was the
    a. rise of fascism.
    b. invention of "talkies."
    c. Great Depression.
    d. spread of literacy in Europe.

41. The logical empiricism espoused by Ludwig Wittgenstein argued that
    a. philosophy is only the clarification of thoughts.
    b. individuals must become "engaged" in modern life.
    c. one must search for moral values and then act on those values.
    d. the concept of God could be adapted to fit within the Einsteinian universe.

42. Challenges to the centrality of rational thought to understand the human condition came from all of the following philosophers *except*
    a. Ludwig Wittgenstein.
    b. Henri Bergson.
    c. Georges Sorel.
    d. Friedrich Nietzsche.

43. Jean-Paul Sartre stressed
    a. the role of emotion in understanding reality.
    b. that individuals must give meaning to life through actions.
    c. the role of religion in human behavior.
    d. that philosophy is only the study of language.

44. Friedrich Nietzsche maintained all of the following *except* that
    a. religious belief provided stability in an absurd world
    b. conventional morality was suffocating self-realization and excellence.
    c. rationality had been overemphasized.
    d. a few superior beings could rise above the masses to become heroes.

45. The Christian revival featured all of the following *except*
    a. a belief in human beings' sinful nature.
    b. the necessity of faith.
    c. a reduced emphasis on the miraculous aspects of Christianity.
    d. the mystery of God's forgiveness.

46. Albert Einstein's greatest contribution to the destruction of the Newtonian universe was his
    a. discovery of quanta.
    b. principle of uncertainty.
    c. discovery of the radioactive properties of radium.
    d. theory of special relativity.

47. Vincent van Gogh's masterpiece *The Starry Night* exemplified
    a. expressionist attempts to express a psychological view of reality and emotion.
    b. the dark side of human nature.
    c. functionalism's combination of fine and applied art.
    d. impressionism's bourgeois values.

48. The popular appeal of motion pictures in the interwar years was a result of
    a. the nationalistic vision typically presented.
    b. their sexual explicitness.
    c. their moralistic messages.
    d. the temporary escape they offered.

49. The British Broadcasting Corporation is representative of
    a. a middle path between private networks in the U.S. and direct control on the Continent
    b. the role of private corporations in the development of radio entertainment.
    c. propaganda value of radio broadcasts.
    d. Britain's direct control of the airwaves.

50. To replace the Dual Entente, France turned to a defensive alliance with
    a. the United States.
    b. Italy and Austria.
    c. the Soviet Union.
    d. the "little Entente."

51. With the U.S. failure to ratify the Versailles Treaty, many French leaders placed their hopes for future security on
    a. strict implementation of the treaty.
    b. the alliance with Great Britain.
    c. the League of Nations.
    d. a closer relationship with Germany.

52. When Germany refused to make its second reparations payment, France and Belgium
    a. declared war.
    b. occupied the Ruhr district.
    c. appealed to the League of Nations.
    d. declared the Versailles Treaty null and void.

53. The hyperinflation of 1923 in Germany had its greatest impact on the
    a. aristocracy.
    b. working class.
    c. middle class.
    d. big industrialists.

54. The political stability of the mid- to late 1920s featured all of the following *except* the
    a. Dawes Plan.
    b. Kellogg-Briand Pact.
    c. Locarno treaties.
    d. Munich Agreement.

55. In France and Germany during the 1920s, the chief target of Communist party hatred and attacks was the
    a. middle class.
    b. socialists.
    c. fascists.
    d. government.

56. During the 1920s Britain's worst problem was
    a. high unemployment.
    b. colonial independence movements.
    c. dangerous class tensions.
    d. significant depopulation.

57. The American stock market crash of October 1929 was primarily the result of
    a. nationalist economic policies in Europe.
    b. too much overseas investment.
    c. an imbalance between real investment and speculation.
    d. the government's Keynesian economic policies.

58. President Franklin Roosevelt's Works Progress Administration attempted to
    a. plan and control the U.S. economy.
    b. solve the problem of unemployment.
    c. establish a social welfare system.
    d. nationalize banks, railroads, and heavy industry.

59. New Deal measures to cope with the agricultural crisis included all of the following *except*
    a. the Agricultural Adjustment Act.
    b. the Works Progress Administration.
    c. abandonment of the gold standard.
    d. devaluation of the dollar.

60. The most fundamental commitment of the New Deal was to
    a. reform the capitalist system.
    b. concentrate political power in the federal government.
    c. resuscitate free-trade economics and balanced budgets as soon as possible.
    d. use the federal government to provide for the welfare of all Americans.

61. Britain responded to the Great Depression by
    a. increasing exports.
    b. large-scale deficit spending policies.
    c. concentrating on its domestic market.
    d. increasing investment in its colonies.

62. The Popular Front was formed in response to
    a. the occupation of the Ruhr.
    b. U.S. isolationism.
    c. the growth of fascism.
    d. the growth of communism.

63. The victory of the Popular Front in the French elections of 1936 indicated the
    a. strength of the extreme right.
    b. weakness of moderate republicans.
    c. weakness of the political left.
    d. underlying political unity of the French republic.

64. John Maynard Keynes's critique of the postwar settlement called for
    a. strict enforcement of the Versailles Treaty.
    b. an enhanced role for the League of Nations.
    c. the implementation of new economic policies.
    d. a complete revision of the Versailles settlement.

65. Leni Riefenstahl's film *The Triumph of the Will*
    a. was a masterpiece of Nazi propaganda.
    b. was a bizarre expressionist masterpiece.
    c. brilliantly dramatized the communist view of Russian history.
    d. starred Charlie Chaplin in his greatest role.

66. The "spirit of Locarno" referred to the belief that
    a. the Great Depression would never end.
    b. God was dead.
    c. capitalism and bourgeois culture were dying.
    d. peace was possible.

67. Besides movies, the most popular form of entertainment among the working classes was
    a. the radio.
    b. the television.
    c. hunting and fishing.
    d. religious revival meetings.

68. According to Freud, human behavior
    a. cannot be understood.
    b. is motivated by rational calculation.
    c. is a compromise between instinct, reason, and moral values.
    d. is controlled by societal norms and moral values.

69. According to C. E. M. Joad, whose view of evil is presented in "Listening to the Past," evil
    a. is caused by economic inequality and injustice.
    b. is endemic in the human soul.
    c. results from psychological maltreatment.
    d. can be eradicated by humane social reforms.

History and Geography

70. Where is the Ruhr Valley and why would France and Belgium occupy this region when Germany refused to make its second reparations payment?

71. Examine Map 28.1. Where was unemployment during the Great Depression the most substantial? Give a brief explanation for the varying levels of unemployment.

CHAPTER 29

DICTATORSHIPS AND THE SECOND WORLD WAR

Key Terms

1. arsenal of democracy
2. "socialism in one country"
3. collectivization
4. Great Purges
5. Black Shirts
6. Lateran Agreement
7. Vichy government
8. Le Chambon
9. Nuremberg Laws
10. "work and bread"
11. *Mein Kampf*
12. Munich conference
13. *blitzkrieg*
14. Final Solution
15. Auschwitz
16. Grand Alliance
17. Stalingrad
18. Pearl Harbor
19. Hiroshima
20. Resistance

Essay Questions

21. Describe Stalin's "revolution from above." What factors prompted Stalin's actions and what were his goals? How successful was the revolution?

    The essay should describe, in significant detail, the main features of Stalin's efforts to transform the Soviet Union: collectivization, centralized planning (especially the five-year plans with their emphasis on heavy industry), and political propaganda and terror, including the purges. Next the essay should identify and assess the relative importance of the causative factors, emphasizing the "cursed problem," the peasants; ideological hatred of the peasant-friendly NEP; economic power of the peasantry through their control of the grain crop; political rival potential; tensions with the capitalistic West - political, economic, ideological, and strategic - that led to this effort. From this discussion of causative factors and actual policies, explain Stalin's immediate and long-range goals. Finally, assess the impact on the Soviet economy, people and political system.

22. Historians and other scholars have offered differing interpretations of the nature of the radical dictatorships of the 1930s. What are these interpretations? Based upon a careful comparison of Nazi Germany and the Stalinist Soviet Union, which interpretation seems most valid?

    The essay should define the interpretations: the concept of totalitarianism; fascism as the unifying impulse; and the limitations of broad generalizations and focus on unique nature of each regime. The essay should then turn to its comparison of the two regimes: similarities include one-party, dominant leader, role of terror, aggression, primacy of state, revolutionary expansion; differences include: Hitler's racism, relationship to private property, ideology, role of women, view of history. Finally, the essay should decide which of the three interpretations is most valid.

23. Some have argued that strong actions by England and France in the mid-1930's would have prevented World War II and that appeasement merely whetted Hitler's attitude. How accurate is this statement?

    The essay should provide a brief narrative of the events leading to the outbreak of war; the narrative should include the factors other than simply Hitler's appetite for conquest: lingering resentment about the Versailles settlement, ardent nationalism. The narrative should also discuss those factors that encouraged appeasement in the West: war weariness, pacifism, fear of the Soviet Union, British guilt over the Versailles settlement. Finally, the essay should return to the basically unappeasable nature of Hitler and the weaknesses of the Western states.

24. "Hitler's diplomatic and military actions—rather than being just irrational acts—seemed to complement the domestic aspects of Nazi totalitarianism." Analyze this assessment by examining both Hitler's actions and motivation in the diplomatic and military arena. What was the connection between domestic and foreign/military policy? How does the Holocaust fit? What clues to this connection can be discovered in *Mein Kampf*?

    This question requires an examination not only of Hitler's foreign and military policies and his motivation but also of how these actions were connected to domestic policies. One should consider both his immediate motivation (that is, what he hoped to gain with each move) as well as his overriding purpose. The essay should identify the impact of domestic needs, before and during the war, on Hitler's decision-making in diplomatic and military affairs. For the Holocaust, reference to Marco Nahon's testimony, reproduced in "Listening to the Past," should be made. Finally, one should examine the main themes of Hitler's overall political views - including *lebensraum*, racism, Versailles revisionism, and the revolutionary dynamic of Nazism - on Hitler's foreign and military policies.

25. The most horrifying aspect of Hitler's ideology and his regime was its violent anti-Semitism, culminating in the Final Solution which claimed over 6 million lives. Describe Nazi policies towards the Jews of Europe, being sure to indicate the basis of Hitler's anti-Semitism. Based on this description, offer an assessment of Daniel Goldhagen's thesis that "ordinary Germans" were Hitler's "willing accomplices."

The essay should describe the early anti-Semitic actions of the Brown Shirts in the 1920s; following 1933, official policy and actions of the Nazis should be described fully: Kristallnacht, Nuremberg laws, etc. With the war, the attempts to make the new German Empire free of Jews should be discussed (the role of collaborator governments could also be included), with an extensive discussion of the death camps and the elaborate empire of slave labor, expulsion, and death of which they were the apex. Goldhagen's thesis should then be considered; the essay can maintain the older interpretation that most Germans were oblivious to the Holocaust or agree that Goldhagen is accurate.

26. The Grand Alliance was a smashing military success. What were the factors that contributed to this success? What were the turning points in the Allies' march to victory?

The essay should identify the assets of the members of the Grand Alliance: population, productive capacity, natural resources, control of the seas, sound leadership. The inherent weakness of the Axis powers, including unstable leadership and shortages of natural resources should be described. The essay should then identify the various turning points: Coral Sea, Midway, El Alamein, Stalingrad, Normandy, Hiroshima/Nagasaki. The good essay would indicate how Allied victories in these turning points reflected the strengths of the Allies and the weaknesses of the Axis powers.

27. What was the impact of industrialization, collectivization, and the purges on the citizens of the Soviet Union? Did the positive aspects justify the suffering brought on by Stalin's revolution? Why or why not?

The essay should describe the impact of Stalin's revolution on the Soviet citizens, rural and urban, of both genders: declining standards of living, increased access to education for men and women, improved employment opportunity for women, a degree of upward mobility based on education, continued pressure on women as both wage-earners and primary care-givers and managers of the family economy. The essay should include a discussion of psychological and physical terror in general and its specific impact on societal groups such as the kulaks and the Old Bolsheviks. In light of this discussion, the essay should provide a reasoned conclusion as to whether or not Stalin's revolution was justified.

28. The leftist interpretation of totalitarianism argues that despite excesses there were positive aspects of the Stalinist revolution. To ascertain the validity of this interpretation, compare the experience of women in the Soviet Union, Nazi Germany, and fascist Italy. Based on this comparison, does the leftist interpretation seem valid? Why or why not? Is this an appropriate and adequate method to assess the validity of this interpretation?

First the essay should provide a definition of the leftist interpretation of totalitarianism. Next, the essay should describe the experience of women in the three regimes as thoroughly as possible, including such topics as property rights, educational and employment opportunities, reproduction, family roles, official and societal views of women. Then, based on this description, the essay should assess the validity of the leftist interpretation. Finally, the essay should offer criticisms of this analytical exercise.

Multiple-Choice Questions

29. The most impressive accomplishments of Stalin's five-year plans occurred in
    a. collectivized agriculture.
    b. heavy industry.
    c. consumer industry.
    d. foreign trade.

30. The strategic decision that most epitomized Hitler's violent and unlimited ambitions was the
    a. invasion of the Soviet Union.
    b. offensive into the eastern Mediterranean.
    c. declaration of war against the United States.
    d. bombing of British cities during the Battle of Britain.

31. Hitler's *Mein Kampf* included all of the following basic themes *except*
    a. living space.
    b. land reform.
    c. race.
    d. the leader-dictator.

32. The Nuremberg Laws
    a. outlawed private property in the Soviet Union.
    b. established the parallel government/party structure of Nazi Germany.
    c. deprived German Jews of their rights of citizenship.
    d. attempted to implement Hitler's promises of "work and bread."

33. The first German act of aggression that could not be justified by self-determination was the
    a. annexation of Austria.
    b. occupation of "rump" Czechoslovakia.
    c. invasion of Poland.
    d. remilitarization of the Rhineland.

34. The regimes of Nazi Germany, fascist Italy, and the Stalinist Soviet Union all shared a
    a. complete rejection of private property.
    b. violently racist ideology.
    c. goal of complete economic transformation.
    d. profound hatred of Western liberalism.

35. For women, life in Stalinist society featured all of the following *except*
    a. sexual and familial liberation.
    b. greater employment opportunities.
    c. great sacrifices, being both wage-earner and mother and wife.
    d. greater opportunities for advancement, through education.

36. At first, Mussolini's program included all of the following components *except*
    a. territorial expansion.
    b. land reform for peasants.
    c. separation of church and state.
    d. social welfare reforms for workers.

37. The British adopted a policy of appeasement for all of the following reasons *except*
    a. guilt over the Versailles settlement.
    b. the strong pacifist movement in Britain.
    c. the belief that Hitler could be used to stop communism.
    d. anti-Semitic sentiments among the British ruling elite.

38. The newer comparative studies of fascism identify all of the following as shared characteristics *except*
    a. alliance with working-class movements.
    b. extreme, expansionist nationalism.
    c. a dynamic and violent leader.
    d. glorification of war and the military.

39. The Grand Alliance was cemented by all of the following policies *except*
    a. a commitment to unconditional surrender.
    b. U.S. adoption of the "Europe first" principle.
    c. postponement of a discussion of the eventual peace settlement.
    d. the decision to exclude France from the Alliance.

40. The most important factor in Hitler's rise to power was
    a. the support of the Social Democrats.
    b. the breakdown of the conservative German government at the time.
    c. the Great Depression.
    d. his political skills.

41. Lenin's New Economic Policy was a political compromise with the
    a. urban workers.
    b. Russian peasants.
    c. White counter-revolutionaries.
    d. foreign capitalists.

42. The Lateran Agreement indicated that Mussolini had the support of
    a. the Pope and the Catholic church.
    b. Italian labor unions.
    c. Nazi Germany.
    d. fascist Spain.

43. The term *Final Solution* refers to
    a. Stalin's industrialization drive.
    b. the Allies' demand that Germany had to surrender unconditionally.
    c. Hitler's suicide as Soviet troops stormed Berlin.
    d. the attempted extermination of European Jews by the Nazis.

44. The battle that ensured U.S. naval superiority in the Pacific was the Battle of
    a. Midway Island.
    b. the Coral Sea.
    c. Guadalcanal.
    d. Iwo Jima.

45. Hitler's popularity was based on all of the following *except*
    a. his establishment of equality for women.
    b. economic recovery.
    c. the perception of greater equality and social mobility for all Germans.
    d. his successes in foreign policy.

46. The turning point in European theater was the Battle of
    a. Britain.
    b. El Alamein.
    c. Stalingrad.
    d. the Bulge.

47. The emergence of traditional conservative regimes in the successor states of eastern and central Europe resulted from all of the following reasons *except* the
    a. lack of a tradition of self-government.
    b. influence of Mussolini's fascist movement.
    c. belief that authoritarian dictatorship would preserve national unity.
    d. large landowners who turned to dictators to protect them from radical political movements.

48. In Stalin's Soviet Union, women
    a. were relegated to agricultural and domestic labor.
    b. were urged to liberate themselves sexually.
    c. shared family duties equally with men.
    d. were able to pursue professional careers.

49. The only eastern European state that retained its parliamentary government through the turbulent 1920s and 1930s was
    a. Czechoslovakia.
    b. Poland.
    c. Hungary.
    d. Yugoslavia.

50. All of the following states were conservative dictatorships *except*
    a. Hungary.
    b. Portugal.
    c. Poland.
    d. Czechoslovakia.

51. Early writers on totalitarianism such as Elie Halévy
    a. asserted that all totalitarian states were closely related.
    b. stressed the differences between fascism and communism.
    c. argued that fascism was a tool of powerful capitalists.
    d. stressed the differences in the historical patterns of fascist states.

52. According to historian Daniel Goldhagen, most Germans
    a. detested the anti-Semitic policies of the Nazi party.
    b. greeted the outbreak of war with resignation.
    c. were Hitler's willing accomplices in the Final Solution.
    d. were indifferent to the Holocaust.

53. Stalin's theory of "socialism in one country"
    a. was originally proposed by Leon Trotsky.
    b. argued that the Soviet Union could build socialism on its own.
    c. maintained that the success of socialism depended on world revolution.
    d. was rejected by the Communist party.

54. One example of the successful resistance of Russian peasants to collectivization was
    a. Stalin's decision to limit the extent of collectivization.
    b. de-kulakization.
    c. grudgingly tolerated family plots.
    d. their control of the Siberian grain and raw materials sectors of the Soviet economy.

55. The ultimate objective of Stalin's five-year plans was to
    a. accelerate industrial development.
    b. prepare for war with Nazi Germany.
    c. destroy private property and political opposition.
    d. create a new socialist humanity.

56. All of the following were factors in the success of Stalin's industrialization drive *except*
    a. a sharp decrease in domestic consumption.
    b. the skill of Soviet economists.
    c. extensive labor discipline.
    d. the use of foreign experts.

57. Mussolini was able to stay in power because he
    a. introduced land and labor reforms.
    b. enforced harsh racial laws.
    c. made a deal with the old conservative elites.
    d. engaged in widespread police terrorism.

58. One of the most important consequences of the Great Purges was the
    a. creation of a new generation of communists loyal to Stalin.
    b. destruction of the Red Army's ability to fight.
    c. elimination of foreign spies and saboteurs.
    d. decline in the international scope of the communist movement.

59. Hitler's aggressive foreign policy was exemplified by all of the following *except* the
    a. remilitarization of the Rhineland.
    b. annexation of Austria.
    c. invasion of Ethiopia.
    d. invasion of Poland.

60. Hitler's promise to create a "third path" between capitalism and communism was directed primarily at
    a. the army officer corps.
    b. the middle and lower middle classes.
    c. big business.
    d. urban workers.

61. Hitler acquired absolute dictatorial powers, through the Enabling Act, as a result of
    a. the Reichstag fire.
    b. a wave of strikes by German labor unions.
    c. the remilitarization of the Rhineland.
    d. the assassination of a German diplomat by a Jew.

62. Hitler purged the SA, the brown-shirted Nazi storm troopers, because
    a. they had been infiltrated by Communist agents.
    b. they resisted Hitler's personal control of the Nazi party.
    c. the army and big business were suspicious of them.
    d. the SA had attempted to overthrow Hitler.

63. Hitler's slogans in the early 1930s included all of the following themes *except*
    a. national rebirth.
    b. expulsion and extermination of the Jews.
    c. crimes of the Versailles treaty.
    d. emphasis on young Germans and the future.

64. Prior to the outbreak of the war, Hitler's domestic policies had resulted in all of the following *except*
    a. a modest degree of social mobility.
    b. the virtual elimination of unemployment.
    c. greater equality for women.
    d. improvements in the average standard of living.

65. The French adopted the policy of appeasement because they
    a. felt impotent without British support.
    b. felt guilty about the Versailles settlement.
    c. believed a strong Germany, under Hitler, could be used to destroy the Soviet threat.
    d. were paralyzed by pacifism.

66. According to Hitler's New Order, the European "race" that was next to the Jews on Hitler's scale of subhumans was the
    a. Latin race.
    b. Slavic race.
    c. Nordic race.
    d. Anglo-Saxon race.

67. By 1945, Hitler and his Nazis had murdered
    a. 600,000 Jews.
    b. 1 million Jews.
    c. 2 million Jews.
    d. 6 million Jews.

68. The story of the villagers of Le Chambon represents the
    a. horror of the Holocaust.
    b. impact of the Soviet collectivization drive.
    c. many others who actively worked to save Jews from the Nazis.
    d. depths of depravity associated with collaboration.

69. World War II was finally brought to an end by the
    a. Soviet capture of Berlin.
    b. Battle of the Bulge.
    c. surrender of the German general staff.
    d. atomic bombs dropped on Japan.

70. According to Marco Nahon's *Birkenau: The Camp of Death*, excerpted in "Listening to the Past," when the Jews of Dimotika learned they were to be deported, most of them
    a. cooperated, believing the Allies would be able to liberate them.
    b. responded with armed resistance.
    c. fled to Turkey.
    d. offered passive resistance, refused to leave Dimotika, and were shot.

History and Geography

71. In *Mein Kampf,* Hitler stressed living space. Where was this living space to be found? Why was Hitler interested in this region and what would be the consequences of this fixation?

72. Why was the defeat of Hitler and Nazi Germany virtually assured by creation of the Grand Alliance?

73. After the German failure in the Battle of Britain, Hitler chose to attack the Soviet Union. What were the strategic problems with this decision? Suggest a more plausible strategy.

CHAPTER 30

COLD WAR CONFLICTS AND SOCIAL TRANSFORMATIONS, 1945-1985

KEY TERMS

1. welfare state
2. Teheran Conference
3. Truman Doctrine
4. Marshall Plan
5. Christian Democrats
6. Berlin blockade
7. managerial class
8. neocolonialism
9. European Economic Community
10. Richard Nixon
11. *Brown v. Board of Education*
12. Nikita Khrushchev
13. Tet Offensive
14. Big Science
15. Bob Dylan
16. "misery index"
17. Margaret Thatcher
18. Ronald Reagan
19. Betty Friedan
20. *The Second Sex*
21. détente
22. Helsinki Conference

Essay Questions

23. The postwar era was a period in which the European states gave up their overseas colonial possessions. Why? How was decolonization accomplished? What is meant by neocolonialism? What have been the consequences of decolonization?

    For this question, factors in Europe and in the colonial empires that fostered decolonization should be identified: economic collapse, crisis of conscience; independence movements, U.S. policy. Second, describe policies and actions of European states. Third, describe the process, which some critics call neocolonialism, by which Western powers, notably France and Britain, have maintained a strong role in their former colonial empires through economic policies, education, political alliances, aid packages. Finally, a good essay should assess the political, economic, social, cultural, and ethnic consequences of decolonization, including, but not limited to, civil war, ethnic strife, dictatorships, and economic decay.

24. The postwar period in Europe has been called an economic miracle. Why? How did the western European states meet the challenge of postwar reconstruction? What was the role of the United States and how does George C. Marshall's commencement address delivered at Harvard University, presented in "Listening to the Past," help us to understand that role?

    First there should be a description of the economic rebirth of Europe, in terms of economic growth, demography, cooperation, and social welfare. Second, outline and assess the importance of state policies on the European economy; a comparison of France (mixed economy) and Germany (free market economy) would help enhance this aspect. Finally, assess the role of the United States (including the Marshall Plan as his commencement speech outlined it and how it worked in practice, as well as the impact of U.S. cold war commitments and Western leadership) in the European economic recovery.

25. Postwar Europe experienced a trend toward unity. What were the successes and failures of the movement? Who were its leaders? What motivated them? What factors explain the successes and failures of the movement toward European unity?

    Initially, a brief narrative of the history of the efforts at unity from the end of the war to 1985 should be presented, indicating the major events of this history, such as the Schumann Plan, the formation of the European Coal and Steel Community, Treaty of Rome, economic unity of the Common Market; the ambivalence of the British and de Gaulle's nationalistic efforts should also be explored. Include in this outline the early leaders (Christian Democrats in general, and specifically Schumann, Monnet, Adenauer, de Gasperi) and their motivations, essentially to prevent future wars in Europe and ultimately the political unity of Europe. Finally, assess the factors that contributed to the successes of the movement toward unity (the horrors of the war, commitment of early leaders, and hard work of average Europeans, role of the United States and the cold war) and those factors, such as nationalism, that have deterred the movement.

26. International affairs in the postwar era were dominated by the cold war. What were the key events in its development? What were the causes and consequences? Which side was responsible? Given the political, military, and ideological situations at the time, was the cold war unavoidable? Support your conclusions.

    The essay should begin with a brief narrative, describing the main events of the cold war (wartime conferences, Soviet coups in eastern Europe, Soviet support of liberation movements around the world, Berlin Wall, Truman Doctrine, Korean and Vietnam wars). Next, describe and assess the causes (political, ideological, strategic) of the cold war. Third, indicate the immediate and long-term consequences, for both world politics and the peoples of the Soviet Union, Europe, the United States, and the Third World. Finally, there should be an assessment of responsibility

27. "After 1945, western European society became more mobile and more democratic; class barriers relaxed and class distinctions blurred." Assess the validity of this quotation. What factors accounted for these changes?

There should be a description of the changes in the European class structure in terms of mobility, access to political rights, educational and employment opportunities, consumer consumption, and recreation. Next, these changes should be accounted for by examining the role of economic and technological transformation (such as the rise of scientific management and decline of family-owned firms, changing composition of the work force from manufacturing to service jobs), demographic shifts from countryside to urban areas, increased political participation, and social welfare polices.

28. After the death of Stalin, the Soviet Union underwent a process of "de-Stalinization." Describe this process. What impact did de-Stalinization have, domestically and internationally? Why did later Soviet leaders re-Stalinize?

    First, the essay should describe the process, beginning with Khrushchev's "secret speech," the dismantling of the repressive apparatus, openness for artistic expression, greater emphasis on the consumer sector of the Soviet economy, thaw in relations with the West. The impact of de-Stalinization on the Soviet Union includes: artistic freedom (Solzhenitsyn, Pasternak), rising standard of living, shake-up in the membership of the Communist Party, relaxation of labor discipline; for the Warsaw Pact countries, the impact included rebelliousness in Poland and Hungary; for the world, the normalization of relations with the West and increased Soviet aid to Third World nations. The backlash resulted from the fear that Khrushchev's policies threatened the power of the party and from Khrushchev's erratic policies towards the West (Berlin crisis, Cuban missile crisis.)

29. The revolutionary surge of the 1960s was primarily a youth movement. Describe this movement. What factors caused it to gain momentum and then explode in the late 1960s and early 1970s? What were the consequences of this movement?

    First, the essay should identify and discuss the origins of the movement : baby boom, mass communications and worldwide travel, postwar prosperity, no punishment for unconventional behavior. Next, there should be a discussion of the general characteristics: sexual experimentation, attraction to romantic alternatives to Western liberalism, rock-and-roll music, fusion with counter-culture movement. The growth of higher education, Civil Rights movement, and the Vietnam war should all be discussed as the factors that explain its growth and later revolutionary activity. Consequences include a greater degree of political participation in general, but specifically the events of May 1968 in France should be discussed as should the antiwar rallies of the United States and the role played by young people in the revolutionary upheavals of the late sixties and early seventies.

30. Describe Willy Brandt's attempt to answer the "German question." What role did the United States and NATO play in Brandt's policies? What was the impact of those policies on the cold war?

    Initially, the essay should define the "German question" (Germany's role in Europe and the world) and Brandt's overtures to the Soviet Union and East Germany. Second, Brandt's motivation behind his "ostpolitik" should be explained. In the next section, the concerns of the U.S. and the NATO allies about possible German neutrality and the manner in which these fears were allayed by Brandt should be presented. Finally, an assessment of the impact of this diplomatic effort on the emergence of détente, the end of the cold war, and, ultimately, the reunification of Germany should be made.

31. What is meant by the term "second wave of feminism"? How did it interact with existing social, political, and economic trends? What have been the consequences?

The essay should begin with a definition, underscoring the difference between the new and the old feminism; include a discussion of tactics, leadership, and results. De Beauvoir's castigation of traditional marriage and her remedy provides a solid example of the new feminism, from one its founders. Next, there should be a description of the existing situation - especially the roles of economic transformation, social mobility, and political empowerment - with which the "second wave of feminism" interacted to achieve substantial results; a discussion of family strategies and economic necessity must be included. Finally, the essay should conclude with a discussion of the consequences, including increased opportunities for and power of women, limits of transformation, and the backlash against feminism.

32. Historians use the term *détente* to describe relations between the Soviet bloc and the Western democracies in the 1970s. How did the policy evolve? What were the key elements of this diplomatic change? What were the limits of détente? What impact did détente have on the subsequent end of the cold war?

The term should be defined; then the essay should trace the course of relations between East and West that led to détente; include Brandt's policies, U.S. foreign policy (including Nixon's overture to China), NATO, and Soviet policy. Next, the essay should describe the changes that took place, such as a reduction of ideological warfare, increased cultural and academic contact, and arms control. The discussion of the limits should include the recognition of spheres of influence, espionage, support of various armed conflicts around the world, and the inviolability of domestic affairs. Finally, assess the long-range impact and support this assessment.

Multiple-Choice Questions

33. The wartime decisions that led to a Europe divided between East and West were made at the
    a. Teheran Conference.
    b. Yalta Conference.
    c. Munich Conference.
    d. Potsdam Conference.

34. The goal of the Truman Doctrine was to
    a. contain communism in areas liberated by the Red Army.
    b. rebuild the European economies.
    c. force the communists out of eastern Europe.
    d. destroy the communist parties in western Europe.

35. In order to foster economic growth, the German Minister of the Economy Ludwig Erhard
    a. dismantled the extensive social welfare network.
    b. retained the Nazi-era economic planning machinery.
    c. emphasized free-market capitalism.
    d. adopted the French model of a mixed economy.

36. After World War II, the Soviet Union
    a. experienced a period of general freedom.
    b. underwent a consumer revolution.
    c. reintroduced Lenin's New Economic Policy.
    d. returned to the totalitarianism of the 1930s.

37. The European economic rebirth in the postwar era can be attributed to all of the following factors *except*
    a. Marshall Plan aid.
    b. nationalistic economic policies.
    c. government policies fostering growth.
    d. growth of western European economic cooperation.

38. The primary reason the United States and Great Britain agreed to Stalin's demands for "friendly" governments in the eastern European states liberated by the Red Army was
    a. to reward the Soviet Union for its role in World War II.
    b. their fear of communist revolution at home.
    c. their fear of resurgent Nazism.
    d. the presence of the Red Army in those states.

39. French decolonization in sub-Saharan Africa
    a. broke all ties with the former colonies.
    b. effectively removed Western influence in Africa.
    c. resulted from long wars for colonial independence.
    d. enhanced economic and cultural ties with former colonies.

40. Khrushchev's de-Stalinization resulted in all of the following *except*
    a. an economy more responsive to Soviet consumers.
    b. ferment among writers and intellectuals.
    c. a reduction of the Communist party's monopoly on political power.
    d. rebelliousness in the eastern European satellites.

41. The basic reason that the conservative opposition overthrew Khrushchev was because
    a. of his failed economic reforms.
    b. of the fear that de-Stalinization endangered Stalin's still powerful henchmen.
    c. he strayed from the true path of Marxism-Leninism.
    d. of the Berlin Wall confrontation with the United States.

42. The Manhattan Project was responsible for the development of
    a. jet aircraft.
    b. radar.
    c. the atomic bomb.
    d. computers.

43. The ultimate goal of Robert Schuman's plan was to
    a. rebuild the European economy.
    b. create a single competitive market in Europe.
    c. reduce the influence of the United States.
    d. bind the members of the Common Market so closely that war would be impossible.

44. The structure of the lower classes in the postwar years featured
    a. growth in the agricultural labor force.
    b. rapid growth in the number of white-collar and service employees.
    c. expansion of the urban industrial working class.
    d. rigidity and immobility in all sectors.

45. The European Economic Community was created by the Treaty of
    a. Paris.
    b. Potsdam.
    c. Rome.
    d. Yalta.

46. The emergence of the international youth culture can be attributed to all of the following factors *except*
    a. mass communication and youth travel.
    b. the postwar baby boom.
    c. economic stagnation and unemployment among young people.
    d. postwar prosperity.

47. The youth culture fused with the counterculture in opposition to the established order for all of the following reasons *except*
    a. the collapse of postwar prosperity.
    b. the rebirth of romanticism and revolutionary idealism among young people.
    c. boredom with prosperity.
    d. disenchantment with the materialistic West.

48. American military involvement in Vietnam
    a. never had much support.
    b. was based on U.S. imperialism.
    c. grew out of the commitment to the containment policy.
    d. was part of a larger strategy to destroy communism.

49. Changes in the structure of the European society were primarily the result of
    a. economic and technological transformation.
    b. rising birth rates among the lower classes.
    c. the slaughter of World War II.
    d. political and social revolution.

50. The wave of social unrest that almost toppled de Gaulle's Fifth Republic was begun by
    a. workers.
    b. peasants.
    c. students.
    d. civil servants.

51. Big Science is characterized by all of the following *except*
    a. large research teams.
    b. less competition.
    c. tremendous specialization.
    d. enormous costs.

52. The growth of the middle class in the postwar era has been attributed primarily to
    a. increased demand for technologists and managers.
    b. the strength of family-owned businesses.
    c. the high birthrate among this class.
    d. increased opportunities for new businesses.

53. The leveling of European society was a product of all of the following *except*
    a. social welfare programs.
    b. increased immigration resulting from decolonization.
    c. a rising standard of living and standardized consumer goods.
    d. higher taxes on the rich.

54. The most surprising leisure-time development since World War II has been
    a. the interest in high culture.
    b. the vast range of commercial hobbies.
    c. the boom in travel and tourism.
    d. television.

55. The leaders of the Czechoslovak reform movement of 1968 attempted to
    a. abolish the Communist party.
    b. remove Czechoslovakia from the Warsaw Pact.
    c. reintroduce capitalism and liberalism.
    d. make communism more humane.

56. The Vietcong and their North Vietnamese supporters won a great psychological victory over the United States with the
    a. Battle of Dien Bien Phu.
    b. Tet Offensive.
    c. capture of Saigon.
    d. completion of the Ho Chi Minh Trail.

57. The first person to attempt to reconcile the Eastern and Western blocs in Europe was
    a. Mikhail Gorbachev.
    b. Richard Nixon.
    c. Leonid Brezhnev.
    d. Willy Brandt.

58. The Helsinki agreement of 1975 called for
    a. the nonproliferation of nuclear weapons.
    b. the reunification of eastern and western Europe.
    c. respect for human rights in the Soviet bloc and the recognition of existing political boundaries.
    d. American de-escalation in Vietnam and Soviet withdrawal from Afghanistan.

59. The main reason most married women remained in or entered the workforce in the 1980s was
    a. personal fulfillment.
    b. economic necessity.
    c. shrinking population.
    d. equality of opportunity in the workplace.

60. The main point, for women's emancipation, of the culmination of twentieth-century trends toward early, almost universal marriage and small family size was that
    a. motherhood occupied a much smaller portion of a woman's life.
    b. population growth slowed dramatically.
    c. marriages became based on romantic attachments.
    d. postwar economic transformation offered increased job opportunities.

61. Simone de Beauvoir argued that women could become more free through
    a. political revolution.
    b. the abolition of marriage.
    c. refusal to have children.
    d. courageous action and self-assertive creativity.

62. The *misery index* is a measurement that
    a. combines inflation and unemployment rates.
    b. measures per capita levels of malnutrition and disease.
    c. combines expenditures for oil and government deficits.
    d. links per capita income to oil imports.

63. The text attributes the lack of U.S. leadership during the OPEC oil embargo to the
    a. Tet Offensive.
    b. student revolts.
    c. Watergate crisis.
    d. Yom Kippur War.

64. The economic problems of the 1970s led to all of the following *except*
    a. lower levels of private debt.
    b. students' growing conservatism.
    c. more women in the workforce.
    d. healthier lifestyles.

65. The founder of the National Organization for Women was
    a. Simone de Beauvoir.
    b. Betty Friedan.
    c. Margaret Thatcher.
    d. Helen Gurley Brown.

66. Ronald Reagan's efforts to control government spending failed for all of the following reasons *except*
    a. his extravagant military build-up.
    b. the harsh recession of the early 1980s.
    c. his generous support of the space program.
    d. his crude antiwelfare rhetoric.

67. The emergence of "second wave" feminism has been attributed to all of the following *except*
    a. changes in the patterns of work and motherhood.
    b. the work of a vanguard of feminist intellectuals.
    c. the organization of dissatisfied women to demand changes.
    d. fewer opportunities for women outside the home.

68. In Great Britain, Margaret Thatcher's efforts to encourage low- and moderate-income renters to buy their apartments
    a. failed miserably.
    b. led to destructive debt levels for poorer people.
    c. was supported by the Labour party.
    d. created a new class of property owners.

69. According to the text, the sharp rise in the number of married women working full time outside the home was a response to
    a. the reduction of home-centered work and child-care responsibilities.
    b. the demands of increased industrialization.
    c. the number of casualties suffered in World War Two.
    d. advances in social welfare.

70. Common strategies of the women's movement included all of the following *except*
    a. efforts at eliminating discrimination in the workplace.
    b. elimination of male-dominated governments.
    c. legislation to legalize abortion and divorce.
    d. support for programs to help single parents.

71. The essence of Willy Brandt's policies toward the Eastern bloc was
    a. to seek peace and reconciliation.
    b. the reunification of Germany.
    c. to reduce the influence of NATO in Germany.
    d. to establish German neutrality in the cold war.

History and Geography

72. Explain why, based on geographic factors, the decision to establish a second front in France rather than invading through central Europe helped create the division between eastern and western Europe.

73. What factors explain Britain's early reluctance to join the European Economic Community (and its recent ambivalent attitude toward European unity)?

74. What geographic factors helped influence Willy Brandt's decision to try to reconcile East and West?

CHAPTER 31

REVOLUTION, REUNIFICATION, AND REBUILDING, 1985 TO THE PRESENT

KEY TERMS

1. Mikhail Gorbachev
2. Saddam Hussein
3. Paris Accord
4. Commonwealth of Independent States
5. New World Order
6. Viktor Chernomyrdin
7. Chechnya
8. Vaclav Havel
9. "velvet divorce"
10. Slobadan Milosevic
11. ethnic cleansing
12. Maastricht Treaty
13. Helmut Kohl
14. Dayton Accords
15. Jacques Chirac
16. Cardinal Karol Wojtyla
17. Gdansk Agreement
18. *perestroika*
19. Nicolae Ceausescu
20. Boris Yeltsin

Essay Questions

21. The Gorbachev "revolution" in the Soviet Union focused on four main areas. What were these areas and how successful was the reform effort? What forces for change were already present? To what extent were Gorbachev's reforms responsible for the revolutions of 1989 and 1991?

    Describe and assess the impact of Gorbachev's reform efforts in the four main areas: economic restructuring, political openness, democratization, cooperation with the West, and encouraging reform in the Soviet satellites. Next, indicate the forces for change, such as increased interaction between Soviet and Western scholars and the increasingly urbanized and sophisticated elite, which already existed and were strengthened by Gorbachev's efforts. Finally, assess the impact of his efforts in the collapse of the Warsaw Pact and ultimately the destruction of the Soviet Union.

22. The year 1989 witnessed an almost unbelievable turn of events in the Eastern bloc. Discuss those changes. What were the long-term causes? What new problems were created?

First, describe the collapse of Soviet control of eastern Europe, the rise of new regimes in the former Warsaw Pact countries, German unification, and the overthrow of the Soviet Union itself. Next, a thorough analysis of the causes, including the long-term political, economic, and social problems and their exacerbation by Gorbachev's reforms and growing nationalism. The efforts of leaders such as Yeltsin to reform Soviet-style economic and political systems should be stressed, being sure to indicate the problems - entrenched elites, cultural reluctance - still facing these areas. The explosive growth of nationalistic conflicts in the region should also be stressed, with emphasis placed on the civil war in the former Yugoslavia.

23. The recent past has seen a quickening of the pace in the process of European integration and unification. Describe this process since 1985. What are the key issues? How have Europeans reacted to the "new Europe"?

This essay should begin with the Single Europe Act of 1985, and its emphasis on closer economic and political integration. Next, the evolution and signing of the Maastricht Treaty, backed heavily by Mitterand of France and Kohl of Germany. Then one should discuss the efforts made to adhere to the Maastricht criteria for inclusion in the European monetary union. The key issues include the balancing act between nation-state sovereignty, British uneasiness, enlargement, economic growth, social welfare reform. Reaction ranges from the full support of European elites to the less than enthusiastic response of average Europeans, evidenced by the close referenda on the new currency proposals, replacement of ruling parties by the voters, and the strike activity to protest austerity measures designed to bring national economies and budgets into line with criteria for inclusion in the single currency club.

24. The collapse of the Soviet Union led quickly to the declaration that the cold war was over. What have been the consequences of this historic event?

Consequences include: the emergence of the United States as the only remaining superpower, evidenced by the Gulf War; a cessation of the nuclear arms race between the U.S. and Soviet/post-Soviet Russia; expansion of NATO; reunification of Germany; resurgence of virulent nationalism and several bloody conflicts in the successor states of the Soviet empire; the adoption of the neo-liberal economic model throughout Europe.

25. In recent years European leaders - east, central, and west - have adopted a neo-liberal, free-market vision of capitalist development. Why? What have been the consequences?

The economic success of the United States is the most important reason for this adoption; mention of Fukuyama's announcement that "history had ended and liberalism had won" would be useful. Consequences include the resounding failure of Russia to achieve economic success following its implementation of liberal, free-market reforms; the relative success of the central European states; reforms of the welfare system in western Europe and subsequent protests.

26. The most disturbing consequence of the collapse of the Soviet Union has been the resurgence of ardent nationalism in central and eastern Europe as well as the border states of the former Soviet Union. Trace nationalistic developments in the former Soviet empire. What signs are there of a peaceful resolution of this problem?

    This essay should begin with the multifaceted civil war in the former Yugoslavia, stressing the role of Slobadan Milosevic and his Greater Serbia concept; special attention should be paid to the events in Bosnia, including ethnic cleansing. Ethnic/nationalistic civil wars in various successor states of the Soviet Union should also be mentioned, especially Chechnya. Signs of a peaceful resolution include: Russia's moderating role in most of the civil wars on its borders; the peaceful "velvet divorce" of Slovakia and the Czech Republic; the Dayton Accords.

27. In your opinion, what does the new millennium hold for the history of the human race?

Multiple-Choice Questions

28. The only Eastern bloc country that responded to the prodemocracy movement of 1989 with bloody repression was
    a. Poland.
    b. Czechoslovakia.
    c. East Germany.
    d. Romania.

29. Soviet actions seemed most contrary to the spirit of détente in
    a. eastern Europe.
    b. Afghanistan.
    c. Somalia and Ethiopia.
    d. Egypt.

30. The Brezhnev era in the Soviet Union appeared stable for all of the following reasons *except*
    a. the coercive apparatus of the state and Party.
    b. the high rate of growth in the consumer sector of the economy.
    c. intense nationalism of ordinary Great Russians.
    d. a gradual rising standard of living.

31. The Brezhnev era saw all of the following changes *except*
    a. the growth of the urban population.
    b. rapid expansion in the number of highly trained specialists.
    c. cultural and artistic freedom.
    d. the growth of Soviet public opinion.

32. Poland differed from the other Eastern bloc states because
    a. its economy was managed effectively.
    b. it retained an independent military.
    c. of its independent agriculture and vigorous church.
    d. of its native leadership.

33. The workers at the Lenin Shipyards in Gdansk demanded all of the following *except*
    a. dissolution of the Communist party.
    b. the right to strike.
    c. economic reforms.
    d. freedom of speech.

34. Gorbachev's economic reforms included all of the following *except*
    a. freer prices.
    b. more independence for state enterprises.
    c. the establishment of profit-seeking corporations.
    d. the break-up of collective farms.

35. The least successful of Gorbachev's reform programs was
    a. Glasnost.
    b. the economic restructuring of the Soviet Union.
    c. the democratization of the Soviet Union.
    d. new political thinking in foreign affairs.

36. In the revolutions of 1989, the first state to elect a non-Communist leader was
    a. Poland.
    b. East Germany.
    c. Czechoslovakia.
    d. Romania.

37. In order to gain Soviet agreement to German unification, the newly united Germany pledged never to develop nuclear weapons and to
    a. withdraw from NATO.
    b. resist European political unity.
    c. provide large loans to the Soviet Union.
    d. protect the former Communist rulers.

38. Privatized companies in post-Soviet Russia
    a. are not allowed.
    b. usually ended up in the hands of former Soviet managers and bureaucrats.
    c. have attracted a great deal of investment from average Russians.
    d. have been bought up by foreign investors.

39. Long-term inflation resulted from Yeltsin's reforms for all of the following reasons *except*
    a. Soviet monopolies simply turned into private monopolies.
    b. criminal intimidation that has hindered the foundation of new firms.
    c. the influx of loans from the West.
    d. the cultural resistance of most Russians to capitalistic enterprizes.

40. For average Russians, Yeltsin's reforms have resulted in all of the following *except*
    a. greater investment opportunities.
    b. widespread unemployment and poverty.
    c. declining life expectancy.
    d. the destruction of pension savings.

41. Russian moderation in foreign affairs is evident in all of the following *except* its
    a. acceptance of the expansion of NATO.
    b. continued decline in military spending.
    c. respect for the independence of the successor states of the Soviet Union.
    d. application to join NATO.

42. Yeltsin and his reformist allies are opposed in the parliament by all of the following *except* the
    a. Christian Democrats.
    b. Communists.
    c. Nationalists.
    d. Populists.

43. The Solidarity movement of the 1980s was led by
    a. Mikhail Gorbachev.
    b. Lech Walesa.
    c. Alexander Dubcek.
    d. Karol Wojtyla.

44. In order to deal with the disastrous economic situation, the Solidarity government in Poland
    a. continued the Soviet-style, command economy.
    b. followed a program of modest reform in small-scale industry.
    c. applied for membership in the European Economic Community.
    d. implemented economic "shock therapy," for free markets and private property.

45. In 1990, Gorbachev was faced with all of the following problems *except*
    a. near civil war between Armenians and Azerbaijanis.
    b. threats of invasion by former Warsaw Pact states.
    c. assertions of independence by the Baltic states.
    d. growing dissatisfaction among the Great Russian masses.

46. The attempted coup by the Communist old guard failed because of
    a. massive popular resistance, rallied around Boris Yeltsin.
    b. Gorbachev's use of the Red Army to crush the rebels.
    c. threat of NATO intervention.
    d. the inability of the old guard to decide on a new leader.

47. The absorption of East Germany by West Germany featured all of the following factors *except*
    a. millions of East Germans pouring into West Germany.
    b. skillful exploitation of the situation by West German Chancellor Kohl.
    c. powerful resistance from the United States.
    d. German affirmation of peaceful intentions and a pledge against developing nuclear arms.

48. The lessening of the nuclear arms race is best indicated by the
    a. Start I agreement.
    b. Salt II agreement.
    c. Paris Accords.
    d. Dayton Accords.

49. The Gulf War clearly revealed
    a. the disunity among the world community.
    b. Russia's continued importance in world affairs.
    c. the lingering resentment of the Arab world against the United States.
    d. American preeminence as the only remaining superpower.

50. The post-Soviet governments of eastern Europe introduced all of the following reforms *except*
    a. free markets and prices.
    b. privatization of state-owned enterprises.
    c. substantial social welfare systems.
    d. establishment of strong currencies and balanced budgets.

51. The shift from welfare state activism to neo-liberal economic practices resulted from all of the following factors *except* the
    a. collapse of the European Economic Community.
    b. success of the United States and Great Britain.
    c. emergence of the wide-open global economy.
    d. ongoing computer and information technology revolution.

52. The successor states of eastern Europe shared all of the following features *except*
    a. efforts to replace state planning with free markets and private property.
    b. the emergence of one-man dictatorial regimes.
    c. the establishment of Western-style electoral politics.
    d. growing social and economic inequality.

53. The successful reform movements in Poland, Hungary, and the Czech Republic resulted from all of the following factors *except*
    a. state control of strategic industries.
    b. considerable experience with limited market reforms before 1989.
    c. flexibility in government policy.
    d. the enthusiastic embrace of capitalism by a new, rising entrepreneurial class.

54. The east European states which lagged behind in reform efforts included all the following *except*
    a. Slovakia.
    b. Romania.
    c. Bulgaria.
    d. Lithuania.

55. Slobadan Milosevic's plan which hastened separatism and civil war in Yugoslavia was known as
    a. Greater Serbia.
    b. the Third Way.
    c. the League of Communists.
    d. the Commonwealth of Independent States.

56. The event which finally galvanized NATO action against the Bosnian Serbs was the
    a. discovery of ethnic cleansing policies.
    b. slaughter of several thousands citizens in Srebrenica.
    c. invasion of Bosnia by elements of the regular Serbian army.
    d. Milosevic's ditching of his Bosnian Serb allies.

57. The Dayton Accords created a/an
    a. ethnically Serbian state in Bosnia.
    b. strong, centralized state dominated by the Muslims.
    c. multinational union of all Serbs in the former Yugoslavia.
    d. loosely federated state, with Serbs, Croats, and Muslims sharing control.

58. The Single European Act of 1986 called for the free movement of all of the following *except*
    a. goods.
    b. labor.
    c. capital.
    d. services.

59. The Maastricht Treaty criteria for joining the monetary union included all of the following *except*
    a. reduced national budget deficits to 3% of GNP.
    b. low inflation.
    c. high employment rates.
    d. reduced national debt.

60. The Maastricht Treaty faced considerable opposition from all of the following groups *except*
    a. ordinary people.
    b. leftist political parties.
    c. Christian Democrats.
    d. old-fashioned nationalists.

61. Opposition to the Maastricht Treaty was based on all of the following considerations *except*
    a. resentment against the proliferation of EU regulations and large bureaucracy.
    b. fear of the undermining of national sovereignty.
    c. the belief that ordinary people would pay for monetary union by reduced social services.
    d. the belief that the new currency would be easily manipulated and controlled by the U.S.

62. French reaction to the austerity reforms introduced to meet Maastricht criteria featured
    a. massive protest marches and a national strike.
    b. grumbling resentment.
    c. waves of political violence.
    d. lukewarm acceptance.

63. In the aftermath of German reunification, the consequences have included all of the following *except*
    a. high unemployment.
    b. diminution of the status of women.
    c. greater role for women in the public sphere.
    d. psychological distress by east Germans who feel humiliated.

64. Vaclav Havel's message, from the "Individuals in Society" feature, emphasizes
    a. nationalistic self-determination.
    b. the power of peaceful revolution.
    c. the continued importance of socialist welfare systems in eastern Europe.
    d. neo-liberal capitalism by east Germans who feel humiliated.

65. Adam Michnik, whose *Letters from Prison* is presented in "Listening to the Past," argued that Solidarity
    a. should pursue a policy of violent confrontation with the Communist Party.
    b. should be dissolved and replaced with a more politically oriented organization.
    c. Lech Walesa sold out the workers for his own political power.
    d. rejected violence for practical and idealistic reasons.

History and Geography

66. After examining Map 31.2, give a brief explanation, based on geography and ethnicity, for the rapid shattering of the Soviet empire.

67. After examining Map 31.4, describe Milosevic's plan for a Greater Serbia. Why would this lead to war?

68. Describe the current thrust of NATO (and future EU) expansion. How will the post-Soviet world react to this expansion?

UNIT, MIDTERM, AND FINAL EXAMINATION QUESTIONS

The essay questions below are designed for use after each four-chapter unit, and for midterm and final examinations.

UNIT 1 (Chapters 1 - 4)

1. Describe the interplay between geographical factors and social, economic, intellectual, and political development in Mesopotamia, Egypt, and Greece. Was geography the dominant factor in the development of civilization in these areas? What other factors contributed to its development?

2. Describe the development of religion among the Sumerians, Egyptians, Hebrews, and Persians. What elements were common to all? In what ways were these religions different? How did Greek religion compare to these other religions?

3. "The exploits of Alexander the Great bridged the classical world and the Roman Empire." Explain this statement. How did Alexander's empire and the successor kingdoms contribute to the rise of Rome? What features of the pre-Alexandrian world did not change?

4. Everyday life changed dramatically over the time described in these chapters. Discuss the evolution of everyday life from the Paleolithic era through the Classical Age of Greece. What were the most significant changes? What factors produced those changes?

UNIT 2 (Chapters 5 - 8)

1. Discuss the evolution—political, economic, and social—of the Roman Republic. What were the most critical factors influencing change in Rome? How and why did the republic collapse?

2. Evaluate the success of the Augustan settlement and the pax Romana. What were the Romans' weaknesses? Their strengths? Were the seeds of the collapse of Roman civilization planted by Augustus Caesar?

3. The rise of Christianity is intimately linked to the fall of Rome and the emergence of medieval Europe. Discuss this historical phenomenon. What was the role of the early Christian church in both the decline of Rome and the development of medieval Europe?

4. The political and economic organization of European society during the early Middle Ages was based on a rigid hierarchy. Describe the organization of European society at that time. How do we account for this type of organization? Did feudalism and manorialism meet the needs of European society during the early Middle Ages? Explain your answer.

5. The textbook states that European civilization stemmed from the fusion of Greco-Roman heritage, Germanic traditions, and the Christian faith. How did these three elements combine to create a

distinct European civilization? What other factors influenced the development of civilization in Europe?

6. The Romans have been described as politically pragmatic. How do the Struggle of the Orders, the Social Wars, the Augustan settlement, and the reforming emperors of the empire support or detract from this description?

MIDTERM EXAMINATION (Chapters 1 - 8)

1. Write a brief history of everyday life from the agricultural revolution through the time of Charlemagne's empire. What were the key events in this history? How did the role of women change? What were the primary agents of change?

2. Religion and philosophy have been major emphases of the textbook to this point. How did both of these areas change over time? How were both related to their own time and place in history? What was the role of political officials in the development of religion? Philosophy? In what ways did these two areas interact with each other?

3. "History to 800 A.D. shows the seemingly inexorable urbanization of Western civilization." Explain this statement, concentrating on the following periods: Mesopotamia to 1200 B.C., Hellenic Greece, the Hellenistic era, the Roman Empire, and the early Middle Ages.

4. The textbook gives examples of many different forms of government. Compare the governments of Hammurabi, the Persian Empire, Athens, the Roman Republic, the Roman Empire, and the Carolingian Empire. What were the most important factors in the development of these governments? What similarities do you find?

5. Military innovations have greatly influenced the course of Western history. How did military institutions reflect the political, social, and economic institutions of the Persian Empire, Hellenic Greece, the Roman Republic, the Roman Empire, and the early Middle Ages?

UNIT 3 (Chapters 9 - 12)

1. Describe European society during the High Middle Ages. How was society affected by economic revival, the development of the modern state, and the crises of the later Middle Ages?

2. Describe the role of the church and clergy in the political development of England, France, and Germany. Was their role positive or negative? Why? What was the impact of the so-called new monarchies on the church?

3. The later Middle Ages has been called calamitous. Why? Describe the impact of the Black Death, the Hundred Years' War, and the decline of the church's prestige.

4. The church between 800 and 1400 underwent periods of revival and decline. Trace the development of the church over this time, and explain the origin and impact of each period of revival and decline. Was the church stronger in 1450 than in 850? Why or why not?

UNIT 4 (Chapters 13 - 16)

1. "Machiavelli's *The Prince* outlined a political philosophy that echoes the main themes of the Renaissance." Explain this statement. How were the ideas of Machiavelli exemplified by the policies and actions of the rulers of Spain, France, and England in the fifteenth and early sixteenth centuries; the political developments in France and Germany during the eras of religious wars; and the development of absolutism in France?

2. Compare the political evolution of France and England from 1450 to 1715. How do we account for the different paths taken?

3. From the Renaissance to the Age of Absolutism (ca. 1415 - 1715), society underwent tremendous change. Discuss that change in terms of religion, economics, and social organization. How did these elements interact with one another? Did the status of women and blacks change over this time? If so, in what ways?

4. Explain the nature of reform and renewal in the Christian church. What were the main goals and tactics of the Protestant and Catholic reformers? What were their successes? Their failures? Why and how did this reforming outburst lead to the religious violence of the sixteenth century? What was the political impact of Luther's movement and the religious civil wars in France?

5. "The Renaissance was in many ways a product of the economic resurgence of Europe." Describe this economic resurgence and assess the accuracy of this statement. How did expansion in the New World create economic difficulties? What can be learned from these two examples of expanded economic activity?

FINAL EXAMINATION, VOLUME 1

1. European civilization has been called a combination of Greco-Roman heritage, Christianity, and Germanic traditions. What were the contributions of these three elements to that civilization? Which of these three had the greatest impact? What other influences helped shape the development of civilization in Europe?

2. The history of Western civilization is closely linked to the phenomenon of urbanization. Discuss the causes and impact of urbanization on the course of Western history to 1715.

3. The relationship between church and state has been a major theme of the textbook. Describe this relationship in pharaonic Egypt, the Hebrew kingdom, the Roman Empire, Renaissance Europe, and Reformation Europe. What are the common threads of this relationship? How has religion supported or detracted from the power of the state throughout history?

4. The course of Western history experienced many profound changes between the dawn of time and 1715. How did these changes affect everyday life for the average person? That is, was everyday life appreciably different for an agricultural peasant or artisan in Babylon than it was for a French peasant or artisan in the seventeenth century? Explain your answer.

5. You have been asked to write a textbook for a history of women from the Neolithic era through the Reformation. Concentrating on the changes, positive and negative, in the status of women,

present a brief overview. In your opinion what caused the secondary status of women throughout this period of history?

6. Western civilization has seen the rise and fall of many empires. Pick four of the empires discussed in the textbook (Hittite, Persian, Athenian, Alexandrine, Roman, and Carolingian) and discuss the reasons behind their successes and failures. What were the common factors in the fall of these empires?

7. Philosophical inquiry is said to have begun with the Greeks. Is this true? Why or why not? What is the enduring legacy of Greek philosophy?

8. Your textbook examines the development of something called *Western civilization*. What are the key characteristics of Western civilization? Which characteristics do you find admirable? Unadmirable? Explain your answers.

UNIT 5 (Chapters 17 - 20)

1. Absolutism in eastern Europe was inspired by the example of France under Louis XIV, but was modified to fit the situation of the respective monarchies in the east. Trace the development of absolutism in Russia and either Austria or Prussia. In what ways were they similar? Different? How do we account for the differences? How did the eastern absolutists react to the Enlightenment?

2. Historians have determined that absolutist monarchs needed the help or threat of some outside agent—war, invasion, civil strife—to establish their regime. Describe the impact of these outside agents in Prussia, Austria, and Russia. How did the example of Poland underscore the necessity of creating a strong, centralized state?

3. It can be argued that the scientific revolution found its practical expression in the agricultural revolution, and that the Enlightenment was expressed in "enlightened government." Consider this argument. How did each theoretical development influence its application? Does the relationship between the scientific revolution and the Enlightenment reveal anything about the relationship between economic development and the role of government? If so, what?

4. What effect did economic development (agriculture, cottage industry, and the Atlantic economy) and the population explosion have on everyday life? What was their impact on marriage, the family, women, and children? What about diet, medicine, and religion?

5. The condition of the peasants in eastern Europe contrasted sharply with that in the west. Describe the differences. What accounts for them? What were the consequences - political, social, and economic - of this social system on eastern Europe? Did the reigns of the enlightened monarchs toward the end of the eighteenth century improve the situation for the enserfed peasants of Austria, Russia, and Prussia?

6. As absolutism in the east was growing stronger, French absolutism was crumbling. Trace this collapse. What factors—economic, political, and social—brought about the breakdown of the absolutist government in France?

UNIT 6 (Chapters 21 - 24)

1. The years from 1775 to 1850 were truly a revolutionary period in European history. How did the political, economic, and social structure of Europe change? Compare the predominant structures of Europe in 1775 to those in 1850. Which of the three areas changed the most? Why?

2. The French Revolution is one of the most hotly debated historical events. Much of this debate revolves around the causes of the Revolution and the roles of various social groups in French society. What were the causes? What social groups were involved? What role did each group play in the Revolution? How does this help explain the different views of the Revolution?

3. The Revolutions of 1848 were motivated in large part by the "isms" of the nineteenth century. What were these ideologies? To whom did they appeal? Where were they influential? How did the French and Industrial Revolutions influence these ideologies and thus the Revolutions of 1848? How do we account for the early successes and subsequent failures of the revolutions all over Europe?

4. How did the face of urban Europe change between 1815 and 1848? What was the impact of the Industrial Revolution? What were the problems brought on by that revolution? How did contemporaries appraise the social costs of the Industrial Revolution? How do modern historians interpret those costs?

MIDTERM EXAMINATION (Chapters 17 - 24)

1. European history from about 1583 to 1848 was one of profound change, with revolutions occurring in intellectual, economic, and political systems. Describe these revolutions briefly, and identify the interplay among the three areas. Which of the three do you think has had the greatest impact on the course of European history? Why?

2. While the Revolutions of 1848 were raging across continental Europe, England and Russia were islands of calm. How were these two very different states able to avoid revolution? What can we learn from this to broaden our understanding of the revolutions in the rest of Europe?

3. The eighteenth and nineteenth centuries witnessed the birth of new ways of looking at the world. Describe the various "isms" that emerged. How do they reflect the impact of the so-called dual revolution in economics and politics? What was their impact on the Revolutions of 1848? Which seems to have been the strongest?

4. Describe the impact of the revolutionary changes in Europe on women and the family. What were the most striking changes?

5. Outline the changes experienced by the laboring classes as a result of the French and Industrial Revolutions. Which of the two had greater impact on the workers and peasants of Europe?

6. How did artistic expression reflect the prevailing trends in European society from the Baroque through the Romantic movements?

UNIT 7 (Chapters 25 - 28)

1. In 1929 the Great Depression began in the United States and spread quickly to Europe. What was the impact of the Depression on the lives of everyday people in the United States and western Europe? How did the Depression affect the lives of Soviet workers? Did the Great Depression and the Soviet experience have an impact on the continued vitality of liberal politics and economics? Explain your answer.

2. Discuss the course of international relations between the end of World War I and the outbreak of World War II. In light of the subsequent developments in the diplomatic history of the interwar years, can we argue that the Versailles settlement "caused" the Second World War? Why or why not?

3. Article 231 of the Versailles Treaty placed full blame for World War I on the Germans. Discuss the long- and short-term causes of the war. In light of that discussion, how accurate was Article 231?

4. The First World War had a tremendous impact on European civilization. What were the positive and negative aspects of that impact? Overall, can you argue that World War I was actually a positive experience for European civilization? Explain your answer.

5. Some historians insist that the First World War killed nineteenth century liberalism. Why? How do the events in Russia, Germany, Spain, and Italy support this contention? Are there any examples of the continued vitality of liberalism?

UNIT 6 (Chapters 29 - 31)

1. The postWorld War II era saw a veritable renaissance in western Europe. What were the most striking accomplishments of the postwar recovery? How was this recovery achieved? How and why was the experience of eastern Europe different from that of western Europe?

2. Hitler's rise to power in Germany seems to have been one of the most improbable events of recorded history. How do we account for it? That is, how did the conditions in Germany, Hitler himself, and the actions of the other European nations all combine to put a madman at the head of one of the most powerful states of all time? How was Hitler able to consolidate and increase his power after 1933?

3. Artistic expression after the First World War has been called a rebellion against bourgeois culture. What does this mean? Describe the revolutionary developments in the visual arts, music, and literature. How did these developments reflect the situation in Europe in general?

4. The Grand Alliance against Nazi Germany was successful militarily but disappointing diplomatically. What were the reasons behind the success and failure of the Grand Alliance?

5. The cold war was a tremendous disappointment after the glorious efforts of the Allies against the Axis powers during the war. Describe the origins of the cold war. Which side - the United States or the Soviet Union - seems most guilty of starting the cold war? Explain your answer.

6. Perhaps the most revolutionary changes of the postwar era have been those experienced by average people in their daily lives. Describe the way in which life has changed since World War II. Have these changes been for the better?

7. The division of Europe began essentially with the success of the Bolshevik revolution in 1917 and was institutionalized after World War II. Trace the history of this division and explain how this division has, in recent years, been healed.

FINAL EXAMINATION, VOLUME 2

1. Since Kievan Rus, the Russian state and society has been dominated by powerful central governments and entrenched elites, seemingly unresponsive to the masses of the people. Trace the history of authoritarian government in Russia and the Soviet Union. Identify the factors which seem to predispose Russia to strong central governments and a lack of concern for individual liberty. What, if any, are the indications that this historical pattern might change?

2. The textbook asserts that Europe began a "dual revolution" in politics and economics in the last years of the seventeenth century. Describe this dual revolution. What were its high and low points?

3. European civilization since 1583 has been shaped by the emergence of intellectual trends and ideologies. Trace the intellectual history of Europe since 1583. What were the most influential ideas and ideologies of the past four hundred years? How have they affected the political, economic, and social history of Europe?

4. Everyday life has undergone a radical change since the seventeenth century. Describe what you think of as the most fundamental of these changes. What factors accounted for these changes? Have they all been beneficial? Explain your answer.

5. Perhaps the most radical change experienced by European civilization has been that of the status of women and the family. Compare the situations of women and the family in preindustrial Europe, Europe in the mid-nineteenth century, in the years between the wars, and in the postWorld War II era. What have been the most profound changes? What caused these changes?

6. There have been three major peace conferences since the French Revolution, all charged with the task of reconstructing the European international system. Compare the goals, the underlying principles, and the successes and failures of the Congress of Vienna, the talks at Versailles, and the Grand Alliance conferences. Which of the three was most successful? Why?

7. Perhaps the most powerful "ism" of the nineteenth century was nationalism. Explain the origins and development of this ideology. What impact has nationalism had on the political and diplomatic history of Europe in the nineteenth and twentieth centuries?

8. One of the themes of the text has been the growing divergence between the elites and the popular classes at least since the fifteenth century. On what is this theme based? Be sure to consider politics, economics, culture, and everyday life. Has this pattern changed significantly in the postwar era?

9. The text asserts that the expansion and redefinition of human liberty has been one of the great themes of modern Western history. Discuss this assertion critically, identifying the key moments in this movement. What were the causes and consequences of these expansions and redefinitions and how did each new achievement lead to subsequent developments? In light of your discussion, to what extent can we argue that the evolution of human liberty was inevitable?

10. A key theme of the history of European international relations has been the "German Question," that is, how German unification would be achieved and what role unified Germany would play in the international system. Discuss this question by examining the efforts at German unification in the nineteenth century and the impact of unification on late-nineteenth and twentieth-century history. What role can the newly reunified Germany be expected to play in the international affairs of the coming years?

ANSWER KEY

CHAPTER 1

27.	b	40.	b	53.	d
28.	a	41.	d	54.	c
29.	c	42.	c	55.	c
30.	a	43.	c	56.	b
31.	d	44.	b	57.	d
32.	c	45.	c	58.	b
33.	b	46.	a	59.	a
34.	a	47.	d	60.	c
35.	d	48.	b	61.	c
36.	a	49.	a	62.	d
37.	c	50.	b	63.	c
38.	c	51.	a	64.	b
39.	a	52.	b		

CHAPTER 2

28.	c	42.	a	56.	a
29.	c	43.	b	57.	d
30.	a	44.	a	58.	b
31.	b	45.	b	59.	c
32.	d	46.	d	60.	d
33.	b	47.	d	61.	d
34.	c	48.	d	62.	a
35.	b	49.	b	63.	a
36.	a	50.	c	64.	c
37.	d	51.	a	65.	b
38.	c	52.	c	66.	b
39.	c	53.	b		
40.	b	54.	d		
41.	d	55.	a		

Answer Key / 279

CHAPTER 3

30.	c	45.	a	59.	c
31.	c	46.	b	60.	d
32.	b	47.	c	61.	c
33.	b	48.	c	62.	a
34.	d	49.	a	63.	b
35.	c	50.	a	64.	c
36.	a	51.	b	65.	d
37.	a	52.	d	66.	c
38.	d	53.	d	67.	c
39.	b	54.	c	68.	d
40.	b	55.	a	69.	a
41.	c	56.	a	70.	c
42.	c	57.	b	71.	b
43.	a	58.	a	72.	a
44.	d				

CHAPTER 4

27.	c	41.	d	55.	d
28.	a	42.	a	56.	c
29.	b	43.	c	57.	b
30.	b	44.	d	58.	a
31.	d	45.	a	59.	d
32.	c	46.	d	60.	a
33.	b	47.	b	61.	c
34.	c	48.	a	62.	b
35.	d	49.	c	63.	a
36.	a	50.	c	64.	b
37.	b	51.	a	65.	a
38.	c	52.	c	66.	d
39.	b	53.	d	67.	a
40.	c	54.	b		

CHAPTER 5

28.	c	41.	a	54.	d
29.	b	42.	b	55.	a
30.	a	43.	b	56.	c
31.	c	44.	d	57.	d
32.	d	45.	c	58.	b
33.	b	46.	c	59.	b
34.	a	47.	a	60.	a
35.	d	48.	c	61.	c
36.	b	49.	b	62.	b
37.	b	50.	c	63.	a
38.	c	51.	d	64.	d
39.	d	52.	c	65.	a
40.	c	53.	a		

COPYRIGHT © HOUGHTON MIFFLIN COMPANY. ALL RIGHTS RESERVED.

CHAPTER 6

28.	b	41.	b	54.	c
29.	c	42.	b	55.	c
30.	b	43.	c	56.	d
31.	b	44.	a	57.	b
32.	d	45.	b	58.	a
33.	d	46.	c	59.	b
34.	a	47.	d	60.	d
35.	c	48.	a	61.	c
36.	d	49.	b	62.	a
37.	c	50.	d	63.	d
38.	a	51.	a	64.	d
39.	c	52.	b		
40.	a	53.	a		

CHAPTER 7

30.	c	43.	c	56.	b
31.	b	44.	a	57.	c
32.	a	45.	c	58.	b
33.	d	46.	d	59.	c
34.	d	47.	d	60.	d
35.	a	48.	c	61.	a
36.	b	49.	a	62.	c
37.	d	50.	d	63.	b
38.	d	51.	c	64.	d
39.	b	52.	c	65.	b
40.	c	53.	b	66.	b
41.	b	54.	a	67.	c
42.	a	55.	d	68.	a

CHAPTER 8

28.	c	41.	d	54.	a
29.	a	42.	c	55.	b
30.	b	43.	a	56.	a
31.	c	44.	d	57.	c
32.	a	45.	c	58.	d
33.	d	46.	c	59.	b
34.	b	47.	b	60.	a
35.	c	48.	d	61.	c
36.	a	49.	a	62.	b
37.	c	50.	a	63.	d
38.	d	51.	a	64.	d
39.	b	52.	b	65.	b
40.	c	53.	d		

CHAPTER 9

28.	b	40.	b	52.	d
29.	a	41.	a	53.	b
30.	c	42.	d	54.	a
31.	b	43.	c	55.	d
32.	b	44.	a	56.	a
33.	b	45.	b	57.	c
34.	c	46.	c	58.	d
35.	a	47.	d	59.	a
36.	c	48.	a	60.	b
37.	d	49.	d	61.	c
38.	a	50.	c	62.	b
39.	c	51.	b	63.	d

CHAPTER 10

28.	a	43.	d	58.	d
29.	c	44.	b	59.	d
30.	b	45.	d	60.	a
31.	c	46.	a	61.	b
32.	c	47.	a	62.	c
33.	c	48.	c	63.	b
34.	a	49.	b	64.	a
35.	c	50.	a	65.	b
36.	b	51.	d	66.	d
37.	d	52.	d	67.	b
38.	c	53.	a	68.	a
39.	a	54.	b	69.	c
40.	b	55.	c	70.	b
41.	a	56.	a	71.	d
42.	c	57.	c		

CHAPTER 11

34.	b	48.	c	62.	b
35.	a	49.	c	63.	b
36.	b	50.	b	64.	c
37.	c	51.	d	65.	b
38.	d	52.	c	66.	d
39.	a	53.	a	67.	a
40.	b	54.	b	68.	b
41.	b	55.	a	69.	a
42.	d	56.	c	70.	c
43.	a	57.	b	71.	d
44.	d	58.	d	72.	a
45.	a	59.	a	73.	c
46.	c	60.	c	74.	c
47.	a	61.	d		

COPYRIGHT © HOUGHTON MIFFLIN COMPANY. ALL RIGHTS RESERVED.

CHAPTER 12

30.	b	44.	b	58.	c
31.	a	45.	c	59.	d
32.	d	46.	a	60.	b
33.	c	47.	c	61.	b
34.	a	48.	c	62.	c
35.	c	49.	d	63.	c
36.	c	50.	c	64.	d
37.	d	51.	d	65.	b
38.	a	52.	c	66.	c
39.	c	53.	b	67.	a
40.	d	54.	a	68.	d
41.	b	55.	a	69.	c
42.	c	56.	a		
43.	a	57.	b		

CHAPTER 13

29.	d	45.	c	61.	c
30.	c	46.	b	62.	a
31.	b	47.	c	63.	d
32.	c	48.	b	64.	c
33.	a	49.	b	65.	b
34.	b	50.	c	66.	c
35.	b	51.	c	67.	b
36.	a	52.	b	68.	c
37.	d	53.	d	69.	a
38.	c	54.	c	70.	a
39.	a	55.	d	71.	b
40.	a	56.	c	72.	d
41.	c	57.	a	73.	b
42.	b	58.	b	74.	c
43.	c	59.	a		
44.	a	60.	b		

CHAPTER 14

29.	a	41.	c	53.	a
30.	c	42.	b	54.	c
31.	d	43.	d	55.	a
32.	c	44.	a	56.	b
33.	c	45.	b	57.	a
34.	a	46.	c	58.	d
35.	b	47.	c	59.	c
36.	c	48.	c	60.	a
37.	b	49.	b	61.	c
38.	a	50.	c	62.	c
39.	a	51.	b	63.	c
40.	d	52.	d	64.	c

Answer Key / 283

CHAPTER 14, continued

65.	a	68.	d	71.	b
66.	c	69.	a		
67.	b	70.	d		

CHAPTER 15

29.	c	44.	b	59.	a
30.	a	45.	b	60.	d
31.	b	46.	c	61.	a
32.	d	47.	c	62.	b
33.	a	48.	d	63.	a
34.	c	49.	b	64.	b
35.	a	50.	a	65.	c
36.	d	51.	d	66.	d
37.	b	52.	d	67.	b
38.	a	53.	b	68.	d
39.	b	54.	a	69.	a
40.	d	55.	b	70.	c
41.	d	56.	d	71.	b
42.	b	57.	a	72.	d
43.	a	58.	b		

CHAPTER 16

28.	c	41.	d	54.	b
29.	a	42.	b	55.	a
30.	b	43.	a	56.	a
31.	d	44.	b	57.	c
32.	a	45.	b	58.	a
33.	b	46.	d	59.	c
34.	b	47.	c	60.	d
35.	a	48.	b	61.	d
36.	a	49.	a	62.	b
37.	b	50.	c	63.	a
38.	c	51.	d	64.	d
39.	c	52.	b	65.	a
40.	d	53.	d	66.	c

CHAPTER 17

28.	c	36.	b	44.	a
29.	b	37.	d	45.	b
30.	d	38.	a	46.	c
31.	b	39.	d	47.	d
32.	a	40.	c	48.	c
33.	c	41.	a	49.	a
34.	d	42.	c	50.	b
35.	d	43.	c	51.	b

COPYRIGHT © HOUGHTON MIFFLIN COMPANY. ALL RIGHTS RESERVED.

52.	a	58.	b	64.	c
53.	c	59.	b	65.	a
54.	a	60.	c	66.	d
55.	b	61.	c	67.	a
56.	b	62.	b	68.	c
57.	c	63.	b		

CHAPTER 18

29.	c	43.	c	57.	c
30.	b	44.	d	58	b
31.	b	45.	a	59.	c
32.	c	46.	b	60.	b
33.	d	47.	a	61.	d
34.	c	48.	c	62.	a
35.	d	49.	b	63.	a
36.	d	50.	b	64.	c
37.	c	51.	d	65.	c
38.	d	52.	a	66.	b
39.	a	53.	b	67.	a
40.	c	54.	c	68.	d
41.	b	55.	a	69.	c
42.	c	56.	c	70.	a

CHAPTER 19

27.	a	40.	b	53.	b
28.	b	41.	c	54.	d
29.	d	42.	b	55.	c
30.	d	43.	a	56.	a
31.	c	44.	a	57.	d
32.	d	45.	b	58.	a
33.	c	46.	b	59.	a
34.	b	47.	a	60.	c
35.	d	48.	c	61.	b
36.	a	49.	b	62.	d
37.	b	50.	c	63.	d
38.	c	51.	d	64.	b
39.	d	52.	a	65.	c

CHAPTER 20

27.	a		41.	b		54.	d
28.	c		42.	c		55.	c
29.	b		43.	a		56.	d
30.	d		44.	b		57.	a
31.	c		45.	d		58.	c
32.	a		46.	d		59.	d
33.	c		47.	c		60.	c
34.	b		48.	d		61.	b
35.	a		49.	d		62.	d
36.	d		50.	b		63.	c
37.	b		51.	d		64.	a
38.	a		52.	a		65.	b
39.	a		53.	a		66.	d
40.	d						

CHAPTER 21

32.	b		46.	c		60.	b
33.	d		47.	d		61.	c
34.	c		48.	b		62.	b
35.	a		49.	a		63.	c
36.	a		50.	d		64.	a
37.	c		51.	a		65.	d
38.	c		52.	c		66.	d
39.	d		53.	b		67.	c
40.	b		54.	c		68.	b
41.	d		55.	d		69.	d
42.	a		56.	a		70.	b
43.	d		57.	d		71.	a
44.	d		58.	c		72.	c
45.	b		59.	a		73.	b

CHAPTER 22

30.	b		43.	c		56.	d
31.	c		44.	b		57.	b
32.	a		45.	d		58.	c
33.	c		46.	a		59.	d
34.	d		47.	c		60.	d
35.	b		48.	a		61.	c
36.	a		49.	b		62.	d
37.	c		50.	b		63.	a
38.	d		51.	c		64.	d
39.	c		52.	d		65.	b
40.	a		53.	b		66.	c
41.	d		54.	a		67.	a
42.	b		55.	b			

COPYRIGHT © HOUGHTON MIFFLIN COMPANY. ALL RIGHTS RESERVED.

CHAPTER 23

28.	a	41.	b	54.	b
29.	a	42.	d	55.	a
30.	c	43.	b	56.	b
31.	c	44.	a	57.	c
32.	b	45.	b	58.	b
33.	b	46.	c	59.	a
34.	d	47.	d	60.	d
35.	a	48.	a	61.	d
36.	d	49.	b	62.	b
37.	c	50.	d	63.	a
38.	c	51.	a	64.	c
39.	d	52.	c	65.	d
40.	b	53.	d	66.	b

CHAPTER 24

29.	a	43.	a	57.	c
30.	c	44.	b	58.	c
31.	b	45.	c	59.	d
32.	b	46.	a	60.	a
33.	d	47.	b	61.	a
34.	c	48.	b	62.	c
35.	c	49.	a	63.	c
36.	a	50.	c	64.	b
37.	b	51.	d	65.	d
38.	a	52.	a	66.	c
39.	c	53.	c	67.	a
40.	a	54.	b		
41.	b	55.	a		
42.	b	56.	b		

CHAPTER 25

27.	b	41.	b	54.	c
28.	d	42.	c	55.	d
29.	a	43.	d	56.	a
30.	b	44.	a	57.	c
31.	c	45.	b	58.	b
32.	c	46.	c	59.	a
33.	d	47.	d	60.	c
34.	a	48.	a	61.	d
35.	d	49.	c	62.	a
36.	b	50.	d	63.	b
37.	b	51.	a	64.	c
38.	c	52.	b	65.	b
39.	d	53.	a	66.	a
40.	a				

COPYRIGHT © HOUGHTON MIFFLIN COMPANY. ALL RIGHTS RESERVED.

CHAPTER 26

29.	b	42.	a	55.	b
30.	c	43.	d	56.	d
31.	d	44.	b	57.	c
32.	a	45.	a	58.	c
33.	c	46.	d	59.	a
34.	c	47.	c	60.	d
35.	b	48.	b	61.	b
36.	d	49.	c	62.	d
37.	a	50.	d	63.	a
38.	b	51.	d	64.	d
39.	c	52.	a	65.	a
40.	b	53.	b	66.	c
41.	d	54.	c		

CHAPTER 27

29.	c	43.	d	56.	a
30.	d	44.	a	57.	b
31.	b	45.	d	58.	c
32.	d	46.	c	59.	d
33.	a	47.	a	60.	b
34.	c	48.	b	61.	b
35.	d	49.	a	62.	d
36.	a	50.	d	63.	a
37.	a	51.	b	64.	d
38.	b	52.	a	65.	a
39.	a	53.	c	66.	d
40.	c	54.	d	67.	c
41.	d	55.	d	68.	b
42.	b				

CHAPTER 28

28.	c	42.	a	56.	a
29.	b	43.	b	57.	c
30.	c	44.	a	58.	b
31.	d	45.	c	59.	b
32.	a	46.	d	60.	d
33.	c	47.	a	61.	c
34.	c	48.	d	62.	c
35.	b	49.	a	63.	b
36.	d	50.	d	64.	d
37.	b	51.	a	65.	a
38.	c	52.	b	66.	d
39.	d	53.	c	67.	a
40.	b	54.	d	68.	c
41.	a	55.	b	69.	b

COPYRIGHT © HOUGHTON MIFFLIN COMPANY. ALL RIGHTS RESERVED.

CHAPTER 29

29.	b	43.	d	57.	c
30.	a	44.	a	58.	a
31.	b	45.	a	59.	c
32.	c	46.	c	60.	d
33.	b	47.	b	61.	a
34.	d	48.	d	62.	c
35.	a	49.	a	63.	b
36.	c	50.	d	64.	c
37.	d	51.	a	65.	a
38.	a	52.	c	66.	b
39.	d	53.	b	67.	d
40.	c	54.	c	68.	c
41.	b	55.	d	69.	d
42.	a	56.	b	70.	a

CHAPTER 30

33.	a	46.	c	59.	b
34.	a	47.	a	60.	a
35.	c	48.	c	61.	d
36.	d	49.	a	62.	a
37.	b	50.	c	63.	c
38.	d	51.	b	64.	a
39.	d	52.	a	65.	b
40.	c	53.	b	66.	c
41.	b	54.	c	67.	d
42.	c	55.	d	68.	d
43.	d	56.	b	69.	b
44.	b	57.	d	70.	b
45.	c	58.	c	71.	a

CHAPTER 31

28.	d	41.	d	54.	d
29.	b	42.	a	55.	a
30.	b	43.	b	56.	b
31.	c	44.	d	57.	d
32.	c	45.	b	58.	a
33.	a	46.	a	59.	c
34.	d	47.	c	60.	c
35.	b	48.	a	61.	d
36.	a	49.	d	62.	a
37.	c	50.	c	63.	c
38.	b	51.	a	64.	b
39.	c	52.	b	65.	d
40.	a	53.	a		